**so you're
going
to court!**

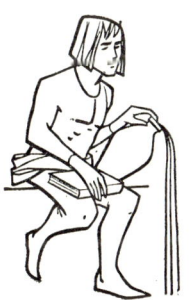

so you're going to court!

The LAW and YOU

by
Robert W. Smedley, LL.B.

INTRODUCTION BY
ADOLF A. BERLE
*Professor Emeritus of Law
Columbia University*

Fountainhead Publishers
475 FIFTH AVENUE, NEW YORK 10017, N. Y.

SECOND PRINTING

Copyright, © 1964 by Robert W. Smedley

All rights reserved. No part of this book may be reproduced in any form or portions thereof without permission in writing from the publishers, except by a reviewer who may quote brief passages in a review to be printed in a magazine or newspaper.

LIBRARY OF CONGRESS CATALOG CARD NO. 62-14231

Published in New York by Fountainhead Publishers, Inc. and simultaneously in Toronto, Canada by Ambassador Books, Ltd.

Manufactured in the United States of America by The Colonial Press Inc., Clinton, Massachusetts

For my own girls
PHOEBE, CARA and MELISSA
because they make things worthwhile

ALL NAMES OF PEOPLE AND PLACES IN THE INCIDENTS MENTIONED IN THIS BOOK ARE FICTIONAL AND ANY RESEMBLANCE TO PERSONS, PLACES AND EVENTS IS PURELY COINCIDENTAL.

AUTHOR'S ACKNOWLEDGMENTS

I acknowledge with thanks the interest of the many persons who encouraged me in the writing of this book, my colleagues of the Bar Associations and of the legal organizations of which I am a member, the courtesies extended to me by the staffs of the various legal libraries, and the patience and skill of the editorial department of Fountainhead Publishers.

CONTENTS

Introduction   xiii

Chapter 1. **You and the Law**   1
What the law is . . . Its ancient origin . . . Hammurabi, King of Babylon . . . The Justinian Code of Rome . . . The Napoleonic Code . . . Definition of law . . . Origin of the jury system . . . The Magna Carta . . . The U.S. Constitution's Bill of Rights

Chapter 2. **Let's Try a Case**   5
Purchasing a retail business . . . failure of consummation of sale . . . hiring a lawyer to retrieve the purchase deposit . . . Motion for Summary Judgment . . . The Jury Trial.

Chapter 3. **Twelve Good and True**   19
Receiving a jury questionnaire . . . Jury system keystone of American independence . . . Jury trial of burglary case . . . Law of Evidence founded on principle jury will hear facts alone . . . Hearsay disallowed . . . Cross examination . . . Jury decides the facts . . . size of jury, responsibility, oath, jury room, instruction to jury, confining a jury, jury system active participation in the processes of government . . . a hung jury . . . Open Venire, petit jury called to try a case in public . . . grand jury hears cases in secret . . . returning an indictment.

Chapter 4. **Swear to Tell the Truth**   39
The witness is the most important person in a trial . . . Interviewing witnesses to a tavern robbery involving death of victim . . . coroner's report, detectives' lineup . . . Automobile accident in which one driver is killed . . .

ix

x · CONTENTS

What makes a good witness? A defendant in a criminal case not forced to testify . . . why a lawsuit is public concern . . . a subpoena . . . insanity does not always disqualify a witness . . . witnesses incompetent to testify . . . when a suspect in a crime is granted immunity . . . when a witness cannot speak English . . . impeachment of a witness . . . the expert witness, the lay witness . . . fictional discrediting of a witness

Chapter 5. **Murder Over Lightly**   58
Homicide . . . detective's presentation of investigation file to District Attorney in case of 'People of the State vs Fred Taylor' . . . the court appointed lawyer . . . examination by psychiatrist . . . pleas of insanity . . . calling a jury . . . District Attorney . . . Defense Attorney . . . Definition of first degree murder . . . involuntary manslaughter . . . Address to the court by Prosecuting Attorney . . . by the Defense Attorney . . . Rebuttal by District Attorney . . . after arguments of counsel . . . reaching the verdict . . . setting bail . . . motion for new trial . . . probation . . . sentencing.

Chapter 6. **Supreme Law of the Land**   90
In an incident of stealing a sign (property of the state) case filed in Justice of the Peace Court . . . Search Warrant . . . Personal privacy . . . Search allowable in case of lawful arrest . . . Constitution's protection against illegal searches and seizures.

Chapter 7. **There Ought to be a Law**   99
Where the law comes from and how lawyers find it . . . Making a will . . . Hypothetical case of an elderly man . . . Appeal to State Supreme Court . . . Legacies provided in a will . . . Annulment of illegal marriage . . . Conservator of estate of deceased testator . . . Probate Court requires mental competency of maker of a will . . . How lawyer handles problem of protracted litigation by settlement . . . Negligence cases . . . necessity of professional counsel and representation.

Chapter 8. **Tell It to the Judge**   116
Traffic courts . . . vicious fee system . . . Traffic charges

Contents · xi

offences against the State . . . must be informed of charge against you . . . Your traffic ticket is a summons . . . Mechanical devices in drunk driving cases . . . Blood test . . . the Breatholizer . . . motion pictures . . . Leaving scene or 'hit run' . . . State compulsory auto liability insurance laws . . . Traffic law enforcement.

Chapter 9. Redressing the Wound 125
1. The Accident 2. Preparation for Trial 3. The Trial Begins 4. The Judge's Ruling 5. Instruction to the Jury . . . Burden of Proof . . . Preponderance of Evidence . . . Damages . . . Expectancy . . . Pre-existing conditions . . . Experts . . . Sympathy . . . General Instructions 6. The Summations 7. The Verdicts 8. The Karen Walters Case

Chapter 10. For Better or For Worse 179
Marriage . . . separation . . . Grounds for Divorce . . . Connivance . . . Court papers including Divorce Restraining Order . . . Divorce is a luxury . . . Traps in Nevada divorce route . . . Property Division . . . Interstate Divorce Problems . . . Due Process of Law . . . Chart of Marriage Laws in 50 States and District of Columbia . . . Chart of Divorce Laws in 50 States and District of Columbia . . . Private Marriage Counselors or Social Workers.

Chapter 11. On the Job 202
Employer-employee relations . . . Formal and Informal Contracts . . . Law of Supply and Demand in Labor Market . . . Employment Contract . . . Labor Legislation . . . Minimum Wage Laws . . . Workmen's Compensation Acts . . . Injunction . . . Trade Union Movement in America . . . National Labor Relations Act of 1935 . . . Labor Unions . . . Discrimination.

Chapter 12. Of Sound Mind 217
Wills and Estates . . . Anti-fraud Statutes . . . Rights of Creditors . . . Types of Property . . . Will must be Probated . . . Executor of a Will . . . Groups having Vested Interest in Property of the Deceased . . . 'Estate Planning' . . . Advantage of insight into the Law of Wills and Estates.

xii · CONTENTS

Chapter 13. **Preventative Law**   227
Role of Lawyer . . . Legal Planning in setting up a Trust . . . Dealing with the eager seller . . . Buying a house . . . Accidents . . . Keeping financial records within a marriage . . . 'Bailment' . . . Necessity of a will . . . Liability Insurance Policy.

Chapter 14. **Crime and Punishment**   238
Criminal Law the Disciplinarian of a Civilization . . . How it operates . . . by whom imposed . . . the Fourteenth Amendment . . . Hypothetical dialogue between the Constitution and the Government as spokesmen . . . Twenty-one Fundamental Rules of American Justice . . . Specializing of attorney in criminal cases . . . Definition of word 'crime' . . . Criminal Negligence . . . Felonies and Misdemeanors . . . Accessory during the Fact and after the Fact . . . Proof of Conspiracy . . . Exceptional criminal . . . Backward criminal . . . Burden of proof on the State . . . Criminal Punishment in America.

Chapter 15. **Home, Sweet Home**   254
Land is Real Property . . . Real Estate Law . . . Ownership . . . Public Records . . . Search of Title . . . Notice of suit in District Court . . . Terminology inherited from Western Europe . . . Rights of Property Owner . . . Public and Private Restrictions and Controls . . . Public Control of Land . . . Law of Zoning . . . The Tax Burden . . . Land Survey . . . *Caveat Emptor* (Let the Buyer Beware) . . . Financial Problems . . . Deposit . . . Conventional Loans . . . Problems of Sellers . . . Brokers . . . Mortgage . . . What is a house? . . . Liabilities . . . Types of deeds . . . Faulty Transfer . . . Surety Bond . . . Significance of True Ownership of Land.

Chapter 16. **Summing Up**   272
107 Questions and Answers . . . Basic Concept of the Law relating to the individual's rights and obligations.

Glossary of Legal Terms   285
From 'Abstract of Title' to 'Zoning'

About the Author   301

INTRODUCTION

The average American is continuously involved with "the law" in practically every phase of his life. Yet his actual knowledge of its mechanics and processes is remarkably scarce. Mr. Smedley's readable, popular and non-technical exposition, written for everyone, therefore fills a plain need.

Almost everyone comes into direct (although usually unwanted) contact with courts, lawyers and law administration in four contexts. A policeman hands him a ticket for traffic violation. Or, involved in some automobile accident, he is involved as plaintiff or defendant in an action for damages, although an insurance company usually handles the proceedings. Or he is called for jury duty. A fourth context—he is dead and his estate has to go through a probate or surrogate's court—brings his family into the picture, although he himself is happily removed from the proceedings. In all of these situations, the individuals find themselves in a different world, dominated by remote power-figures known as judges, operated by technically trained lawyers, and oddly controlled by far-away mandates set out in statutes ("laws") or by past decisions of courts which unaccountably settle what happens to him. More often than not all the public knows about this strange world is derived from dramatic tales or self-told lawyers' tales of brilliant devices to win verdicts or from gruesome detective stories. Well, in a probate or traffic court there rarely is a jury, and the drama-content is usually nil. Even in criminal cases, the detective or district attorney (commonly the villains of the tale) is surprisingly matter-of-fact. The whole process often seems frustrating.

Our plain American citizen is torn between an age-old desire (chronicled by Shakespeare) to kill all lawyers, and a strong desire to have a lawyer working for him whose magic can be relied on to pull him through.

Unhappily, the first-rate lawyers and great law schools of the United States which train them, increasingly draw away from our average citizen. Their graduates hope to become (and usually do become) members of an elite group at the bar, lucratively engaged in dealing with large corporate or property interests. Somehow at the level at which most men encounter the law in action—the traffic courts, magistrates courts, probate courts dealing with small estates, or domestic relations courts dealing with divorce, alimony and custody of children—the best of the bar appears to be somewhere else.

In these cases—there are millions of them every year—the court-processes can be set out in clear, non-technical English. This is what Mr. Smedley has endeavored to do. The mysterious world encountered by anyone drawn on a jury panel or called as a witness loses much of its terror when its workings are simply explained. The obligations of the individual as juror, as witness, or perhaps as plaintiff or defendant are not incomprehensible. The job of the judge (who in his courtroom is just as human as anyone else) can be plainly described. The legal operations occasionally impinging on your life and mine have little magic in them. Once that element is eliminated, machinery of the law, although it loses some of its terrors, acquires more dignity and commands more respect. Consequently Mr. Smedley has performed a real service in explaining it.

In writing this introduction, let me add one *caveat*. Mr. Smedley's simple explanation should not tempt anyone to go lightly to court. One of the greatest of Federal Court judges, the late Justice Learned Hand, once observed that, next to a serious illness in the family, an extended law suit was the greatest personal misfortune a man could suffer. This is still true. Courts are intolerably congested. The cost of a lawyer's service is frequently out of proportion to the benefit received. More often than not, a bad settlement is more advantageous than a good law suit. Of the judgments for damages in accident cases (they run into hundreds of millions, perhaps billions, in each year), little more than half ever reaches the claimant, and the costs of the party whose insurance company pays, show up in steadily rising rates for automobile insurance. The American bar and the legal technicians have a long, long way to go to transform justice —which should be a right—into a readily available service instead of a costly and dangerous luxury. But this problem, one may note, has been with us at least since the days when, after the Parthenon was built, an Athenian court tried Phidias on a charge that he had stolen some of the gold sheathing the Parthenon's statue of Pallas Athena.

The task of simplifying justice, expediting it and making it inexpensive nevertheless will be helped if the processes are understood. Mr. Smedley is entirely right in approaching the subject, not from the lawyer's angle, but from the point of view of the individual who becomes involved.

ADOLF A. BERLE
Professor Emeritus of Law

COLUMBIA UNIVERSITY, NEW YORK
September, 1964

**so you're
going
to court!**

Chapter One

YOU AND THE LAW

The intangible force that makes freedom and progress possible is, of course, law. It is law that brings order into the affairs of men—that enables them to lift their sights above mere survival, to accumulate possessions, to develop the arts, to pursue knowledge, and to enjoy life among their fellows. Law gives the individual a security that he could obtain in no other way; it protects the family and other groups organized for the advancement of common interests; it permits the growth of great cities and the development of vast enterprises. In other words, it is the cement that holds our free society together.

Curiously enough, the average person knows less about the law than other basic tenets of communal life. He knows how his children should be educated. He knows about religion, and attends the house of worship of his choice. He is conversant with local and national politics. Today, through the various media of communication: newspapers, magazines, radio and television, he is acquainted with international affairs. And he knows how to socialize with other members of his community. But about the law, which affects every facet of his life, day in and day out, he often knows little or nothing. The purpose of this book, therefore, is to acquaint you with what goes on behind the doors of courtrooms throughout the land. And although legal procedure is ancient and dignified, there is no need for you to be hesitant about entering. Remember, the law's intent is the administration of equal justice to all.

The vast complexity of the law, like Rome, wasn't built in a day. Originally, laws arose from the instinct that certain regulations had to be made in order to promote the best interests of the community. Honest citizens had to be protected from harm and, to accomplish this end, evildoers had to be punished.

History recognizes Hammurabi, King of Babylon—circa 1900 B.C.—as the originator of one of the earliest written codes of law. It was carved on an eight-foot slab of black stone and, by the miracle of archeological preservation, you can see it in the Louvre Museum in Paris today. About 2,000 years later, Rome developed an excellent legal system. However, by the time of the Byzantine emperor Justinian (483-565 A.D.), it was cluttered with conflicting opinions and outdated legislation. He therefore ordered its revision, and the Justinian Code has been the foundation of most European law up to the present.

The last famous legal code set down was that of Napoleon Bonaparte, and the Napoleonic Code is still the law of Louisiana, which is the only state in the Union not grounded on English Common Law. A number of American laws are older than the United States because they were brought here by the colonists who migrated from England. American law does not have as its basis any written code, but arises from the system of English Common Law, which grew out of the continuous addition of judges' decisions over the centuries. English Common Law consists of customary law and judge-made law as opposed to statute law created by legislatures. And even today the use of precedent by judges adds to the body of statute laws.

"The law is the last result of human wisdom acting upon human experience for the benefit of the public."

—SAMUEL JOHNSON

The law is a set of rules for living laid down by society for the conduct of its members toward one another. In addition, there are many rules of conduct that society expects its members to obey, which are not enforceable in a court of law.

The freedoms we enjoy: free speech, free assembly, and freedom of religion—incorporated in the first amendment to the Constitution

—must be limited in order to be preserved since we cannot have freedom of belief for ourselves unless we are willing to allow it for those holding other beliefs. The middle of the road between complete freedom from law (anarchy) and complete submission of freedom (dictatorship) is democracy, where the law affords the necessary protection to individual rights, and insures as little interference as possible to individual initiative and freedom of action. In a democracy, the law is on the side of the people.

"Equal and exact justice to all men, of whatever estate or persuasion, religious or political; freedom of person under the protection of the habeas corpus; and trial by juries impartially selected, these principles form the bright constellation which has gone before us, and guided our steps through an age of revolution and reformation."

—Thomas Jefferson

The jury system, which provides the right to be judged by our peers, goes back nearly a thousand years. In England, in 1075, twelve men were asked to give their opinions regarding the facts in a case concerning the ownership of property. This is believed to be the first recorded jury trial. In 1215, King John of England signed the Magna Carta, which instituted trial by jury. It guaranteed that a man could not be harmed or imprisoned without the judgment of his equals, and by the law of the land. An original of the Magna Carta can be seen in the British Museum. Although the ink has faded away so that it can no longer be read, this historic document still preserves, in a democracy, the right of every person to be judged by his or her fellow citizens.

Every person's rights are also respected and protected by the Bill of Rights, the ten original amendments to the Constitution. Here, in brief, are the articles expressly applicable to the individual's involvement with the law and the courts:

Article 4—The right of the people to be secure in their persons, houses, papers, and effects, against unreasonable searches and seizures.

Article 5—No person shall be held to answer for a capital or other infamous crime unless indicted by a grand jury (federal guarantee only); nor tried twice for the same offense; nor be forced to testify against himself; nor be deprived of life, liberty or property without due process of law.

Article 6—In all criminal prosecutions, the accused has the right to a public trial, to be confronted with the witnesses against him, and to have the assistance of counsel for his defense.

Article 7—The right of trial by jury.

Article 8—The right to be free under bail.

"The interpretation of the laws is the proper and peculiar province of the courts. A constitution is in fact, and must be regarded by the judges, as a fundamental law."
—Alexander Hamilton

The Constitution and the Bill of Rights were written to protect our democratic society and the rights of all of its members. We could not function as a free people without them. You and every American enjoy these liberties. However, they can only be maintained by the eternal vigilance of the law. In a courtroom, whether you are a plaintiff, defendant, witness, juror, or simply a spectator, you will see that while the mills of the law grind slowly, they grind exceedingly well. No detail is overlooked in the attempt to dispense justice fairly, reasonably, and with compassionate understanding of the frailties of mankind. Lawyers and judges are human, too, as you will discover. The panorama of humanity, its struggles, failures and triumphs, is no better displayed than in the pulsating life of the law as it proceeds, day after day, in our courtrooms.

Chapter Two

LET'S TRY A CASE

George and Louise Smith, who desire to obtain extra income, decide to purchase a small retail business which Louise could run. George would help her during his off hours. They consult the want ad columns of the newspaper and under "Business Opportunities" find an ad: "TOT & TEEN children's wear, 314 Holly. Owners forced to sell this attractive and profitable business. A real opportunity. Low down payment. J. J. FLEESON, Business Broker, G L 4-2875."

Mr. Fleeson is contacted and George and Louise view the shop. The owner says he has "family sickness" and must leave the state. The shop will need a little decorating, but it appears to fit the bill, and the terms are satisfactory—$3,000 down and the remainder on time payments, which can be easily met through income. The account books happen to be at the auditor's office, but the store is operating fairly profitably, and the books and the balance sheet will be available to George and Louise before the final closing of the sale.

George and Louise decide to buy the shop. Response from the ad seemed to be rather brisk, so they make up their minds quickly. Mr. Fleeson says that a $3,000 certified check payable to him will be required for the down payment, so they transfer their savings to a checking account, sell some common stock, and obtain the certified check. They sign a "business purchase agreement" and turn the check over to Mr. Fleeson as the agent of the owners. They are still concerned about the earnings and request again to see the store books, but they are not yet available. At any rate, to be sure, they insert the following language in the contract: "purchasers may examine store accounts before closing." This occurs two days after they answered the advertisement. Mr. Fleeson assures them that they have made the smartest decision of their lives.

While the sale is pending, Louise arranges to spend a few days in the shop getting acquainted with the business. It soon becomes obvious to her that things are not as favorable as they had been led to believe. She notices, among other things, that parking is very awkward for the customers—that they must park at the shopping center across a busy street and then bring their small fry to the shop. She also sees that a national chain store close by has comparable merchandise at generally lower prices. The "family sickness" of the sellers becomes increasingly vague each time the subject is mentioned.

George and Louise resolve that unless the accounting books are produced promptly and show satisfactory earning, they simply cannot go through with the deal. Each request for the books is met with a stall. Finally, ten days after their decision to purchase, they call Mr. Fleeson and request return of their deposit. The deposit is not returned. The "closing date" passes and no closing takes place. George and Louise refuse to purchase the shop because the owners and their agent, Mr. Fleeson, fail to live up to their agreement to produce the accounting books. They are convinced that the place is far from what was represented as to earnings and value.

The problem now is to secure the return of their $3,000 deposit. This should be automatic, they reason, because the sellers refused to live up to their agreement, and, therefore, they are entitled to back out of the agreement to purchase the store.

George and Louise then confidently begin what is to become one of the most frustrating periods of their lives, trying in vain to get hold of Mr. Fleeson and, harder still, to get some satisfaction from him. Up until this point they couldn't believe that a person in business would be so hard to contact. They telephone his office time and time again. He is busy in conference, or out of town, but they are always assured that he will call back. He never calls back. George takes time off from his job and plants himself in Fleeson's office.

Fleeson arrives and is a bundle of apologetic innocence. "I told my secretary to mail you that check," he says. "She'll mail it this afternoon and you'll have it in the morning." But the check never comes.

George and Louise ask the owners about their money and are told that Fleeson never turned any part of it over to them. Again they are on an interminable chase after Mr. Fleeson with the same routine as to phone calls and the same type of broken promises.

Finally they realize that they have to go to a lawyer. One of the first things the lawyer asks to see is their purchase agreement. He reads it and points out some language of which neither George nor Louise had been fully aware. "Should either party fail or refuse to complete this agreement, the down payment made hereunder shall be retained by the undersigned agent as liquidated damages for his commission." The lawyer further points out that their inserted provision, "purchasers may examine store accounts before closing," does not state that the contract will be void, entitling them to the return of their money, if the books are not produced.

George and Louise explain to the lawyer that great and glowing statements were made about what a wonderful business the TOT & TEEN shop was, and how reluctant the owners were to give it up but had to because of family sickness, and that the income was very good. "We wouldn't have signed it," they say, "if it hadn't been for all of the promises."

Their lawyer sympathizes but explains that when you have a written agreement or contract, the language in writing governs, and all the sales talk that went on before would not even be considered by a court. He goes on to explain, however, that when an ambiguous or unclear provision appears in the written instrument, the Court can inquire into the oral conversation of the parties to determine their intent, and if they could show that everyone had agreed that the deal would be off if they weren't satisfied with the accounting books, then they might have a chance to get their money back. In short, they then realized that they had a lawsuit on their hands.

Here is a dispute as to facts, as to law, and as to the relative rights between parties. Obviously, a Court, and only a Court, could decide this dispute. George and Louise are firmly convinced that

Fleeson stole their money and should be put in jail. Fleeson feels he has a legal right to keep the money. This is the stuff that cases in court are made of.

George and Louise retain the lawyer by paying him an advance fee for his time and for the costs of filing a case. On his advice they decide to sue Fleeson. Their lawyer starts the suit by drafting two legal papers, the Complaint and the Summons.

What is a Summons? It is a paper showing the court and the title of the lawsuit, in this case, *George Smith and Louise Smith, the Plaintiffs, versus John J. Fleeson, the Defendant,* and informing the defendant that he must answer the charges of the Complaint in court within a certain time (usually 20 days) or default judgment can be taken against him.

What is the Complaint? It is the plaintiff's charge against the defendant. In this case it will outline the facts, that Fleeson received the $3,000 and that he refuses to return it, and will demand the money back plus interest and, perhaps, damages in addition for wrongfully taking the money.

When Fleeson is served, he takes the suit papers to his lawyer, who must file a "responsive pleading" in court. This may be a motion or various motions, if the lawyer feels they are justified, such as "Motion to Dismiss for Failure to State a Claim upon which Relief can be Granted" or "Motion for More Definite Statement." If such motions are filed, then the 20-day period to answer is extended until they are argued by the opposing lawyers before the judge and decided by him. Then, usually within 10 days after the motions are decided, Fleeson's lawyer must file an Answer.

What is an Answer? It is the denial filed in court by the defendant's lawyer. In this case Fleeson, through his lawyer, will probably admit that he received the $3,000 but will deny that he wrongfully kept it, claiming that by the terms of the written contract he had a right to keep the money as "liquidated damages."

Fleeson's lawyer will explain to him, if he doesn't already know, that the term "liquidated" means pre-determined. The amount of damages for breaching the contract is set by its own terms rather than leaving the issue of the amount of damages to be determined by a Court or jury on the basis of monetary loss to the parties. Fleeson's lawyer will probably explain, also, that if the Smiths can show that the sellers agreed that the deal would be off if the account books weren't satisfactory to the purchasers, then he would lose the case. The lawyer might suggest that Fleeson offer to pay back a portion of the claim, say $1,000, so that the case can be settled without a fight. In any case, Fleeson will also have to retain his lawyer with an advance fee for time and suit costs.

Let us assume that Fleeson's lawyer, upon examining the copy of the contract which his client shows him, feels that he has legal cause for a judgment in his client's favor based on law alone without a jury. The lawyer realizes that if and when he ever becomes required to argue the case before a jury, his client will be in a less sympathetic position than the Smiths because, after all, he is claiming a commission for a sale that never took place, and he is in a business, whereas the Smiths were drawn in and persuaded to sign a contract and give up their savings and did not, in fact, receive anything in return.

Fleeson's lawyer knows that written contracts mean what they say, regardless of the sympathies, and that even though the Smiths claim that the contract was to be void if they weren't satisfied with the accounts, the written contract itself does not say this. The lawyer realizes further that he can strongly contend before a judge that the Smiths are really in the wrong in that they agreed to purchase the shop and then refused to do so. The fact that they now desire to back out means nothing under the law. The agreed intention of both sides at the time of signing is what controls. Otherwise, contracts would be meaningless. People could sign them and then say they had changed their minds, or they could agree to things in writing, cause other people to rely on their promises, and then claim the writing doesn't mean what it says.

Based on these contentions, Fleeson's lawyer files his Answer in court and, along with it, a "Motion for Summary Judgment." To this he attaches a photocopy of the contract and refers to it as "Exhibit A." In the motion he claims that the case contains no legitimate factual controversy whatsoever and that the judge should, as a matter of law, decide the case in Fleeson's favor without allowing a jury to decide it.

Fleeson's "Motion for Summary Judgment" is then set for hearing on a particular date and time in the court room. The clients, the

Smiths and Fleeson, may or may not be present at this time. They are generally not required to be in court because the arguments before the judge pertain to legal matters only, and it is assumed that the judge will make his decision based on the law alone and won't be impressed, one way or the other, by Louise's pretty hat or painful tears.

The issue at this point is clear-cut—is there or isn't there a factual question for a jury? The Smiths' lawyer says there is, and Fleeson's lawyer contends there is not. This points up one of the most important functions of a judge. Before he can present any case to a jury, he must first sift it to determine if there is any factual issue upon which reasonable minds can differ under the law. If there is such an issue or question, a jury must decide the case. If there is not, the judge must decide it under the law alone.

Where is the line drawn between a legal question and a factual question? Needless to say, this is a difficult concept for one not trained in law; however, it is the sort of thing which answers itself when sufficient knowledge is present. Take these basic legal principles, which the judge knows he cannot change, nor can he allow a jury to change them: (1) Written contracts mean what they say. (2) The intention of the parties at the time of signing is what governs, not their intention now. (3) Unless the contract is ambiguous on its face, or unless there is definite proof of fraud in obtaining the signature on the contract, the law will not even allow any jury to hear testimony tending to prove the parties' intention was different than that clearly stated in writing.

Taking these rules into account, the judge denies Fleeson's Motion for Summary Judgment. He finds that the language "purchasers may examine accounting books" is unclear and requires some explanation outside the written contract as to whether or not a denial of the privilege would render the contract void. Also, the judge notes that in the Smiths' complaint they allege, through their lawyer, that various statements were made to them about the wonderful profits of the shop, and it was to confirm these that they wanted to see the books.

At this point, the judge does not decide the truth or falsity of the Smiths' allegations, but merely decides that they should be given an opportunity in the trial to try to prove them. In denying Fleeson's

Motion, the judge finds that the dispute as to what the contract means may be a real dispute. In other words, the judge says that if the Smiths prove what they say they can prove, that the whole deal was tied to a showing as to earnings, then reasonable minds could differ, under the law, as to who should win the case.

If this is so, a jury will decide the case. But after all the facts have been presented in the trial, the judge will then again have to decide whether the jury will be allowed to make the decision. This will depend on the nature of the evidence presented.

After disposition of Fleeson's "Motion for Summary Judgment," the case is then set by the judge for pre-trial conference. Since the judge has already become familiar with the case, and since both sides have admitted the existence of the contract, the pre-trial conference is a very brief procedure. Its purpose is to pinpoint the issues and to require each side to disclose the identity of the witnesses they intend to call, to present the exhibits they propose to offer in trial, and to list the legal cases and authorities they will rely on so that the judge and the other attorney will have an opportunity to study them.

Pre-trial conferences are required by many courts and are intended to take some of the sporting character out of trials as well as to save time when the trial commences. By requiring opposite sides to outline their testimony and display their exhibits in advance, the surprise element is eliminated.

All trials are adverse proceedings. As in a boxing match, the parties oppose each other. Otherwise, if there weren't any points of contention, there would be no trial. However, the Courts strive to minimize trickery and strategy in battling out a lawsuit. The purpose of a trial is not to decide who has the best lawyer or into how many traps the other side can be led. Its purpose is to ascertain the truth, so far as is humanly possible, and fairly to adjudge the rights of the parties. This is justice.

Obviously, both sides cannot win, and someone is going to feel that justice has been denied. But if both sides are treated fairly, without prejudice, and if the facts are allowed to be presented fully, and if a fair and impartial jury decides the factual questions, which, as in this case, usually determine the outcome, then justice will result insofar as human beings are capable of devising it. Pre-trial conferences are most important in the long and complicated trial. They are often conducted two to three months before the trial in order to give the lawyers and the judge a chance thoroughly to digest the matters presented by the other side.

After the pre-trial conference, the case is set for trial. The trial date may be from perhaps five months to one year or more after filing of the case. In some large cities it takes three to five years to get to trial. Virtually all of this time is spent just waiting in line on the court docket until the case's turn comes up.

Fleeson is on the "slow side" of the case, that is, he is the one being sued, and he doesn't care if the case ever comes to trial. Obviously, extended delay in getting to trial works to the advantage of the wrongdoer and frustrates the rights of the aggrieved party. So if this case occurred in a city where such delay is prevalent, he could just sit back and wait. Perhaps the Smiths will have to move far away, or time can cause any number of things to happen which will diminish the chances of a worthy plaintiff. At the very least, the sting of the original hurt is lessened when the case finally comes up.

Fleeson might eventually be charged interest for the waiting period, but this is only 6 per cent in many states, and the many advantages of delay to him make possible interest assessment a bargain.

Upon being informed of the long wait for trial and the possibility of a further extended delay if Fleeson should decide to appeal the case to a higher court, the Smiths might throw up their hands in despair and, even though in their opinion they have a 100% worthy cause, would accept whatever token settlement Fleeson might offer.

Lawyers and judges are fully cognizant of the injustices caused by court congestion and delay in some of our large metropolitan areas. Correction of this situation is close to the number one public service project of all responsible members and groups in the profession. The fact is that the judicial branch of the government is often denied its rightful share of the tax dollar in relation to the service it performs. The administration of justice is expensive, but it is one of the most essential governmental services, and the amount it costs is infinitesimal, as compared to other governmental projects, in light of the great service it offers. Without justice, civilization is a lie. Hitler supplied all the governmental services one could ask for, but he

denied justice. This is why it is so essential that our courts be well equipped, supplied with fair, impartial and well-trained judges, and be readily available to our citizens.

In places where trial delay is long, it is often the practice of the lawyers to preserve evidence through the practice of taking depositions of various important witnesses so that, if they should die or be otherwise unavailable, their deposition can be presented in lieu of their testimony at the trial. In order to understand this practice, it is necessary to know what the term "evidence" means. Evidence is the testimony of witnesses given under oath. A witness can be anyone who has actual knowledge of any fact pertaining to the case.

Exhibits can also be used as evidence. An exhibit is any object, document, paper, photograph or other physical thing which may, by its existence, tend to prove an issue in the case. For instance, the contract is an exhibit in the Smiths' case against Fleeson. The elusive account books, if any, might be an exhibit. The Smiths' lawyer could direct George, or an independent investigator, to take a movie showing the bad parking situation at the shop. This might become an exhibit to be shown to the jury. Some of the merchandise in the shop, a little girl's dress for example, might conceivably become an exhibit in the case if Fleeson and the sellers had claimed as an inducement for the Smiths to sign the contract that only a certain high quality merchandise was included in the stock and this item showed the statement to be false.

A cash register tape for one day's operation might become an exhibit to indicate that, at least on that day, sales were not what they were alleged to be. The lease under which the sellers held the store building, which the Smiths were to assume, might be an exhibit to show that the terms were not quite as favorable as stated. A copy of the newspaper ad the Smiths answered might be presented as an exhibit. In a recent case, a telephone pole was hauled into court and displayed to the jury to show that it was defective, causing the plaintiff's fall and resultant injuries.

But only in rare instances does an exhibit stand alone. It cannot be simply brought into court and shown to the jury. All exhibits must be identified by a witness under oath who can give certain facts which tie the exhibit into the case.

An exhibit must meet the same tests as testimonial evidence. It must be relevant, material and competent. And the courts are careful to prevent an unfair advantage to be gained by one side or the other through the use of exhibits. It must be clearly established through sworn testimony that the exhibit has not been doctored or changed in any material way since the event which involved it in the fact situation concerned.

For example, the Courts generally hold that anything which would be allowed to be described in words may be shown by a photograph, but a witness must testify that the photograph truly and accurately shows the scene as he saw it when the photograph was taken. Also in cases involving accident injuries or cases of criminal violence, such as murder, the Court may not allow unduly gory pictures unless they have some probative value other than simply showing the extent of the defendant's violent handiwork.

The Courts feel that such vivid photographic displays often tend to excite the passions of juries to such an extent that they will be inflamed and prejudiced against the defendant and will not consider any mitigating factors in his favor, or any failure in proof of the charges against him. However, such pictures are often introduced to show the identity of the deceased, or to show the extent and location of the impact in an accident case, or some other relevant issue.

Testimony is not given by merely turning a witness loose in the presence of a stenographer. It takes the form of questions and answers. A deposition is merely the preserved testimony of a witness. It is given under oath, as is testimony in open court, and may be taken in a lawyer's office with attorneys for both sides present. Generally, the rules of direct and cross-examination apply also to depositions.

Besides the preservation of testimony, depositions have another important function. They are used for what lawyers call "discovery." Discovery is a search for facts regarding a case. Great latitude is allowed to the opposing lawyer in "fishing" for weak spots in the witnesses' testimony. In lawsuits involving a lot of money, where the expense is justified, depositions are often taken for this purpose alone. Should such a deposition ever be presented in the trial because of the unavailability of the witness, then the fishing expedition parts of it, probably containing many irrelevant and immaterial matters, would be screened out and not read to the jury.

Depositions have another important aspect. Once the witness has made a certain statement upon deposition, he must adhere to it. If he changes his story, the deposition can be brought in to "impeach" him; that is, to discredit his testimony because he changed his story.

Other discovery methods are to submit a "Request for Admissions" as to some pertinent facts or "Written Interrogatories" to the opposing side. These must be answered in writing under oath, and answers given bind the side giving them. These methods are often used in cases in which the litigants cannot afford the expense of depositions. Also, "Motions for a More Definite Statement" or for a "Bill of Particulars" are often used to garner additional facts as to the contentions of the opposing side. The courts encourage all legitimate discovery methods short of outright harassment of the other side.

The Smiths' lawyer might well seize on the fact that Fleeson, before he had consulted his lawyer, had stated that he would return the money. A "Request for Admissions" is prepared and mailed to Fleeson's lawyer requiring Fleeson personally, under oath in writing, either to admit or deny that he had stated, "I will have my secretary mail you a check and you'll have it in the morning." A truthful answer would constitute a damaging admission that, at least at one time, Fleeson acknowledged owing the money.

Now let us assume that a trial date has been reserved by the Court for *Smith vs. Fleeson*. The attorneys have hopefully informed the Court that the trial should be completed in two days. The Smiths have demanded a jury, as is their right. The court probably has one or two other trials scheduled to begin the same day. Obviously, it cannot try more than one case at a time, but cases are so often settled on the court house steps or continued for one reason or another that it is necessary to overload the docket in order to assure full usage of court time.

Jurors, witnesses and litigants are often frustrated and chagrined at being summoned to court and then told that the trial has been put off to another day. They may have taken time off from work, causing them to lose income. But these misfortunes are difficult to avoid. Many different people are involved in almost every trial and the sickness or unavailability of any one of them may cause delay. A previous trial might run longer than expected, imposing on other trials. Most lawyers have heavy trial schedules themselves, and they must be accommodated fairly.

As a result of all these factors, the management of a court trial docket is one of the most agonizing administrative tasks that has ever beset mankind. There is no real solution except a continual willingness to get down to business on the part of all concerned.

If, by chance, everything happens to be shipshape on the morning of the trial, the Smiths arrive and meet their lawyer in the court house. They seat themselves in the court room and await the arrival of the judge. At the appointed hour, probably nine o'clock, the bailiff's gavel sounds and he loudly states, "Everyone rise."

Whereupon the judge, black robe flowing, strides into the court room and places himself behind the bench.

While the judge stands momentarily, the bailiff announces, "This division of the District Court is now in session. Please be seated."

The clerk loudly calls the case, "Smith versus Fleeson, Case Number 60894."

The judge asks, "Are the parties ready?"

"The plaintiffs are ready for trial, your Honor," says the Smiths' lawyer.

"Defendant is ready, your Honor," says Fleeson's lawyer.

"Call the jury," says the judge.

The prospective jurors, possibly twenty-five in number, are at this time seated in the spectator portion of the court room.

The clerk shakes a small box containing tickets with the names of the jurors on them. He draws a ticket and calls out the name of the juror chosen. "Mrs. Priscilla Butler, please take Seat Number One in the jury box."

Mrs. Butler rises and is directed to the first seat by the bailiff. The clerk repeats this lottery process until fourteen prospective jurors have been called.

The case will be tried by six jurors, which is the usual number for civil cases. Each side has four "peremptory" challenges, that is, they can excuse four jurors without stating any cause. This is why fourteen jurors are originally called.

The jurors are then asked to rise and raise their right hands for an oath, as follows:

"You and each of you do solemnly swear by the ever living God that you will true answers make to such interrogatories as shall be propounded to you, touching upon your competency to serve as jurors in the cause now on trial before this court."

The jury is examined by both lawyers and the judge to determine if any must be excused for "cause." This is called the *voir dire*, a term meaning "to speak the truth."

After both sides have passed the fourteen jurors for cause, the peremptory challenges are then exercised. Beginning with the plaintiff, each, in turn, excuses four jurors, leaving the jury of six.

Making the correct choices as to jurors may be the most important thing done in the trial. And yet it is largely guesswork. Jury questioning does not afford a good opportunity really to get acquainted with the people. The procedure is formal and public, causing most jurors to be rather stiff and unexpressive about their attitudes. The juror who does open up by asking questions or volunteering some statement becomes a likely candidate for challenge because he or she invariably says something to worry one side or the other.

The six jurors are then sworn to try the case:

"You and each of you do solemnly swear that by the ever living God that you will well and truly try, and true deliverance make between Louise and George Smith and John J. Fleeson, and a true verdict render, according to the law and the evidence."

The Smiths' lawyer then gives his opening statement, which is supposed to be nonargumentative, merely an outline of what he intends to prove by the evidence. Fleeson's lawyer may then give his opening or may reserve it until it is his turn to put on evidence.

The testimony is then presented and the exhibits identified for introduction into evidence. Each witness is then required to take an oath or affirmation, as follows:

"You do solemnly swear by the ever living God (affirm) that the testimony you are about to give in the cause now on trial before this Court, shall be the truth, the whole truth and nothing but the truth?"

Probably the only witnesses will be the parties themselves and the store owners. The lawyer calling a witness conducts direct examination and the opposing lawyer cross-examines. After all of the evidence is in, both sides "rest" their case.

With the aid of the lawyers, the judge prepares the instructions of law, and reads them to the jury. Then the attorneys give their jury summations, the plaintiffs' lawyer first, then defendant's lawyer, and finally rebuttal by plaintiffs' lawyer. After the summations, the jury retires in custody of the bailiff. When they have all agreed on a verdict, they ring a buzzer and are returned to court.

The judge says, "Ladies and gentlemen, have you agreed upon a verdict?"

The foreman says, "We have, your Honor."

The judge, "Kindly hand it to the bailiff."

The bailiff then hands it to the judge and he reads it in open court. At no point have George and Louise felt less confident of victory.

However, the verdict reads, "We, the jury, find the issues herein joined for the plaintiffs, and assess the amount owing in the sum of $3000."

/s/ Henry Carver
Foreman

Thus ends the trial. You see, the judge is the referee, the jury is the fact finder, the lawyers are the advocates, the litigants are the contenders, the witnesses provide the facts, the clerk keeps the records of the court, the reporter records the entire trial, and the bailiff helps keep order.

Few trials are as simple as this one. Usually, many more involved issues are present. But the foregoing is a basic outline which holds true in all trials.

Chapter Three

TWELVE GOOD AND TRUE

We have examined a court case from the viewpoint of the litigants. Now let us look through the eyes of a juror.

Dorothy Bender is a housewife in her early forties. She has two daughters, age 16 and 14. Her husband, Carl, is an engineer employed by Twentieth Century Construction, Inc. Dorothy was a government clerk prior to her marriage and for three years afterward. She has not been employed since then and has devoted her life to homemaking with a sprinkling of community activity in the P.T.A. and Girl Scouts. She still remembers the principles she was taught in high school civics because this has been her only formal exposure to government study. She believes in the duty of a citizen to vote, pay taxes and obey the law.

When Dorothy receives a jury questionnaire, it is reminiscent of that memorable day when a bona fide market researcher came to her door to probe in depth about her home world and the color of soap boxes. "Well, they finally got to me." Dorothy Bender is a registered voter, she owns a house and a car with her husband. She is a taxpayer, having filed joint state income tax returns with him. Carl's name appears in the telephone book and he is in the City Directory, a commercially prepared volume supposedly containing the names and occupations of all residents. All or some of these sources are utilized by the Jury Commission of her county in selecting jurors.

The Commission is required by statute to maintain a "wheel," exactly what the name implies, and which looks like the object they cart on stage for bank night at the movies. Periodically, the Commission scans the voting list or the City Directory and draws every tenth or twelfth name. They first note the occupation of the individual and, if the person is an attorney or a volunteer fireman, or the wife or an employee of an attorney, or some other category excluded by law, they then go to the next name, and continue on down the list. To each of the people so selected, they send a jury questionnaire, or a request to come in for a personal interview.

The selector takes great care to avoid any distinction based upon nationality, race, creed, color, religion, economic status, place of residence within the city, or any other factor which might be considered unfair or discriminatory to any person, group or class of persons. The basic underlying principle of chance selectivity is scrupulously maintained.

The questionnaire received by Dorothy Bender contains 23 questions ranging from her name, address, present occupation and age, to her hearing ability, whether or not she is opposed to the American form of government, and if she has ever been convicted of a felony. She fills out the questionnaire and mails it in, expecting to achieve immediate status as a purveyor of justice in some important and fascinating legal "who done it." But she still has a long way to go.

The Commission reviews her answers to see if there is any reason why she could not serve. If she appears qualified, her name is typed on a small card, which is folded shut and then placed in the wheel. It contains the names of approximately one percent of the population, and is kept in a locked vault. On the wheel itself there are three hefty padlocks, each with separate keys which are in the possession of three different people, designated by statute as the presiding judge, the jury commissoner, and the county clerk. All of these officials must be present when the jury wheel is opened, and the wheel is so constructed that no names can be placed in or removed from it without all three padlocks being unlocked. In addition, sealing wax may be utilized to prove that unauthorized entry has not been made.

Why are these precautions stipulated? Because once the names are placed in the wheel, the people named are then distinct from the rest of the inhabitants. They are the potential deciders of all legal controversies in the community for the statutory "life of the wheel," which may be six months, one year or some other period of time as set by law.

Many of the cases will be relatively unimportant, but there is the constant possibility that some really big cases will come up concerning life or death or millions of dollars in property. One maxim in law is that when the stakes are high the noises are loud. The size of a case doesn't change the principles, but more things will be explored with more energy by more people when the outcome is extremely important to someone. When much is involved, man is capable of infinite ingenuity.

Periodically, the presiding judge of the court appears in the jury commission office at an appointed hour. He, the jury commissioner, and the city clerk ceremoniously enter the vault and crank the wheel. They then open it and draw out the names of as many jurors as they anticipate will be needed during the upcoming jury term, usually two weeks in duration. Let us assume that Dorothy is among the lucky "winners." Her name is printed on a jury list and she is summoned to appear in court.

The summons is either sent by Certified Mail, Return Receipt Requested, or is personally served by Sheriffs' Officers of the county. The summons is an order of the court which Dorothy must obey unless she arranges in advance with the judge or commission to be excused for some good cause. The few individuals who do choose to ignore summonses may be arrested and penalized for doing so.

Dorothy appears in Court as directed, but not without first having talked things over with friends and acquaintances who may have had jury experience or whose second cousin's next door neighbor was locked up on that sensational murder case last fall. She wouldn't go without having a general idea of what she was in for. They tell her to be prepared for the old Army game of hurry up and wait, and hope, for her sake, that she won't draw that creepy lawyer they had who talked so long that he forgot what he had said at the beginning so he had to say it all over again. A typical reaction is, "I wouldn't volunteer to do it again very soon, but I'm glad I went through it for the experience, and I learned a lot."

Dorothy finds herself in a group of 100 or more jurors answering roll call administered by an elderly chap who looks as if he undoubtedly has political connections. After that, the man she had been summoned to see, Judge White, presents himself, robe and all, behind the bench and delivers some words of greeting with a volubility indicating that he may have said the same thing before.

Judge White explains that our jury system is the keystone of American jurisprudence, that jurors perform essential services which only they can perform, and that the time they spend in jury service, for small remuneration, could not be better spent in the service of their nation and community. He further explains that criminal and civil cases are scheduled for trial and that the group will be divided up and assigned to different courts for the day. After Judge White's remarks, the jury clerk calls out the names of forty-five jurors, Dorothy Bender included, and directs them to follow him. They comply and are escorted to another court room designated District Court, Criminal Division, and are seated in the spectators portion.

A trial is held which follows the same basic pattern as described in other chapters of this book. The title of the case is "People of the State versus John Caleb and Harold Downey." The charge is burglary and conspiracy to commit burglary. It seems that in the early morning hours of a certain day a tavern was burglarized, tripping off a silent alarm. Before the police arrived, the burglars had escaped, having taken a small amount of change from the cash register and an unknown quantity of cigarettes from behind the bar.

The defendants were arrested as they were walking on the street about an hour later. They had about $7 worth of change in their possession, and each had a full carton of cigarettes of the brand taken in the burglary. They were booked as suspects and questioned by the police. They denied any implication in the burglary, stating that the cigarettes had been given to them by a man they had met about a half-hour earlier, whom they had never seen before and could only vaguely describe. In due course, they were charged with the crime of burglary in court and their case had come to trial. During the trial, they both made the same assertion they had given the police—that they were not guilty and had nothing to do with the burglary, and that the items they had on their possession were innocently acquired.

Dorothy finds herself burdened with the task of deciding the fate of these men. It is not easy for her. The story they tell could very well be true. It sounds a little unusual that a stranger would walk up and present them with two cartons of cigarettes, and they failed completely to describe this benefactor, but still if they actually were guilty, why would they be walking around on the street where they could be so easily picked up? Is it fair to convict these two boys of a felony on that type of evidence? Dorothy doesn't know, but after a difficult period of deliberation with her fellow jurors, they return a verdict.

To the criminal courts, nothing could be more typical or routine than this case, and yet to Dorothy, and to John Caleb and Harold Downey, it is anything but routine. To the defendants it means everything. It means whether they will be convicted felons or not, unless of course, they happened to be confirmed ne'er do-wells, in which case, sooner or later they will be convicts anyway.

To Dorothy it is a world and a responsibility apart from her daily life. In a sense it is her finest hour as a citizen, for what she is doing concerns the very foundation of government. It is easy to suppose that we could have democracy without the jury system; that we could have these cases decided by a panel of judges or by a group of professional jurors or arbitrators. It would be much cheaper and less cumbersome. It would save untold man hours of time spent by the jurors themselves, and by the courts in administering our jury system, and we could show, too, that the results would be much the same. Given a thousand cases, the professional jurors would do about the same thing in 980 of them as would the lay jurors, and it could be said that a professional jury would be less inclined to make errors, to be carried away by irrelevancies and emotional arguments, to be distracted and confused by complicated instructions of law. But let us hope that this never happens.

Simplicity is worth while when it can be achieved without sacrifice of principle, but the day our jury system is replaced with some easy alternative is the day that democracy and freedom will die. Virtually every law suit, be it criminal or civil, contains important factual elements which someone must decide.

The law of evidence is founded on the most disarming of principles, that the jury will hear facts and facts alone. But it becomes immensely complex in all of its various applications. Rules of evidence make or break most lawsuits. These rules are not found neatly and conveniently bound in a small, precise volume. Rather, they run all through the thousands and tens of thousands of law books containing rules and exceptions to the rules, and exceptions to the exceptions to the rules. Few lawyers and judges consider themselves evidence technicians or claim to know all the rules in advance as to every situation which may arise. Rather, they try to cling to reason and truth as a trial proceeds.

One of the fundamental rules of evidence is that a witness will not be allowed to give hearsay. Hearsay is second-hand information. Suppose your next-door neighbor told you that the man across the street slapped his wife. You ask her how she knows this and she says that Mrs. Gridley, next door to her, told her so. Your next question is: How does Mrs. Gridley know? It seems that the lady who got slapped told her so. Could you then be asked to get up in court, under oath, and say that the man across the street had slapped his wife? No. You didn't see it and you have no way of knowing that it is true. Your information is not only second-hand but, in this instance, it is fourth-hand. Could your next-door neighbor swear to the fact? No. She didn't see it either. Her information is third-hand. Could Mrs. Gridley swear that the man slapped his wife? Not unless he saw it, because she heard it from someone else. Her information is second-hand and is hearsay just as surely as yours is. If the man slapped his wife when only the two of them were in a position to see what happened, then there would be just two people in the world who could testify to that fact, the man and his wife. They are the only people who know of this of their own knowledge, who were able to perceive the event by utilization of their own senses.

Say that you, your next-door neighbor and Mrs. Gridley were all standing on your front lawn, talking, and that while you were there you heard a scream from the house across the street and immediately the lady ran out and came over to you. She displayed a fresh bruise on her cheek and her glasses were broken. All three of you then could testify as to just what you saw and heard, that is, you heard the scream and you saw her in this injured condition. Could you testify that the man slapped his wife? No. You did not see that.

The rule excluding hearsay recognizes that a story takes on a bit of the character of the teller each time it is told and wanders further away from the truth. It also recognizes the impossibility of cross-examining somebody who is stating only hearsay.

Cross examination is immensely important for the jury. Why? Because it requires the witness to support his testimony with sound reason and logic when faced with the penetrating questions of the cross-examining attorney. And the only sure way to contend successfully with the cross examiner is to give truth and more truth in answer to his questions. But if hearsay were allowed, the cross examiner would be helpless. The witness could fearlessly make some bland statement as to a supposed fact and then neatly sidestep all further inquiry.

The cross examiner has a fertile field in which to uncover inconsistencies and untruths. In some instances, it might well be argued that the jurors do not need the protective hand of the court to exclude hearsay for them because they, as reasonable people, should be able to spot hearsay as well as the judge and disregard it as worthless. But unfortunately, this is not true as a general rule because hearsay takes some very insidious forms. It has a way of cloaking itself in respectability, requiring the trained mind of a judge to distinguish between it and direct proof.

One can, for example, readily discern the danger if detectives or other investigative officers were allowed merely to present their neatly drafted reports in court without presenting themselves as witnesses and without bringing the actual witnesses to the crime into the courtroom to stand examination under oath. The determination of guilt or innocence of an accused would thereby be transferred from the courtroom to the street or to the detective bureau of the police department. This could never be allowed. The witnesses themselves must be in court.

We do not place a detective on the witness stand to say, "I interviewed Henry Smith and showed him a picture of the defendant. He said that the defendant robbed him." Quite the contrary. We have Henry Smith in court to point out the defendant in person and say, "That man robbed me." The defense attorney then goes through his cross examination, "How do you know it was that man?" "How were you able to see his face?" "How far away from you was he?" "What was he wearing?" "Had you ever seen him before?" "How long did you look at him?" "Describe the clothes he was wearing." and so forth.

Printed matter, such as appears in a newspaper, is an extremely dangerous form of hearsay. This type of thing is never allowed in a trial to prove the facts it may purport to state. The fact that somebody had it printed does not make it credible. Yet many people have a tendency to believe some alleged fact just because it appears in print. Perhaps they think there must be some law requiring everything printed to be true. There are libel laws, of course, but these have only a limited scope and by no means give news material an infallible status.

In one way or another, you and I rely on hearsay every hour of our lives. We could not possibly keep in touch with the world by the direct use of our own senses alone. What we read or hear about world events is purely hearsay to us. Even the warning label on a bottle containing poison is hearsay, and the word we receive that Congress has passed a certain law which we must obey is hearsay. Even your birth date is hearsay to you.

Why is it that we are expected to heed hearsay and govern ourselves accordingly in the conduct of our everyday lives, yet the courts will not allow it? It is because courts are directly concerned with narrow factual issues which must be absolutely reliable.

The entire body of American law is based on the jury system. Case after case concerns some point of evidence or procedure in handling the jury, some decision as to what the jury should or should not be allowed to do and hear. The most common problem of a judge is not to decide the ultimate merits of a case, but rather to decide when and how the issues should be put to a jury.

The judge decides the law and the jury decides the facts. This is a definite and clearly established division of authority and responsibility, and yet it has not always been so clear.

Although the jury as adopted in the United States Constitution was at that time fundamentally what we have today, there still continued argument that, particularly in criminal cases, the jury should determine the law as well as the facts. This proved unsatisfactory in practice because the jury found itself befuddled by lawyers' arguments on intricate questions of law which they by training background and experience, were in no position to decide. It's hard enough for them to understand the law as presented by the judge and then apply the facts to it. It was not until the 1880's that the United States Supreme Court finally and thoroughly disposed of the contention that juries should also determine the law. It is still the rule in some states, particularly in Justice of the Peace courts, that the jury will determine both issues, but this anachronism, as well as the Justice of the Peace courts themselves, is fast becoming obsolete.

Historically, a jury verdict must be unanimous. This rule has been modified in some places, allowing nine of the twelve jurors to rule. It has often been argued that requiring a unanimous verdict necessarily places the jurors in a position of compromising their principles, but nevertheless, a unanimous verdict is by far the most prevalent rule.

A criminal jury is a jury of twelve, but this number may be reduced in size by agreement of the parties; should they want to be tried by a lesser number, this will be done and the verdict will be legal. In civil cases, the most common number used is six, although a greater number may be requested by one side or the other upon deposit of the fees for the extra jurors by the party requesting them. Minor criminal offenses are often tried by a jury of three. Strange as it may seem, the number in the jury appears to make very little predictable difference in the outcome of a case. Lawyers who have experimented with the use of different sizes of juries can seldom make confident assertions that this or that number will be most favorable for any particular type of case.

One fortunate thing about our juries today is that we call upon the female population. This was not always so, and it opens up a fertile field of good, available and interested jurors. It is unfortunate that some of the most qualified men, the heads of businesses or professional men, will oftentimes manage to get themselves excused because of their heavy duties and responsibilities. This sometimes gives a jury an imbalance, where the people who don't have anything better to do are the ones who are called upon to make weighty decisions, and the most highly qualified classifications are not represented.

You may have heard the expression "Ignorance of the law is no excuse." This is more than an expression. It is actually a very clearly established rule of law which precludes, for example, a defendant in a criminal case from coming into court and avoiding criminal responsibility by stating, "I didn't know any better." And by the same token, it prevents a person from avoiding his legal responsibilities to his fellow men in civil cases by making the excuse that he did not realize what his duties were. The rationale of this rule is quite obvious. People must be held to some standard of responsibility as to their conduct, and this cannot be made dependent upon their success in pleading ignorance of what that responsibility is. Mental inacapacity to know right from wrong is recognized as a defense to a crime, but unvarnished ignorance is not a defense.

The universal test of knowledge and of conduct is that a person must know and do what an ordinarily reasonable and prudent person would do under the circumstances. This test includes knowledge of the law.

"Ignorance is no excuse" takes on an interesting quirk in the case of jurors. As Dorothy Bender drives down to the courthouse, she is charged with knowing the law. If, the day before, the Mayor signed an ordinance passed by the City Council that it is illegal to make a right turn at a red light, changing the law that had existed for years before allowing such a turn, she is charged with knowing this the minute it becomes law, whether she actually knows it or not. Carrying this to its logical conclusion, we may say that since she does not know all the law applying to the case of "People of the State versus John Caleb and Richard Downey" she would, therefore, be incapable of serving. But this is not the case. When she walks into the courtroom and becomes a prospective juror, she is not expected to know the law surrounding the case at trial; in fact, it is better if she does not know it, because then she will have an open mind, enabling her to follow the law as decided and given by the court. So ignorance of the law is no excuse for jury service.

Strangely enough, often the most intelligent and eager juror will inadvertently get himself excused by his deep thinking. It is perhaps a sad commentary that a really profound thinker should be rejected, but let us examine an exchange which might take place:

Attorney (to prospective juror): Now, sir, you understand the defendant must be proven guilty beyond a reasonable doubt?

Juror: What is reasonable?

Attorney: It is a word presumed to have a universally understood meaning.

Juror: That is a fallacy. Are you applying the subjective or objective test to the word?

Attorney: I hadn't thought about it, but I assume it would be an objective test.

Juror: I doubt if there is such a thing. Reasonable is only what every man thinks it is.

Attorney: Well, sir, do you feel that you can follow the Court's instruction which will state that while you are not to find the defendant guilty if you entertain a reasonable doubt of his guilt, you are not to search for a doubt?

Juror: What is a doubt?

Attorney: Well, that is a question in your mind which gives you pause.

Juror: Everything gives me pause. I am a very cautious man. I pause not because of doubts, necessarily, but to analyze and examine the situation.

Attorney: Do you consider yourself a reasonable and prudent man, sir?

Juror: You are dealing in a fiction. Reasoning is different in each person, depending upon his background, experience and intelligence. Kant pointed that out very clearly in his "Critique of Pure Reason."

Judge: (impatiently) All we are trying to find out, sir, is if you think you can be a fair and impartial juror and follow the instructions of law.

Juror: Your Honor, I would try to, but I am a purist, and if a proposition is put to me that I do not agree with, then I do not feel bound to accept it.

Judge: The juror will be excused. Call the next juror.

Whether this man is really the most profound and intelligent person on the scene, or whether he is engaging himself in a fanciful pretense of intellectuality, no one in the courtroom will ever find out, because the courts do not have time to indulge in mere mental exercise. It is clear why an experienced judge would excuse this individual because he has seen through the years that juries, by and large, render reasonable and proper verdicts; but those that depart from reasonableness are juries which have been carried away by some irrelevant point not directly related to the true merits of the case. Skilled lawyers in their advocacy often emphasize small points, out of proportion to the really important ones. It is the duty of the opposing attorney to clarify the issues, and it is the duty of the jury to sift the evidence as reasonable people, not necessarily as profound people, and to do substantial justice. In fact, it could well be said that one of the most common mistakes of juries is attempting to be too profound about their verdict.

In criminal cases, for example, juries do not decide the total justice of the case. They do not ordinarily decide the penalty. If they try to be profound by supposing what the penalty will be, they are going outside their scope of responsibility and they are, necessarily, speculating because, since they are not to decide this issue, they are given no information about it.

Jurors are held to the same degree of respect, honor and truthfulness in their relation to the court as are all other people. The jurors are given an oath before they are examined by the attorneys and by the court. In this oath they solemnly swear that they will "true answers make to such interrogatories as may be propounded to them bearing upon their qualification to serve as jurors in the cause at hand." Should they then lie in answer to questions, they could be charged with perjury, just as a witness is subject to perjury; and perjury is a serious crime designated as a felony with a possible penalty of imprisonment in the penitentiary. Should a juror conduct himself capriciously or with open disrespect to the court, he can be held in contempt. Contempt is the power of a court to enforce its own orderly processes and to maintain its dignity. Should one interfere with these processes, the judge will then find the person in contempt.

For example, let us assume that a man is called on the panel of prospective jurors to try an important criminal case. After undergoing a tedious morning in the courtroom, and while the jurors are out for the lunch hour, he is overheard to say: "This whole thing stinks. You can tell that guy is guilty just by looking at him. Why don't they hang him from a tree and let us get out of here." It would be the duty of fellow jurors who may have overheard this remark to report it to the judge. The judge would then call this juror into chambers and inquire as to his statement. If the judge became convinced that he had actually said this, the juror would then be held in contempt for subverting the processes of the court and offending its dignity. This juror would likely find himself serving a sentence in jail and paying a substantial fine. Such a remark might also cause the judge to declare a mistrial in the case if it were felt that the juror's remarks might have contaminated the panel with unfair and improper ideas. When a mistrial is declared, all of the jurors are excused and the case is set over for commencement of an entirely new trial before a different group of jurors at a different time.

When a jury is selected to try a case, they take another solemn oath. The jurors all rise together, raise their right hand and solemnly swear that they "will well and truly try and true deliverance make between the parties on trial and will deliver a verdict according to law and the evidence." Should a juror wilfully ignore or disregard this oath, he could be held in contempt.

What would constitute a violation of this oath? Fortunately, this question seldom arises because few jurors are obtuse enough to violate it openly. Obviously, assuming a stand regarding the merits of the case, even though it may be directly contrary to the opinion of all the other jurors and the judge, would not be a violation of this oath. Every juror is entitled, in fact obligated, to arrive at his honest opinion.

Let us refer again to the case on which Dorothy Bender served —*People of the State vs. Caleb and Downey*. Suppose that the jury went into deliberation and that one of the men on the jury made this statement in the jury room: "I don't think the policemen are telling the truth. I don't believe the bar owner, either. I don't even believe that this place was burglarized, and therefore I will not find these men guilty of anything." This statement would in no sense be a violation of the oath because here the juror is passing upon the credibility of the witnesses and the merits of the proof, which he is entitled to do. But assume, instead, that this same juror makes the following statement: "I don't care who is telling the truth and who isn't. I don't believe in cigarettes and I don't believe in bars, and I'm not going to find anybody guilty of burglary for stealing some cigarettes from a bar." Should the juror persist in this view, Dorothy and the other jurors would be entitled to report this attitude and these remarks to the judge, in which case the juror making the remark could be held in contempt and could be fined and imprisoned for violating his oath wherein he promised to "render a true verdict based on the law and the evidence."

A jury room has a very definite sanctity about it and it is extremely rare that any inquiry whatsoever is made as to what went on during the deliberations. This is a remarkable thing. At all other stages of the trial, the jury is closely supervised by the judge. Yet at what is perhaps the most important stage, the deliberation, wherein they decide upon their verdict, they are totally unsupervised. For example, the judge tells them that the first thing they must do is pick a foreman, but he does not spoonfeed them by telling them how. Jurors are presumed to be reasonably intelligent people, and part of this is knowing how to pick a group leader in some acceptable way. There are no particular rules for picking a foreman as a foreman is always deemed as necessary. Virtually all Americans have a natural understanding of the rudiments of democratic group action.

Jurors are carefully instructed that during the trial they are not to discuss the case with anyone until they go into deliberation. After they have rendered their verdict, they may discuss it with anybody they like, but they are not required to do so if they choose not to. Many times lawyers like to talk things over with a juror after the case is over in order to build their professional skill by seeing what mistakes they may have made during the trial. By and large, jurors are a bit wary of this practice, although there is no real reason why they should be; there is nothing wrong in it either from the standpoint of the juror or the lawyer.

Juries are sometimes confined during the entire trial, from the moment they step into the jury box until they render a verdict in open court. This practice is usually reserved only for capital cases, that is, where the possible penalty imposed would be a death sentence or life imprisonment in the penitentiary. It would not usually be done in a civil case. However, the judge has the discretion to order confinement in most any case should the circumstances require. If jury confinement is ordered in a civil case, the parties must pay the dormitory cost and the meals for the jury. The reason for confinement is to assure that the jury will not be subjected to attempts at improper influence during the trial, and such danger usually exists only in large, important or sensational cases.

The term "confined" does not mean literally that. It means that the jury is at all times kept together under the supervision of the bailiffs and not allowed to intermingle with the general populace. They go to meals together at public restaurants but are not allowed to speak to anyone except their fellow jurors. They give their meal orders to the bailiff and the bailiff communicates with the waiter. They sleep in the jury dormitory. They cannot communicate with their family and friends by telephone or otherwise, and any messages they want to give to their family are transmitted by the bailiff. All conversation they have among themselves must be based on everything or anything but the case, and the only time they are allowed to discuss the case even among themselves is after they have gone into deliberation. The bailiffs are charged with the duty of attending to the conduct of the jurors in this regard.

Overall, jury service is not an onerous citizenship duty because its burden is spread so thin, and it would be unusual to find an individual who had spent more than one month during his entire life as a juror. Yet, in terms of numbers, more people are involved in jury duty than in any other lay involvement in the courts.

The jury system is of great educational value. It is an active participation in the process of government. The ordinary citizen will pay his taxes and vote; he may even contact a representative about some proposed legislation; he may rise and speak at a town meeting, or write a letter to the local newspaper referring to some governmental issue. He seldom however utilizes his whole person in a governmental activity as he does when he becomes a juror. Here, he is making a decision for the government rather than trying to tell somebody else what it should be. Most of us are completely preoccupied with our own little world of personal activities and survival. Yet as jurors we are confronted with a solemn duty to decide something independent of ourselves. Though perhaps few jurors would admit it, this has the makings of a most healthful and satisfying action. A juror cannot escape the conclusion that, "Here I am, and I must be good for something or I wouldn't have been chosen to decide this worrisome problem. It makes not a particle of difference to my little world what the result is, but I have a regard for truth and justice, and I am going to do the best I can."

Here we have a true personal fulfillment for the individual juror. And this is certainly the average reaction, as most people want to do the right thing. But herein lies the real hardship of jury service. One can easily forget about the inconvenience and the loss of time, but the compromise of strongly held principle is a difficult experience to go through. Necessarily, because the verdict must be unanimous, and because there will always be a difference of opinion to begin with, somebody is going to have to concede some point.

Any lawyer has seen juries walk into their jury room, unworried, even jaunty, happy that the tedious presentation of evidence and long-winded oratory by the lawyers are finally ended. Hours later, these same people drag out of the jury room, harried and mean, worried and cross, bleary-eyed, yet with a stalwartness and strength about them. They have argued and fought for what they believe. They have pleaded and cajoled and, perhaps most difficult of all, they have listened and tried to see the viewpoint of others; finally they have resolved to do a certain thing that they can and will live with in their own conscience. They have done this for somebody and something having nothing whatsoever to do with their personal problems. The satisfactions of this experience lie in its difficulty and selflessness.

What happens when a jury simply cannot agree upon a verdict? This is called a hung jury. One might think that, with the strict requirement that a verdict be unanimous, hung juries would be very common, but they are not. They result in much fewer than five percent of all jury trials. Juries see the large amount of time, trouble and expense involved in getting the case to them, and their natural inclination is to make every effort to do their part, no matter how difficult.

Deciding when a jury is hung is not entirely within their power. For example, a jury might start out in substantial agreement with the exception of one individual who announces with a great display of determination that he is going to do a certain thing and that nobody will ever change him. The other jurors might well be inclined to ring the buzzer and ask to be excused because they are in a hopeless deadlock. Whether or not to discharge the jury at that point is entirely within the discretion of the judge, and most judges require a jury to deliberate for many hours, perhaps days, before accepting their statement that there is no chance of a verdict. Some judges will give what is commonly called the "third degree" instruction in part as follows:

"On the other hand, if a majority are for acquittal, the minority ought seriously to ask themselves whether they may not reasonably, and ought not to, doubt the correctness of a judgment from which so many of their number dissent, and distrust the weight or sufficiency of that evidence which fails to carry conviction to the minds of their fellows.

"And, while at the last each juror must act upon his own judgment concerning the evidence in the case and not upon the judgment of his or her fellows, it is your duty, guided by the foregoing and by all of the instructions heretofore given in this case, to decide the case, if you can conscientiously do so.

"It is accordingly ordered by the court that you be returned to your jury room for further deliberation."

If a jury is actually deadlocked and cannot arrive at a verdict, then a mistrial is declared by the judge and the case retried.

There are as many types of jurors as there are people. Those with long experience close to jury trials can seldom state that they have ever seen a corrupt juror. It is a heartening commentary on American citizens that, almost without exception, juries are sincere and honest in what they do. Every judge and lawyer has had occasion violently to disagree with the jury's verdict, but it is seldom, indeed, when a jury displays a lack of integrity in its actions. Virtually all people have a consuming regard for justice, and the verdicts with which you and I might strongly disagree usually represent only a difference in opinion as to what is justice in a particular case.

Do you realize that you could be walking down the street one day and suddenly feel the tap of a deputy sheriff's finger on your shoulder? You turn around, and before you can say anything, you are asked the question: "Do you live in this County?" You answer, "Why, yes." The Deputy then very courteously says, "Come with me." You say, "What for?" He says, "You are on the jury." This is known as open venire.

Before jury selection procedures reached the sophistication we have today, this was the only method of selection. When a trial came up, the judge would direct the officers to go out on the street and bring in a given number of prospective jurors. Now it is seldom used, but is always available if needed.

Suppose, for example, that a court was in the process of choosing a jury for a rather important case which had been fully covered in the news media. One hundred and fifty jurors were called into the courtroom to be examined, but juror after juror was excused because they had to say in all honesty that they had formed an opinion as to the merits of the action and couldn't render a true verdict only on the evidence and the law presented in court. Near the end of the day, the panel of prospective jurors is exhausted. What does the judge do? He can order an open venire where jurors are picked up from the street under force of law. Naturally, the courts try to avoid this necessity because it is so disruptive of people's lives, but it is entirely legal and proper.

Very seldom are members of a petit jury allowed to interrogate any witness. The only people who ask questions of witnesses are the attorneys and occasionally the judge. The reason for this is that a juror, being untrained, might say something considered prejudicial to one side or the other, or might open the trial to hearsay or other improper evidence. Ordinarily, if a petit juror desires to question a witness, he is requested by the judge to put his question in writing so that the judge may examine it to determine whether or not it would be proper before it is actually said.

Our discussion has so far concerned juries called to try cases. This is known as the petit jury, as distinguished from the grand jury.

The grand jury is chosen from the same jury wheel, or it can be obtained "off the street" in an open venire, but it is quite a different body, with different functions to perform. The reason why it is called "grand," and why a jury called to try a case is called petit, is only because historically the grand jury consisted of a larger number than the petit jury. Today the grand jury is often no larger than the petit jury, the most common number being twelve, but in some places as many as twenty-three jurors comprise the grand jury.

A jury trial is public; grand jury hearings are secret. The grand jury is an investigative body which is empowered by law to return indictments against individuals who they feel are guilty of some crime. Grand jury hearings are usually conducted under supervision of a judge and the district attorney, but they are not bound by what the judge or the district attorney brings before them, and they make their own independent investigation of supposed criminal activities in the community. Their deliberations are in private. Usually a vote of three-fourths of the grand jury is sufficient to return an indictment, sometimes called a "true bill." If they decide not to indict, they return a "no bill" to the court.

"Returning an indictment" means presenting a criminal charge to the court. In this way they create a criminal case which must then, at a later time, be tried by a petit jury. The grand jury does not finally determine guilt or innocence, and need not be convinced beyond a reasonable doubt of the guilt of the accused. Rather, they need only find that there is probable cause to believe that the accused is guilty. The grand jury may hear witnesses in secret who must come and testify under oath, and the jurors themselves may examine the witnesses by their own questions.

An indictment has the same legal effect as an information, or a criminal complaint. It is nothing more or less than a charge, and the fact that an indictment has been returned is no proof that the crime actually has been committed.

The oath of a grand jury is as follows:

"You and each of you do solemnly swear that you will diligently inquire, and true presentment make of all such matters and things as shall be given you in charge or otherwise come to your knowledge, touching the present service: the counsel of the state, your own and your fellow men you shall keep secret unless called on in a court of justice to make disclosures: and you shall present no person through malice, hatred or ill will, nor shall you leave any person unpresented through fear, favor or affection, or for any reward or hope thereof, but in all your presentments you shall present the whole truth and nothing but the truth according to the best of your skill and understanding."

Secrecy is enforced to avoid harm to persons who may be investigated but not indicted. Grand juries have a very important historical purpose, which continues to be important as the years go on. Every County with a substantial population is usually required to have at least one grand jury impaneled per year, and the grand jury may stay in session for a period of months. During this time, they meet once a week or perhaps oftener.

The real reason for grand juries is to expose the administration of public affairs in the community to scrutiny by an impartial body of citizens. Informations, which have the same legal effect as indictments, may be returned by the district attorney alone on his signature or on the signature of his deputy. The periodic conferring of this great power on a group of citizens has a distinctly salubrious effect on the honesty and integrity of the public officials in the community. State and federal courts have their own jury systems, and some municipalities also have their own petit jury selection framework. A person, therefore, may be subject to call by all these levels of government.

The Honorable Harlan F. Stone, former Chief Justice of the United States Supreme Court, once said:

"Jury service is one of the highest duties of citizenship, for by it the citizen participates in the administration of justice between man and man and between government and the individual."

For jurors, lawyers, judges and all citizens, there is a world of real human fascination in our jury system. It is real and not imaginary— our finest expression of the dignity of man.

Chapter Four

SWEAR TO TELL THE TRUTH

Who is the most important person in a trial? Is it the judge? The lawyer? The defendant? The Plaintiff? A juror? It is none of these.

The most important person in a trial is a witness. Why? Because without a witness, there is no justice. A court cannot operate in a vacuum. It must have facts to go on. And the only source of facts is through a witness.

The day is December 20. The scene is a small neighborhood tavern. It is 3:00 o'clock in the afternoon. There are nine people in the place at that time, the bartender Ornus Bean, a waitress, and seven customers. Among the customers are an old-age pensioner named Clarence Hodgson and his wife. They are seated at the bar, having a glass of beer. A masked man enters the tavern with a gun. He orders everyone to stand at the back of the room. Clarence Hodgson, not realizing what is going on, slowly swings around on his barstool and mumbles, "Hey!" The robber shoots him. He falls to the floor and soon expires.

The robber proceeds, eventually locking up all the customers in a walk-in refrigerator, and absconding with money from the cash register and safe.

When the police arrive to interview the witnesses, they find that none of them can identify the robber because of his mask. To solve the crime, the police turn to other investigative means. They find a fresh tire track in the mud in the alley in back of the establishment.

They make a plaster cast and trace it to a certain tire recapping shop.

The coroner's pathologist performs an autopsy on the body of Clarence Hodgson. He removes the spent bullet from the body and turns it over to the police laboratory, where it is determined to be of a certain caliber. The police scan their gun purchase records to determine if any known dangerous criminals have purchased such a gun in the city within the past few months. They take the general description given by the patrons as to size and manner of the man, and study their files on convicts of known violent and dangerous tendencies to determine if any seem to fit the general description given.

The tire shop records show that one Perry Sty very recently purchased some retreads matching the description of the cast. He also fits the general description given by the customers, and is known to police as a parolee from the State penitentiary, having been twice convicted for crimes of violence.

It isn't much to go on, but the facts fit together well enough to justify an arrest. Perry Sty is picked up at his home, just a few blocks from the tavern. Except to deny that he robbed the tavern and killed the old-age pensioner, he refuses to say anything to the police.

The detectives conduct a line-up. They bring all of the tavern patrons, the waitress and Mr. Bean into the police building and place Perry Sty along with four or five other men on a brightly lighted stage behind a screen which prevents the subjects from looking out into the audience. The witnesses are asked if they see the man who robbed the tavern. They all say that Mr. Sty might be, but because the robber was masked, they cannot make any identification.

At the line-up, the detectives notice that Mr. Bean, the bartender, is very nervous, and they decide that he should be watched. The detectives assigned to this duty note that later that afternoon, while walking to his business establishment, Bean places a letter in a mail box. Time is running out on the police because they cannot hold Perry Sty indefinitely without making a charge. However, they hold him one more day.

The next morning, an anonymous letter arrives at the police

building containing no return address and bearing a city postmark. It is typewritten on a small piece of plain paper and states as follows: "Perry Sty did it." The police immediately go to Mr. Bean's home and ask to be admitted. Mr. Bean still displays the nervous tendencies shown before. The detectives ask if he has a typewriter. He says yes, and they ask to see it. After a quick comparison of the typing in the letter and the type produced by this typewriter, they know they have hit on something.

Under close questioning, Mr. Bean finally admits that he does recognize Perry Sty as the man who shot Clarence Hodgson, and that he recognized him the minute he walked in the tavern, as he had known him ever since Perry was a boy in the neighborhood. Why didn't he tell? The answer to that is fear. Ornus Bean is a law-abiding citizen. He runs his business. He does not want anything to upset his world. He is not overly bright. He has a limited social conscience. He knows that he is the only witness who can identify Perry Sty, and he remembers the vicious tendencies that Perry has shown ever since he has known him. He has a genuine fear that should he be the one to cause Perry Sty's conviction for this crime, and should the defendant ever get the opportunity, he, Ornus Bean, might very well be the next victim.

Mr. Bean does not have a thorough understanding of the processes of the law, but he has heard and read of instances in which people charged with crimes, even serious crimes such as murder, have later been allowed to go free on parole. He fears for himself and his family, and does not believe that he should take the entire burden on his shoulders of seeing that justice is done in this case, yet something prompted him to write the letter. How the police were to gain a conviction without his testimony, he didn't know nor care.

Ornus Bean is forced to testify in court against his wishes, and Perry Sty is convicted of murder and sent to the penitentiary for life. But if the police had not been able to uncover this witness, Perry Sty would have had to be released. And the crime would never be solved.

This instance is by no means rare. Consider its implications. Here, the entire dignity of the State as to this terrible crime rests on the shoulders of one individual, for the courts do not have any means whatsoever to produce their own fact material. They are dependent entirely upon witnesses.

Consider another case. Two cars collide at an intersection controlled by a traffic light. Each car contained only the driver; there were no passengers in either car. The accident occurred late at night; there were few people around. One of the drivers is killed, the other survives. The family of the deceased driver files a law suit against the other driver, claiming damages in the sum of many thousands of dollars for wrongful death. The surviving driver contends that the dead man went through a red light while he had a green light. If there is no other witness available, the defendant would win the case.

Suppose you saw this accident and knew that it was the defendant and not the deceased who ran the red light, and suppose you were the only disinterested witness. Consider how immensely significant your testimony would be. It would mean thousands upon thousands of dollars for the deceased's family, to which they are by justice entitled if the defendant was the negligent party in the accident.

Neither is this situation by any means rare. "Let George do it" is an indefensible attitude for an essential witness in a trial. But just as the role of the litigant and the juror has its frustrations, the role of the witness also contains many perplexing and aggravating elements. Most of these are due to the refusal of the processes of justice to fit into the real or imagined convenience of people.

We all know that satisfaction or dissatisfaction with a particular situation is a state of mind more than anything else, and the most disconcerting events are those that somehow do not fit into the preconceived pattern which we have mapped out for ourselves. People like Ornus Bean do exist, but the more common type of individual is the one who wants to be a witness and a good witness. Unfortunately, this person can clash with justice as seriously as Ornus Bean. Why? Because he does not understand the role of the witness.

Nature inclines us to want to control all things with which we are personally involved. A key witness in any case necessarily has an idea as to the justice of the case and, in spite of himself, desires a certain result. If he is a disinterested witness, without any stake in the outcome of the case, he will be less concerned than if he is the litigant; but even disinterested witnesses often allow their idea of the right or wrong of the case to carry them beyond the scope of their responsibility. Their duty is to tell the truth as they know it from use of their own five senses, no more and no less. They are to tell what they did, what they saw, what they heard. They are not to give their conclusions as to what occurred. Making conclusions as to the facts is the responsibility of the jury. They are not to be advocates for one side or another. That is the duty of the lawyers. And they are definitely not purveyors of the law. That is the job of the judge.

A lawyer doesn't choose his witnesses. The facts of life choose them for him, and he is stuck with them. They may be good, bad or indifferent, but he has to take them as he gets them. They may be stupid or smart, over-eager or under-eager, credible or incredible. Fate seldom places the best witness in a position to see all of the important transactions of a case. The more usual luck is to have the world's worst witness in a position to see everything that transpired. This is particularly true in criminal cases involving acts of violence, and it plagues the prosecution and the defense with equal frequency.

What makes a good witness? The answer to this question may be summed up in a single word—integrity. The dictionary definition of integrity is "honesty, sincerity, uprightness, wholeness, completeness, perfect condition, soundness." If you are trying to learn how to be a good witness, this tells you very little, because the word integrity and its definition contain only the most general guidance. Lawyers often try to school witnesses as to how to avoid typical mistakes. This is quite different from "coaching" a witness as to what to say. Coaching of that type is not only improper but impossible. The lawyer cannot change what a witness does or does not know about a case, and he does not try to do so. Neither can anything be done about the general personality of the witness, or his intelligence. As a result of these factors, all the lawyer can really hope to do is point out certain do's and don't's and, unfortunately, the accent is always on the negative.

"Don't chew gum; don't overdress; don't argue or become angry with opposing counsel; don't be flippant; don't memorize your story.

Don't cover your mouth with your hand; don't laugh or talk about the case in the halls or rest rooms of the courthouse; don't volunteer information not asked of you.

"Don't be a smart aleck; don't be cocky; don't try to analyze every question; don't be too pat; don't act nervous; don't lose your temper; don't ask the judge for advice; don't hedge; don't expect your attorney to help you answer a question.

"Don't look worried; don't mumble; don't exaggerate; don't give your answer until you've thought what you are saying; don't stumble and hesitate; don't answer the question unless you understand it; don't try to be an advocate; don't mimic the attorney; don't pull on your earlobe; don't scratch your nose; don't rub your eyes; don't frown; don't smile to make an impression; don't laugh; don't cry—if you can help it.

"Don't hold back, don't be cagey; don't be officious; don't be pretentious; don't be presumptuous; don't be silly; don't answer until the question is completed; don't try to anticipate the next question; don't say 'I imagine,'; don't say 'I guess,'; don't say 'You'll have to ask So and So,'; don't answer a question with a question.

"Don't wear a funny hat; don't wear your overcoat to the witness stand; don't complain; don't act shocked; don't try to outwit the attorney; don't volunteer answers; don't answer yes or no unless that is a complete answer to the question; don't answer a question 'Of course.'; don't answer a question 'Naturally,'; don't try to sneak an answer in; don't try to conjure up a look of contempt; don't appear disgusted; don't be pious; don't be coy; don't let your eyes wander.

"Don't shout; don't clear your throat—unless you have to; don't wear your best clothes; don't wear your worst clothes; don't forget what you are there for; don't ask for special favors; don't think about the fact that your testimony is being recorded. Don't stumble as you get in or out of the witness box; don't look downcast and worried as you leave the witness stand; don't look elated and triumphant as you leave.

"Don't be smug; don't shake your head in answer to questions; don't loiter around the courthouse; don't apologize for your testimony; don't answer a question starting with the words 'In my opinion,'; don't try to engage in a personality exchange with the opposing lawyer; don't display any prejudices; don't be jaunty;

don't try to engender sympathy; don't try to be a strategist; don't interrupt others; don't wear an unusual hairdo; don't shake your head as you leave the witness stand; don't stop and shake hands with anybody as you leave the courtroom; don't pull out a cigarette before you have left.

"Don't stop and speak with your lawyer in the jury's presence; don't throw up your hands in disgust; don't try to involve politics in your testimony; don't try to involve religion in your testimony; don't try to be somebody you are not. Don't fear to be yourself, don't leave the witness stand until you are told to do so. Don't put your tongue in your cheek; don't be tense; don't disobey the Court; don't be contemptuous; don't try to be a star witness; don't fear to be a witness, or refuse to be a witness. Above all, don't lie."

This free-form type of negative admonition could easily go on and on. It is remarkable because each and every one of these "don'ts" is a valid observation. Under a given circumstance, any one of these mistakes might be enough to destroy the credibility of a witness. Obviously, nobody could memorize all of these points and consciously be on guard against them. The witness would be so confused by "don't's" that he would forget the "do's." Most of all, though, he would forget the very simple reason why he is in court, which is to convey some information through the means of a truthful and honest answer to questions. Such a task can best be done simply.

Being a witness requires strength, the strength afforded by truth. The courtroom might be thought of as a big polygraph machine. A lie detector is an electrical device which records disturbances in the subject's pulse rate and nervous system while undergoing questioning. It has been shown that a person caught in a lie will, in spite of himself, cause some variance to show up on the machine. The results of polygraph machine tests are not admissible as evidence in courts because their effectiveness depends so much on the individual operator of the test, and because they are not sufficiently trustworthy. The analogy is made here only to show that oftentimes the eyes of the jury record involuntary quirks or twists in the actions of the witness which may belie his truthfulness. This is not to say that every time a witness scratches his nose or picks at his earlobe or does any of the other don't's which we have listed, he is necessarily being untruthful, but all of these things have a way of distracting from the testimony, and if they are done under certain situations, at a certain timing during the testimony, and in a certain manner, they might cause an unfavorable inference in the jurors' minds as to what the witness is saying.

This list is given here to show the futility of trying to bundle oneself up with all of the world's advice. The "don't's" are usually emphasized because the lawyer cannot re-do his witness, except perhaps to send him to the barber shop, or direct her to wash a particularly wild shade of rinse out of her hair. A lawyer can veto a flashy suit or an unusually low-cut dress; he can remove the dangling key chain and the blue-tinted hose by his well-meant suggestions. But he cannot correct idiosyncrasies, and he cannot change the general personality of any person. In fact, he would not want to, if he could, because a person's own basic personality is always the best on the witness stand.

The "do's" are much more important than the "don't's." Be truthful and straightforward; dress conservatively; pay attention to the oath, and say "I do" so that you can be heard; speak up to the members of the jury; be frank, open and aboveboard; be polite; listen carefully to the questions; create a mental picture of what you actually saw, and answer; be positive and definite when you can; relax; be your normal self, confident in the truth of what you are saying.

If you attend to these simple suggestions in the positive, the "don't's" will take care of themselves.

Surprisingly enough, the quality of a witness which is wrapped up in the term "integrity" does not align itself with any class or educational hierarchy. When lawyers become witnesses, they often do quite badly, especially when their testimony is being questioned in any way. They have trouble accepting the role of a witness. The lawyers' code of ethics strongly disfavors a lawyer becoming a witness in a case in which he is counsel. If he is personally in possession of the controverted facts in issue, he should withdraw from the case and allow another attorney to represent the client. But of course, lawyers are often witnesses to automobile accidents or other occurrences which place them in the category of any other witness.

Highly educated people or those in a position of power or leadership are sometimes less credible in their total presentation than are the humblest citizens. As a group, their nature leads them to want to control the proceeding, to decide it themselves and get it over with. Although lawyers like to think that they can judge in advance how a witness will stand up in court, and what effect tattoos or weird haircuts might have, they are often fooled in this respect. The best witness is the one who has, and shows he has, nothing to hide and no reason to lie.

You may not find this in the dictionary, but the most important ingredient of integrity as a witness is genuineness. Before you can be believed as a witness, the jury must see the genuine article that you are. This is particularly true for the witness who is also a party to the lawsuit. The fact that a person is suing or being sued does not in any sense disqualify him from being a witness. In fact, the parties are often the major witnesses because they know the most about the case.

A defendant in a criminal case may not be forced to testify, but he may if he chooses to do so. If he does not testify, the jury is then explicitly instructed that they are not to hold this fact against him and are to allow no implication as to his guilt or innocence to enter their minds because he did not testify. This is an anomaly of the law because it goes contrary to human understanding. As a matter of fact, silence may be taken to mean assent in other fields of law. If, for example, a person accuses another of causing an accident by not watching where he was going, and the accused individual says nothing, this may be taken as an admission of the truth of the charge made. But this rule does not apply to the accused in a criminal case because of the constitutional protection against self-incrimination—the so-called Fifth Amendment right.

If the jury were allowed to infer guilt by the exercise of this right, then there would be no such right. But whether the jury can actually follow the mandate of this instruction in their minds, no matter how they might try, is quite another question. Juries often become confused on this point. Some simply think, "If he didn't do it, why didn't he just say so." Others incline too far the other way and mistakenly read the instruction that they can't infer guilt even from proof. They credit the defendant by his silence with exculpatory remarks which he may or may not be able to produce in a believable way.

If the defendant does voluntarily choose to testify, he then becomes like any other witness in the case. He is subject to both direct and cross examination, and the jury must evaluate his testimony as to its truthfulness. In this instance, the jury is also entitled to consider the fact that the defendant has a great personal interest in the outcome of the case, and if they feel that this self-interest is coloring the defendant's testimony, they may take it only for what they feel it is worth.

Parties to a civil action are in quite a different position. They may be forced to testify by the other side, and they may be cross-examined from the very start. Parties are usually the ones who receive the most heat on the witness stand because they are utilizing the courts in an effort to have some grievance resolved in their behalf, and they have to shoulder the responsibility for what they contend. Their lawyer is present in court, but he cannot testify for them. They must mount the lonely witness chair and ride it out. Before they are through, they may feel as if they are in the center of a rodeo arena trying to ride a bucking bronco. The only way to win the prize is to stay loose and reel with the lurches until the buzzer sounds.

Non-party witnesses are often served with a subpoena, which is an order that they appear in court to testify. A subpoena may be served by a process server or by the sheriff or his deputy. Ignoring a subpoena may have the same consequences as ignoring a summons for jury service or any other order of the court. The individual who chooses to do so may be arrested and fined, or given a jail term for his transgression.

Even though a lawsuit may be a private matter between litigants, it is of public concern in that citizens must have a means to obtain justice in private as well as public matters. It is of public concern that justice prevail. This is why the courts are provided at public expense to determine private matters, and why the absolute sanction of governmental authority is given to the court in its subpoena power. The courts could not, and do not in any sense, rest upon the voluntary participation of witnesses. If this were so, the

Swear to Tell the Truth • 49

indifference, or lethargy, or lack of understanding of an essential witness could frustrate the processes of justice.

Often witnesses appear voluntarily, without subpoena; but the reason for their cooperation is often based on the fact that the power of subpoena exists and may be readily imposed on them, rather than any enlightened desire to be of voluntary service.

A subpoena is issued over the signature of the clerk of the court. It states the name of the lawsuit, the place and time when the witness is to appear, and recites which party is demanding the presence of the witness. Usually the witness receives a carbon copy. The subpoena is a printed form, but the particulars as to the case are typed in. The original of the subpoena is filed with the court, and on it the process server writes a certification that at a particular time and place he personally served the copy on the witness. The parties involved in a case are seldom served with subpoenas, as they are present in court and available without this instrument of enforcement.

A subpoena is in no sense a prerequisite to a witness being qualified to testify. With or without subpoena, a witness comes under the power of the court and assumes the role the minute the oath is administered. Virtually any person may be a witness.

A word often used in evidence is "incompetent." This generally refers to a type of testimony which is inadmissible and improper in a court. For example, a hearsay or conjecture is incompetent testimony.

The word "incompetent" is also used as to the witness himself. For example, a child who is too young to understand the nature of an oath is incompetent as a witness. It is for the judge to decide whether or not the child shall be allowed to testify.

An insane person is not necessarily incompetent as a witness, although he may be, depending upon the circumstances. The term "insanity" is subject to much confusion of thought because it has no universally applied meaning, either in law or in medicine. Criminal insanity, for example, means exactly what the statute on that subject says it means—no more and no less. The jury addresses itself only to the defendant's mental condition with respect to the particular issues of the criminal case.

The term insanity is still sometimes applied to civil commitment procedures where a person who, for some reason, is not mentally competent to attend to his own affairs may be made a ward of the State and confined in a mental hospital or cared for under some other program under the supervision of the court. But this may be done because of alcoholism, or suicidal tendencies, or some other defect in the person's mentality which would in no sense disqualify the person to be able to perceive facts and truly relate them. The mental capacity tests which are applied in both civil and criminal cases are not at all similar to the tests applied in determining whether a witness is competent to testify in court. Therefore, a witness may be "insane" or "mentally incompetent" and at the same time be a competent witness. For example, an elderly woman might be declared a ward of the state due to senility. Her mental state does not qualify her to enjoy the rights or carry the responsibility of free citizenship; yet she may be perfectly competent to relate the fact that her roommate set fire to the bed and burned down the nursing home. Or a man may be a hopeless alcoholic and be declared incompetent due to his mental disease. He may then be held as a ward of the state for the protection of himself and of the public, yet while he is so held without access to liquor, he can see what is going on just as well as anyone else and can truthfully relate the facts in court.

A class of witnesses who are incompetent to testify because of public policy are those in a position to receive privileged communications. For example, communications between husband and wife are privileged. This means that the one cannot be forced to testify against the other as to matters related in confidence. The reason for the privilege is to encourage the confidential relationship between spouses, and to promote its closeness, by removing the fear that things privately disclosed could then be publicly exposed. This rule does not apply where the spouses are suing each other, such as in a divorce, or where a crime has been committed by one spouse against the other.

Sometimes a suspect to a crime is granted immunity from prosecution in exchange for his testimony. For example, a young man was arrested and found to be under the influence of a narcotic drug. He is guilty of a crime and can claim his right against self-incrimination by refusing to admit he had taken drugs and by refusing to disclose the source of the drug. It is of greater public concern that the peddler be caught and prosecuted than the victim. The District Attorney may apply to the court for leave to grant him immunity from prosecution for his crime in consideration for a truthful disclosure of the source of the drug. The right to grant such immunity is conferred by statute in a very limited number of cases as public policy demands.

Modern law tends to be liberal in its rules as to who may testify and who may not, but this was not always the case. At one period in the development of English common law, there was a long list of scandalous characters who were excluded from testifying because of their infamy. Among these were prostitutes. But an exception arose, creating a maxim in old English law that "in matters pertaining to the brothel, prostitutes are competent to testify." Now, prostitutes and convicts of all types are competent to testify in court. However, if the witness has been convicted of a felony, then this fact may be brought out to the jury as bearing upon his or her reliability and credibility as a witness.

Religious belief used to be a prerequisite for any witness. It was thought that unless the person believed in a Supreme Being, who was a rewarder of truth and an avenger of falsehood, he was incapable of taking an oath and, therefore, of testifying. Now this test has been completely abolished because the state has no constitutional right to interfere with or judge a person because of his religious belief or disbelief. Often the oath still contains the words, "swear by the ever living God," but the witness may request an affirmation instead. "Do you solemnly affirm that you will tell the truth, the whole truth and nothing but the truth?"

At one time a witness was considered incompetent to testify if he had any interest in the outcome of the case, as a party or otherwise. A treatise published in 1824 explained this as follows: "This rule of exclusion considered in its principles, requires little explanation. It is founded on the known infirmities of human nature, which is too weak to be generally restrained by religious or moral obligations when tempted and solicited in the contrary direction by temporal interest."

Generations of experience showed that this rule did much more injustice than justice because the interested parties are naturally most often the only people in possession of the facts. Many a just grievance died for lack of any means to prove it. One application of this rule still survives, and that is the so-called "Dead Man's Act." This prevents a person from making a claim against an estate by testifying as to some alleged transaction with a deceased person. For example, let us assume that Hattie Hand is a housekeeper for Seth Bower. Seth dies and Hattie eagerly awaits the reading of the will, as she expected to receive a bequest in consideration for her years of selfless service to him. The bequest reads, "To my faithful housekeeper, Hattie Hand, I leave all of my monogrammed handkerchiefs which she ironed so well."

Hattie is crushed. She comes into court and asserts that Seth had promised to will her the sum of ten thousand dollars because she had been so nice to him. If Seth were still around to give his side of the story, such an assertion might be allowed in court, but since death has sealed Seth's lips, the Dead Man's statute evens things up by sealing Hattie's lips. She is incompetent to testify as to this alleged transaction. However, if Hattie could get other people to testify that Seth had made this promise around town and these people were not in a position to benefit from the alleged oral contract, she might prove her claim.

What happens where a witness cannot speak the English language? An interpreter may be used. In this case, the interpreter takes the solemn oath that he will accurately translate the foreign tongue into English, and vice versa.

We have concerned ourselves with those who are competent or incompetent to be witnesses. The next question is what may be done about a witness who is legally competent to testify but is not telling the truth. A witness may be impeached in a number of ways. This is the province of the opposing attorney.

Impeachment of a witness is based on any factor which tends to show his untruthfulness. A common way to impeach a witness is to show that he has made a prior statement which is inconsistent with the one he makes in trial. The prior statement need not have been made under oath; it is sufficient to show that at one time he said one thing, and at the trial he said another. It is then for the jury to decide when he was telling the truth, or whether his word is entitled to any credit at all. This is known as self-contradiction.

Another method of impeachment is to show that the witness is biased or interested in the outcome of the case. This does not render him incompetent as a witness but involves his credibility, which is a matter for the jury to decide. This may be shown during cross-examination of the witness, or by calling other witnesses who establish the fact of bias or prejudice or interest of the witness.

Another impeachment method is to show the bad reputation for truthfulness of the witness. This may be done by calling to the stand members of the community in which the witness lives.

There are definite limitations on the extent to which one can go to impeach a witness. This is one of the most important things for litigants, and witnesses themselves, to understand. The courts do not allow impeachment by disclosure of unfavorable personal facts about the witness. The witness cannot be assailed with indiscretions of his past, such as arguments he has had with his family or neighbors, traffic tickets, or the time he was jailed for a college prank. The line must be drawn somewhere, not only to protect the witness from undue harassment, but to prevent the trial from getting off track on an endless succession of charge and countercharge regarding matters not related to the central issues.

Even the reputation witness is limited to his "yes or no" and "good or bad" answers. Unless asked by the opposing attorney, he cannot say, "Well, he lied about this, and then he lied about that, and then he lied about the other thing," back somewhere in the past. And prior inconsistent statements attributed to the witness must concern matters at issue in the trial to which he has testified.

Say a person is on trial for the misdemeanor charge of passing a short check; he voluntarily assumes the witness stand and states that he didn't intend any wrong because he thought he had enough money in the bank when he wrote the check. The District Attorney can then try to contradict the witness by showing that he had written checks amounting to much more than his last deposit in the bank. But the prosecutor cannot show all the red ink on the defendant's bank ledger. Other short checks written in the past, not related to the offense charged, are irrelevant and immaterial to the case.

They would be prejudicial to the defendant and would constitute a denial of due process of law, as he is entitled to be tried only on the offense charged. But should the defendant be so unwise as to volunteer a statement that "I never had any trouble like this before," he would then have expanded the scope of impeachment by his own indiscretion and the District Attorney could then prove his falsehood by showing that he had often had this difficulty with checks.

An attorney and his client vouch for the credibility of any witness they call. They cannot impeach their own witness. This rule is based on the sound principle that one should not be allowed to use a witness for what they like to hear and then discredit him as to the part they don't like.

No discussion of witnesses could be complete without mentioning the expert witness. In this connection, let us first ask ourselves what a juror brings to court with him besides his clothes? He brings his brain power and the common knowledge of all men. He reaches his factual conclusions based on this common knowledge and the evidence and law he hears in court. The ordinary witness is not allowed to make these conclusions for the jury; that is their job, and their job alone. But assume that a factual question in a lawsuit depends on knowledge which is not commonly within the grasp of the man on the street.

What does a doctor do when he makes a diagnosis? He takes a history of the patient's complaints and makes a physical examination. He then applies his specialized knowledge to these facts, and comes up with a conclusion as to the nature of the illness. Assume that an illness or an injury is a factual question in a trial, which it often is. If the plaintiff has been in an automobile accident and has received an injury to her neck, the jury is in no position to listen to her complaints, physically examine her person and to decide whether or not she has an injury and, if so, its nature and extent. Rather they must rely on the opinion of someone who has made a special study of diseases and injuries. This would be a doctor who would be brought into court and sworn to tell the truth the same as any other witness.

His similarity with other witnesses then ceases. First he is qualified as an expert. That is, the attorney calling him will ask a series of questions regarding his professional study and concentration of effort and experience in a particular field of endeavor which takes him out of the realm of common knowledge of the general populace as to that subject. If the judge determines that he is qualified by special experience and training, he will then be allowed to testify as an expert, giving opinions as to some of the ultimate factual questions of the case. If he examined the injured plaintiff, he would have some of the pertinent facts within his personal knowledge, and he could testify to them as well as giving his opinion on the nature of the injury.

But an expert is sometimes allowed to testify, even if he does not have actual and personal knowledge of any of the facts in the case. Doctors are by no means the only experts allowed. Experts need not have any particular college degrees, nor need they be extraordinarily brilliant. The possession of specialized knowledge is the sole test, and it is up to the sound discretion of the judge to decide whether a person is qualified.

Let us say that we have an engineer who has been qualified as an expert at a trial concerning the quality of the construction of a building. He could testify even though he may have never looked at the building, and had nothing to do with its construction. This is done by presenting him with a hypothetical question containing all of the facts in the case upon which he is going to apply his expert opinion. It might go as follows:

Q Now, sir, assume that a two-story schoolhouse were built, containing 40,000 square feet of space on each floor, that the basic structure was steel I-beam construction, with brick curtain walls; that a single I-beam measuring 12 inches in depth, 8 inches in width and 50 feet in length was utilized to span a 47-foot ceiling with no center support. Would this, in your opinion, constitute a safe construction practice?

The engineer would then answer yes or no, and give his reasons why.

A favorite subject for opinion testimony is the question of sanity or insanity. Although the study of psychiatry has reached a high degree of sophistication whereby a number of common mental disturbances may be identified with some degree of certainty, it is still not an exact science. We often find diversity of opinion among the psychiatrists.

Juries are not bound to accept the opinion of any expert, but are told that their function is merely to use the expert testimony for what they feel it may be worth in arriving at their conclusions. Unfortunately, some expert witnesses not only become experts in their chosen fields of endeavor, but become experts as expert witnesses. Some psychiatrists and some orthopedic physicians, particularly, seem to work themselves into this category by gaining a reputation for more or less reliably taking a certain attitude about certain types of cases. The lawyers help them build their reputation by calling upon them when they need this answer to a case.

For instance, if an orthopedic physician in a city of any size arrives at the idea through his long study and experience that the common whiplash type of neck injury in a rear end automobile collision is usually the basis of malingering, he will then find himself in great demand by attorneys representing insurance companies who are defending this type of lawsuit. A psychiatrist might gain a reputation for liberality in finding that those charged with crimes are suffering some disease which renders them incapable of distinguishing right from wrong. He would then be in continuous demand from defense attorneys. Unfortunately, this type of witness develops a certain trial expertness, just as do lawyers, and their reputation builds to a point where they feel they have something to protect by trying to win the case. Trials become a battle of the experts.

Just as the lay witness should not be an advocate, neither should the expert witness be an advocate and try to take sides in a case. His testimony should be based on a sound and impartial evaluation of the facts relayed to him without regard to who called him as a witness, or what effect his opinion might have on the outcome of the lawsuit.

Some of these experts forget the limitation of their duty and thereby seriously subvert the processes of justice. They attempt not only to give their opinion on the subject in which they are supposed to be particularly competent, but they try to unduly influence the verdict. They are well paid for this work and this may be brought out by the opposing attorney; but, of course, the fact that a doctor or an engineer gets paid for his time does not, in and of itself, destroy his credibility.

A popular theme in fiction dwells endlessly on the mistaken idea that what happens to a witness when his credibility is destroyed in court is this: He or she breaks down on the witness stand in front of everyone, and confesses to the crime. The fact that this chilling phenomenon has never actually hapened in court to the knowledge of experienced judges and lawyers seems to be no deterrent to its tedious repetition. The trouble with it is that it goes absolutely contrary to human nature. Witnesses are ambushed in court every day of the year in every state of the Union. Their credibility is destroyed before their very eyes and before the eyes of everyone else in the courtroom. But nature inevitably impels them in the exact opposite direction from a breakdown and confession in court. It is true that there is a natural compulsion to confess, but not under these circumstances, in open court. The natural thing, if they have gone this far, is to cling to their untruth in spite of everything, and to try to maintain the things they first said.

So when you go to court, please don't expect such an unlikely event to take place before your eyes. Instead, consider the remarkable being a witness is. He is the eyes and the ears of justice. He has the ability to perceive an event and then relate it to you. And the truthful witness is justice's best friend.

Chapter Five

MURDER OVER LIGHTLY

Homicide has always fascinated mankind. The gory book cult shows no sign of receding in size. But the typical "Who-Done-It?" thriller concerns just that, and when the guilty culprit is uncovered, it is then blithely assumed that he will receive his just punishment.

No less fascinating is the subject of homicide in trial. Here, the question is what did he do, why, and what is going to happen to him? To the uninitiated, these questions may seem easy enough to answer: "He killed his wife and he should hang."

But the courts do not view such cases in this summary fashion.

Carl Decker is a regular and sensible fellow who pays his taxes and goes about his business without fanfare. While reading his daily paper, he spots a headline: "Man Kills Wife." He scans the story and reaches a hasty conclusion: the accused is a cold-blooded murderer and should have been put to death before sundown. Then he gives no further thought to the matter. As it happens, Carl received a jury questionnaire some months before, which he filled out, sent in, and forgot about. He didn't know that at that moment a card with his name on it was merrily tumbling around in the big jury wheel down at City Hall, and one day a finger might very well pluck it out.

The man who prompted the newspaper story is Fred Taylor. He is 40 years old, and had been married to Matilda for twelve years. Fred worked as a laborer at a nearby air base and they lived in a small apartment in an unattractive section of town. Matilda was seven years younger than Fred and had, on occasion, liked to go to dances on Saturday night while Fred preferred to be with the boys for a little poker. They had been estranged on various occasions and divorce papers were filed twice. Each time they had reconciled before actually ending their marriage.

The disaster occurred in the early morning hours of Sunday, May 19. Fred, who had been drinking, arrived home about one o'clock, and found Matilda was still out. He began fuming and, after waiting about an hour, he noticed, watching out the window, that a car pulled up, driven by a man, and that Matilda made some gesture towards him which Fred could not quite see but interpreted as an act of affection. She got out of the car and came inside. An argument ensued.

According to Fred, Matilda had a large, heavy pair of scissors in her hand and came at him with this instrument. The autopsy showed that Matilda was choked, and the cause of her death was suffocation by strangulation. The bruises and marks on her neck indicated the use of extreme force applied by large and powerful hands, so extreme, in fact, that a cartilage was broken in her neck.

When Fred found the limp form of his dead wife in his hands, he stood momentarily in disbelief. Suddenly he dropped her and fled out into the street in terror. He walked around aimlessly for about an hour in a frantic daze. Finally he found a place to get a drink and had some more whiskey. He could not go back to the house that night so he rented a cheap hotel room, and flopped down to sleep off his condition.

The landlady found his wife's body that Sunday afternoon. The police were immediately alerted and a pick-up call went out for Fred Taylor. He was arrested later that night.

Fred had served a prison term for burglary during his twenties but, by and large, had managed to steer clear of involvement with the law. He was not a murderous looking individual, and in a way appeared quite pleasant. He spoke in a low voice and seemed to be of average intelligence. He responded in what the police considered a satisfactory manner to their interrogation, but he managed to paint a picture of justification for what had happened. He displayed both grief and instinctive self-preservation by swearing that he did not know what had happened until it was all over, that he did not intend to kill anybody, and that he was preserving his own skin because he was being threatened with an instrument of death. He was able to display a scratch about one and one-half inches long on his right forearm, which he contended was inflicted by the scissors.

One point which concerned the police was that the scissors were found in the apartment, and brought into the laboratory for examination, but showed no signs of blood. Also, they were lying on a desk rather than on the floor or in some position indicating that they had played a part in the violence. When confronted with this information, Fred stated that he must have picked them up and put them back on the desk.

Fred was duly booked in the police records as a murder suspect. His photograph and fingerprints were taken, and he was placed in jail.

The following Monday, a team of detectives spent the day completing their investigation of the case. They interrogated the other tenants of the building, the neighbors, the people where Fred worked, and those who saw him the night before the death. They also looked into the whereabouts of Matilda that night and located the man who had brought her home in his car. Upon interrogation, he denied that there had been improper or immoral activities on the part of anyone.

After the evidence was duly gathered, the detectives presented the complete investigation file to the District Attorney, who drew up a criminal complaint charging murder in the first degree. The Deputy District Attorney who received the case was glad that it was not up to him to decide the degree of homicide. The statutes of the state say that the proper charge in a case of this type is murder in the first degree, and that the court and jury will decide whether it was in fact that type of murder or some lesser degree of homicide as defined by law.

On Wednesday of that week, Fred Taylor was brought into the District Court by the Sheriff's officers at 9:00 o'clock in the morning. He was escorted into the courtroom along with several other prisoners who were being handled in various matters preliminary to trial. The previous afternoon, his case had been filed in court by the District Attorney and had been assigned a number. The District Attorney had requested that the defendant be held without bail.

First degree murder is one of the few offenses where bail or, as it is sometimes called, bond, is not allowed, although this is not a hard and fast rule and in certain circumstances, even though the charge be first degree murder, a court may, upon sufficient showing that the presumption is not great nor the proof evident that the verdict will actually be first degree murder, allow the defendant to be released on bail.

Shortly after Fred Taylor is brought into the court, his case is called out by the clerk, "People of the State versus Fred Taylor, Criminal Action Number 40638." Fred rises from his seat in the prisoner's box as directed by the Sheriff Deputy, and walks up in front of the judge. The clerk then reads the charge as follows: "Hiram Dillon, District Attorney in and for the Second Judicial District of the State informs the Court that on the 19th day of May, 19—, Fred Taylor did unlawfully and feloniously kill and murder Matilda Taylor, contrary to the statute in such cases made and provided and against the peace and dignity of the people of the State."

How do you plead, Guilty or not guilty?

Fred mumbles something, but before he can speak, the judge addresses him as follows:

Do you have a lawyer?
No, sir, I don't.
Do you intend to get a lawyer?
I don't think I can.
Why not?
I don't know any lawyer, and I don't have any money.
Are you working?
Yes, sir, I work when I can find a job.
Do you have a bank account?
No, sir, I do not.
Do you own a car?
No, I—well, yes, I have a car, but you see I owe more on it than it's worth.
Do you own a house?
No, sir, I don't. Judge, all I really own is the clothes on my back and a little bit of furniture we have, which is mortgaged.
Are you telling the Court that you cannot hire your own lawyer?

I couldn't get a lawyer. I wouldn't have no means to get a lawyer.
The Judge then states:

Very well. The Court is satisfied that this accused is indigent and that a lawyer should be appointed to defend him at the expense of the State, which the Court will do. This Court does not receive any pleas or consider any action in a case of this type unless and until the accused is represented by competent counsel. All right, Mr. Taylor, I will appoint a lawyer and have him come to the jail to confer with you and your case will be set over until one week from today at this same hour, when you will be brought into court for a plea.

The lawyer appointed by the Court goes to the jail and confers with Fred Taylor. Fred has had little experience with lawyers and, at first, he is somewhat suspicious and refuses to give all of the details. However, the lawyer appointed is extremely competent and experienced in these matters and, after a few minutes' discussion, he wins his client's confidence. Fred tells him just about what he told the police, that he was really mad when he saw his wife driving up in a car with some other man and that he got in an argument with her; that she came after him with the scissors; that he never intended to kill her; and that when he found what had happened, he ran away in terror.

The lawyer suggested to him that he should consider entering a plea of insanity. At first this sounds ridiculous to Fred because he had never thought of himself as crazy and, to his knowledge, neither had anybody else, but the lawyer explains that according to the laws of the State, there is such a thing as temporary insanity, as exhibited by an irresistible impulse, and this is a legal and proper defense and should most likely be pursued along with all of the other defenses available to him. Fred finally agrees, putting his trust entirely in the lawyer.

The lawyer confers with him several more times in jail before the hearing date comes up, in order to confirm his first impressions and to further gain the confidence of his newly acquired client. When the case is called one week later, the Judge says, "Are you ready to plead?" The lawyer says, "We are, your Honor. We will enter a plea of not guilty, and not guilty by reason of insanity at the time of the alleged offense." "Very well," the Judge says, "pursuant to the plea of insanity, it will be the order of this Court that the defendant be taken to the State Hospital for examination, his stay not to exceed thirty days in length, and be returned to this Court for further proceedings." Whereupon, Fred is taken to the State Hospital and given examination by a psychiatrist employed there by the State.

The psychiatrist thoroughly examines Fred by conferring with him for a long period of time, taking his entire life history, observing his reactions, evaluating his intelligence, and also discussing the events leading up to the difficulty now facing him in court. He is also given a complete physical examination and various psychological tests to aid the psychiatrist in his findings.

From all of this study, the psychiatrist arrives at his opinion, which is that since he did not have a history of mental infirmity or disease, Fred was sane at the time of the alleged offense. The psychiatrist has had experience with the criminal law and therefore he concerns himself not only with the question of sanity but also with the question of intent as applied to the act.

After the examination, the psychiatrist writes a letter to the Court, informing it that in his opinion the defendant was sane at the time of the alleged commission of the crime. Fred is then returned to the County jail and presently brought into court for another hearing. His lawyer has examined the letter from the State psychiatrist but believing that he is entitled to further psychiatric aid, requests the Court to appoint a private psychiatrist to examine the defendant. The Court refuses to do this at State expense. However, the lawyer feels so strongly that he should urge this point further, he takes it upon himself to engage a psychiatrist to examine the defendant in the jail. The psychiatrist's fee will eventually be paid out of the lawyer's state paid fee. The private psychiatrist also takes a complete history of Fred's life, and that of the events leading up to the crime. He arrives at a conclusion different from the State psychiatrist's, and believes that at the time of the offense Fred Taylor was suffering an irresistible impulse. This, according to the psychiatrist, is exhibited by the extreme force which he used in breaking a cartilage in the neck, and in the fact that he was stunned and did not know what he had done until it was all over with. He calls it "obsessive compulsive psychoneurosis."

The case at this point contains two different and inconsistent pleas. The plea of not guilty is a general denial which puts the District Attorney on his proof of all of the essential elements of the crime, that is, the identity of the deceased, the fact that the deceased died, the fact that the defendant was the one who caused the death, and the intent of the defendant to do what he did.

The plea of insanity, on the other hand is, legally, a confession and avoidance, that is, the defendant, by entering this plea through his lawyer, states, in effect, "All right, I did it, but because of this special circumstance of my mental incapacity, I should not stand the usual criminal penalty for what I did." Even though these two pleas are inconsistent, it is permissible for the judge to set both matters for trial at the same time, before the same jury, which he does in this case, the trial being set approximately six months later. Fred will have to spend all of this time confined in the jail since first degree murder is not a bailable offense. His lawyer might seek bail on the grounds that the proof is not evident nor the presumption great that this is really a first degree murder case. But he decides not to do so because they have asserted a plea of insanity and the Judge might not look kindly on the idea of letting a madman out on bond. The lawyer tells Fred that the time he spends in jail might well be worth it in the long run.

About ten days prior to the trial date, our friend, Carl Becker, the prospective juror, receives a jury summons by certified mail, return receipt requested, his little card in the jury wheel having found itself on the top of the pile and been grasped in the hand of one of the people entrusted with that wheel. Carl arrives at the courthouse not knowing what he is in for and goes through the usual experience of beginning jurors. About mid-morning of his first day of service, he finds himself in the Criminal Division, along with approximately 120 other prospective jurors, listening to the call of Case Number 40638, The People of the State versus Fred Taylor. The Judge states, "Call the jury." Whereupon the clerk shakes his little box and, by lottery, calls up thirteen of the panel members who then seat themselves in the jury box. The Judge then makes some remarks directed to the thirteen, but asking the rest of the jurors to also listen carefully, as they might very well find themselves in the jury box before too long.

The Judge reads the information indicating that it is a murder case, and asks if any of the jurors in the box have heard or read about the case. Carl and two or three other jurors raise their hands. The Judge then asks Mr. Decker whether or not he has formed any opinion as to the guilt or innocence of the defendant. In all honesty, Carl has to say that his memory of reading about the case in the newspaper is very vague indeed, and that he may have formed an opinion at the time he read it but he does not now remember what the opinion was, if he had one. The Judge then says, "Well, sir, even though you may have read something about this case at one time and formed an opinion, do you honestly feel that you could act as a fair and impartial juror and decide the issues presented to you solely upon the law and evidence here in the courtroom?" To such a question, Carl answers, "Yes." The other jurors who remember something about the case also answer that they feel they could be fair and impartial.

The Judge then goes on to introduce the attorneys for either side, to point out the defendant, and to name off the witnesses who have been endorsed on the information for the People. He asks if any of the prospective jurors are acquainted with any of these people; if so, to please raise their hand. One juror raises his hand and states that he is acquainted with one of the Deputy District Attorneys in court. The Judge then inquires as to how well he knows this attorney and how long he has known him, and whether or not the association would affect his deliberation one way or another. If the juror says that it would not, then the Judge leaves the juror on and goes on to the next point. If one of the jurors is acquainted with a prospective witness, then the Judge informs the juror that at the proper time in the case, they will receive an instruction stating that the credibility of the witness is for the jury to decide, and asks if the juror feels that in spite of his acquaintanceship he would consider this witness's testimony in the same way as any other witness with whom he is not acquainted and not be influenced one way or another. If the juror states that he feels it would not affect his thinking as to the credibility of that witness, he is left on the panel.

The Judge then gives a brief explanation of the procedure in the trial and points out some of the stock rules of law which are included in any criminal case and which will be presented to the jury. He asks if any of the jurors are in disagreement with these rules so that they could not follow them. The Court then turns the jury examination over to the attorneys.

First, one of the Deputy District Attorneys rises and introduces himself and begins to ask questions. His questions concern the instructions of law which will later be given, and various issues in the case, in an attempt to determine the attitude of the prospective jurors, and whether or not, in his opinion, they would be good jurors for this cause. The law of the State provides that in a first degree murder conviction, the penalty shall be either life imprisonment or death, and that the choice as to this penalty will be made by the jury. Because of this, he asks each prospective juror individually whether or not he or she has any conscientious or religious objection to the imposition of the death penalty in a proper case. When this line of questioning commences, it becomes apparent why so many jurors were called to court because approximately one-third of the jurors assert that they could not impose the death penalty by their verdict under any circumstances. When they so state, they must be excused for cause and another juror called up to replace them. By the questioning, the jurors are made to understand that twelve of them will finally try the case and that their verdict as to guilt or innocence and as to the degree of homicide must be unanimous. Also, their verdict as to the penalty in the case of a first degree murder conviction must be unanimous. Therefore, the verdict in that regard is the verdict of each and every one of the jurors as well as the verdict of the jury as a whole. When asked this question, Carl states that he is not opposed to capital punishment and could be a party to the imposing of it in a proper case.

When the defense attorney makes his jury examination, he concentrates on the issue of insanity and carefully elicits from the prospective jurors their attitude regarding this plea. He asks them whether they have any feeling against the plea, and whether, in a proper case, if proof is presented, they would find a defendant not guilty by reason of insanity. He also inquires carefully about their feeling toward psychiatrists and whether or not they would take the opinion of a psychiatrist regarding the mental condition of an accused at the time of the alleged act. When any juror is excused for cause and another is called up from the panel, the District Attorney gets an opportunity to rise again and ask more questions. He will counter some of the questions asked by the defense attorney on the issue of expert psychiatric testimony to point out the instruction of law on this subject which will be given by the judge at a later time in the trial, informing them that they are not bound by the testimony of the psychiatrist and can canvass his testimony just as they canvass and judge the credibility and weight of the testimony of any other witness in the case, making up their own mind on this issue.

The defense attorney plans his tactics and decides that he will most likely place the defendant on the stand as a witness during his defense, although the defendant is not required to testify in his own behalf and, if he does not testify, the court will provide an instruction which tells the jury that they are not to hold this fact against him and not to make any inference of guilt from the fact that he remained silent. The defense attorney knows that his client has had a previous felony conviction many years prior, and that the District Attorney will be allowed to bring out this fact as bearing upon the credibility of the defendant as a witness. So the attorney attempts to disarm the District Attorney by bringing this out in the open in his own questioning of the jury, asking them if they would find the defendant guilty merely because he was convicted of a separate crime at some different time in the past, to which all of the jurors, being very honest and fair-minded, state that they would not necessarily find him guilty of this crime because of that, but would only consider it in the light of the instruction on that point as given by the court. If any juror says that the fact that the person had been convicted of some other crime before would prejudice him against the person and make him feel that he probably actually did commit the crime he is charged with, even if not fully proven, then that juror is excused for cause.

The defense attorney realizes that a weak point in his case is the conduct of the defendant after the death of his wife in fleeing the apartment and not notifying the proper authorities. He asks each juror individually whether this circumstance would, in and of itself, so prejudice them against the defendant that they would necessarily find him guilty as charged. The attorney says, "You realize, of course, that a so-called consciousness of guilt need not be the only motive for running away—it could be fear, stupidity or any number of other things, isn't that right?" When the question is so carefully presented to them, they, being intellectually honest, must say that this fact alone would not be enough to prove him guilty. Thus the defense attorney seeks further to disarm the District Attorney and deprive him of the power of surprise and drama in his presentation.

The District Attorney anticipates the defense tactic of trying the deceased and presenting her in the light of an unworthy wife. He then seeks to disarm the defense attorney on this point by pointing out that it is the defendant who is on trial here and not the deceased, and gaining commitments from the prospective jurors that they would not treat the case any differently because of any inference of immorality or other characteristics of the deceased, pointing out strongly that regardless of her character, she had a right to live.

During the course of this examination, all of the jurors are asked whether or not under all of the circumstances then known to them, they honestly feel that they could be fair and impartial jurors and could render a verdict based solely upon the law and evidence as presented in court, to which the great majority of the jurors answer yes.

The jurors are further questioned and given a full opportunity to state whether or not they have any family, business or health problems or concerns which would distract them in their full attention to the case. Since this is a capital case wherein the possible punishment could be death or life imprisonment, the jurors will have to be confined at all times and will not be allowed to disband during mealtime or at night. They will stay in a jury dormitory and will be escorted to all meals in the custody of the special bailiffs, a man and a woman, who are provided for this purpose. The attorneys give their best estimate as to the length of the case, saying that it should last approximately five days and, for example, this being Monday, they could expect to be away from their work until Saturday. It is also pointed out that during their deliberation stage they will also be confined and nobody can say how long it will take a jury to arrive at a verdict.

After considering all these factors, a number of the jurors think up a very good reason why they could not serve, such as having small children at home, or a big business problem coming up next week, or any number of things. It is up to the judge to decide on an individual basis whether any of these reasons will justify the juror being excused. If there are any health problems among the jurors, such as ulcers, a bad cold or the flu, they will be excused for this reason.

The jury examination could well consume two full days of court time. In addition to the challenges for cause, each side is entitled to fifteen peremptory challenges, that is, they can excuse up to fifteen jurors without stating any cause therefor, and upon each excuse of a juror another must be called up in his place and examined just as all those before.

After the jury examination is completed, then thirteen jurors are sworn to try the case. The extra juror is provided in case one of the other jurors becomes ill or otherwise incapacitated during the trial. It has become a practice in some courts to use two extra jurors for this purpose rather than just one. If all of the jurors in the first twelve seats have survived up to the point when the deliberation begins, then the extra juror or jurors will be excused and only the twelve will deliberate.

Let us assume that Carl Decker survives all of this and is finally sworn as one of the jurors to try the case. Both the District Attorney and the defense attorney then present their case in due and orderly fashion. The District Attorney makes his opening statement outlining the facts as presented at the beginning of this chapter. He calls his witnesses to the stand, proving all of the essential elements of the crime, proving the fact of death and the identify of the deceased, the agency of the defendant in causing the death, and presenting the State psychiatrist to prove that the defendant was not insane at the time the crime was committed. The defense uses both psychiatrists to elicit opinion as to the degree of the defendant's criminal intent when the matter occurred.

The source of complexity and fascination in homicide as a subject is that the degree of culpability of one accused of killing a fellow human being is not dependent upon the fact of death or even the means used in causing the death, but *is* dependent on a complex and elusive thing, the state of mind of the accused at the moment the death was inflicted. This is a fact question to beat all fact questions, because it is seldom subject to direct proof. On the contrary, it depends upon many factors, often including the entire life history of the defendant's mental condition plus the provocation which may have been present at the time of the crime. It involves all of the facts and circumstances, and in the modern trial, it also includes the brain work of our helpmates in law, the psychiatrists.

After the facts are in, the defense attorney moves for a directed verdict of not guilty. This is a lengthy legal argument where the law of homicide and the facts proven are bandied about at length between the attorneys and the judge.

The defense attorney argues vociferously that this could not possibly be a first degree murder case. He argues that if Fred killed his wife, it was a mistake and unintentional; at the very most, it was a crime of passion, which would not be first degree murder; that there was an indication in the proof that he was acting in self-defense; that it was not a willful and premeditated killing with a deliberate intention to take the life of a fellow creature; and that there was no design or intent to kill formed and devised in the cool state of the blood as is required for a finding of first degree murder. However, the prosecuting attorney points out that the premeditation required for the first degree murder need not exist for any particular length of time before the killing; that it is not necessary that the killing should have been considered, brooded over, or reflected upon for a week, a day, or an hour; that it is sufficient if there was a design and a determination to kill distinctly formed in the slayer's mind at any moment before the act which caused the death, that the slayer acted upon such design and determination, that it matters not how short the interval between intent and act, if it was sufficient for one thought to follow another.

The judge sees much in the defendant's argument, but he points out that by the defendant's own statement he watched his wife from the window, while she was in the car with another man, and noticed her make a gesture towards him, and that was when the defendant became very angry. An argument ensued and, before it was over, the wife was dead. From this, the judge feels that a reasonable jury might decide that the defendant resolved to kill his wife when he saw her with the man in the car. The judge assures the defense attorney that he is cognizant of the evidence that the wife came at the defendant with a pair of scissors. However, he points out, very correctly, that this evidence is only from the defendant's lips and is exculpatory in character. The judge cannot take this as having been proven conclusively and it must be determined by the jury whether or not they will believe the testimony, and if so, what weight they will give to it.

Now begins the action for Carl Becker and his fellow jurors. The judge prepares forms of verdict as follows: Guilty of first degree murder, penalty of death; guilty of first degree murder, penalty, life imprisonment; guilty of second degree murder, guilty of voluntary manslaughter; guilty of involuntary manslaughter; not guilty by reason of insanity; and not guilty.

The judge and the attorneys also prepare written instructions stating that the jury must first determine the sanity of the defendant and, if they find him insane, they shall return that verdict. If they find him sane, they shall then determine whether he is guilty of murder in the first degree, and if so, shall set the punishment. If they do not find him guilty of this offense, they shall then determine whether or not he is guilty of murder in the second degree, and so on down the line. If they find him not guilty, they shall return that verdict. They are also informed that the burden of proof is upon the people through their legal representative, the District Attorney, and that he must prove each and every essential element of the crime beyond a reasonable doubt.

The term insanity and all the different degrees of homicide are carefully defined. Let us take up this interesting question of insanity. The state doctor had testified that the defendant was sane, and that in his opinion he was faking insanity. On the other hand, the private psychiatrist testified that the defendant in his opinion was impelled to do what he did by an irresistible impulse. This doctor said that he found evidence of a brain injury because the defendant had told him that he had blacked out in his youth on various occasions. The instructions state that "a person shall be found not guilty by reason of insanity if he is so diseased in mind at the time of the act as to be incapable of distinguishing right from wrong with respect to that act, or being able so to distinguish has suffered such an impairment of mind by disease as to destroy the will power and render him incapable of choosing the right and refraining from doing the wrong, and such insanity may be manifested whether by irresistible impulse or otherwise, but care should be taken not to confuse such mental disease with moral obliquity, mental depravity, or passion growing out of anger, revenge, hatred, or other motives and kindred evil conditions, for when the act is induced by any of these causes, the person is accountable to the law."

One thing the jury is not told is that if they find the defendant not guilty by reason of insanity he will be confined, not in the penitentiary, but in the state hospital where he will be kept until "cured," when he can be released upon an order of the court after a hearing to determine whether he has been restored to reason. Few areas of law have created more public ire than the insanity plea in a criminal case.

The remarkable thing about homicide is that in this case, for example, any one of the verdicts could be rendered by the jury and they would still be acting as reasonable people under the law and the evidence. This is because the defendant's mental state is the central issue, and one could hardly find a subject more susceptible to difference of opinion.

First degree murder is willful, deliberate and premeditated. As the judge pointed out, when ruling on defendant's motion to dismiss, reasonable people could so find under these facts. Second degree murder is an unlawful killing with malice aforethought, but without deliberation or premeditation, and the malice is implied when no considerable provocation appears, or when the circumstances of the killing show an abandoned and malignant heart. Surely reasonable people could find that this was the case when Fred Taylor's wife met her death. As Carl Becker hears each of these instructions read, his mental inclination is to say "Ah, there is the answer," until he hears the next instruction read. He hears that voluntary manslaughter is killing as a result of a sudden and violent impulse of passion supposed to be irresistible and as a result of provocation. Seeing his wife consorting with another man is certainly provocation, and the passion element is here, no doubt about that. "Maybe this is it," Carl thinks to himself.

He then hears about involuntary manslaughter, which is a killing without any intent to do so in the commission of an unlawful act, or lawful act which probably might produce such consequences in an unlawful manner, provided, however, that if such act is done with a felonious intent showing malice, the offense shall be murder. This is not the case, Carl thinks. It sounds like causing death by reckless driving or something of the sort. But he has not yet heard the instruction regarding self defense, and he has yet to hear the impassioned plea which the defense attorney will later give. Justifiable self-defense makes a killing no crime at all, and although the instruction is strongly worded that it will not be justified unless the defendant exercised all reasonable means to avoid causing a death, it still says that a person is entitled to protect his own life and to kill if necessary in that lawful pursuit.

"You are further instructed that, while you are not to find the defendant guilty if you entertain a reasonable doubt of his guilt, you are not to search for a doubt. The doubt referred to must be such a doubt as would naturally arise in the mind of a reasonable person upon review of all the evidence in the case. It means a serious, substantial and well-founded doubt, and not a mere possibility of a doubt. It is such a doubt as, in the important transactions of life, would cause a reasonable and prudent person to hesitate and pause. And when you can say, after considering all the evidence in the case, that you have an abiding conviction of the truth of the charge, then you are in law satisfied beyond a reasonable doubt."

After hearing the instructions read, Carl thinks to himself: "The insanity is out. It sounds to me like something between first and second degree murder, although I couldn't say for sure just now. I'll have to listen to the attorneys argue, and I'll have to take those instructions and read them over a little more carefully to see what it really is."

The prosecuting attorney makes the opening portion of his closing argument as follows: "Ladies and Gentlemen of the jury, we have been through a long and arduous trial together. I am not going to waste any more of your time by thanking you at length for your careful attention or by apologizing for the many delays. I am sure you understand that legal matters were carefully considered out of your presence at various stages of the trial.

"Here we have a man who is a previously convicted felon, who kills his wife and tells you that she was trying to hurt him with a pair of scissors. Are you going to believe that? Is there any corroboration for that defense? Are you going to allow this man who strangled the life out of his wife to come in here and defile the character of the dead woman who is not here to defend herself and, thereby, try to achieve some leniency from you? Are you going to buy the story of this psychiatrist who was brought in here to tell you that the defendant was suffering under some type of a sickness?

"Ladies and Gentlemen of the jury, this is a case of premeditated murder. This is a case of malice. This is a case of the defendant taking the law into his own hands in the most violent and destructive way possible. Unfortunately, he had no weapon at his disposal that night. So what did he use? He used his powerful hands with muscles and tendons made strong from years of work as a common laborer. We are not here to judge Mrs. Taylor; we are here to judge the defendant. But consider if you will the form of justice she received as compared to that the defendant has received. Here is the defendant in a public trial, conducted by a fair and impartial judge, being tried by an open-minded, fair and unprejudiced jury, provided with an attorney, provided with his own psychiatrist to come in here and talk about irresistible impulses. Did she receive all that? No, Ladies and Gentlemen of the jury. She received the treatment of Fred Taylor who set himself up as the judge, the jury and the attorneys, who set himself up as the legislature, as God. 'I the jury, I decree that you die.' Why? 'Because you won't stay home and mend my socks while I go to play poker and drink with the boys; because you want to live too. Because you want to go out to a dance. That is why you must die.'

"How did he expect her to get home? Did he want her to walk? She took a ride. He imagines he saw something. He did not see anything. There was nothing that transpired between that man and his wife. She could not explain the innocence of her actions. Why? Because there was nothing there in that room to explain anything to.

There was only a murderous, villainous, violent and designing criminal who resolved then and there to execute his design to kill.

"You are going to hear an argument about self-defense and alleged insanity. They are hauling out everything in the books in the hope of influencing you, to plant some notion in your minds of justification for snuffing out the life of a fellow human being in one deliberate violent, hateful act.

"Neither you nor I knew this defendant prior to this trial, and we are entitled to judge his criminal capabilities by his conduct since his arrest and relate them back to that hateful night and see whether or not we believe these excuses, or whether we believe that a murderer stood at that windowpane and resolved to do what he did do a few minutes later. In fact, we can go further than that. We can see what his actions were immediately after the killing. What did he do? Did he call the authorities? Did he call an ambulance? No. There may have been some life in that body, still a chance to save life. He threw her on the floor and fled out in the street, and finally ended up in a hotel room away from it all. These are the acts of a murderer. And when he was arrested, what did he do? He made up an excuse. 'She was coming after me with some scissors. Oh, I must have placed them back on the desk after it all happened.' Is that an act of blind passion, if in fact it did happen?

"Then, what has he done since that time? He has done everything to save his own skin. He has sat calmly in jail without remorse, scheming and designing as to how he was going to gain some advantage in this trial.

"Remember, Ladies and Gentlemen, that this same scheming, designing, cool individual was the man who stood at the window that night, and the instructions of law tell you over and over again that when a killing is perpetrated with design, malice and revenge, it is first degree murder. Revenge for what? For a mistaken notion on his part that his wife was doing something she shouldn't. Whereas, in fact, he was doing what he should not do and had brought the situation on himself. Are you going to allow this villain to be released to kill again? No, Ladies and Gentlemen of the jury, that is not justice. That is not honesty with yourself, that is not doing right by society and by the dead Matilda Taylor."

It is then the defense attorney's turn. He rises and speaks as follows:

"Ladies and Gentlemen of the jury, Freddy Taylor has asked me to give you his personal thanks for being here, and for your careful attention to the trial. I want to thank you too. And, if you will excuse a little pretension, I should like to here thank God for all juries and for this wonderful jury system, because we have just seen an example of what would happen if we didn't give the final say in these things to juries and, instead, left the decision up to some public official.

"I don't know how things can be so black and white to some people, and I don't know why every homicide case has to be first degree murder or nothing. That isn't what the law says, but some people seem to want to look at it that way in spite of the fact that every civilized country makes a distinction between justice and retribution. It's beyond me how anyone could find an element of revenge or malice in these facts, but even more shocking than that is to hear an urgent, and I submit insincere, demand that these orderly court processes be turned into a ruthless vendetta.

"I don't know where the District Attorney presumes to get his information that the defendant has sat in jail without remorse these past few months. I am the one who has been conferring with Mr. Taylor, not the District Attorney, and I know the exact opposite to be true. This tragedy has cut the heart out of a man. It has wrenched his soul beyond belief. Far from being concerned with his own skin, his mind has been obsessed with this awful tragedy, and his constant desire has been the impossible—to bring her back. Truth is the only ointment for this type of pain, and that, ladies and gentlemen, is why we have tried to bring out the truth to you.

"The fact that we have been able to bring out some of the true facts regarding this terrible mistake has done Fred Taylor more good than anything I have been able to tell him before. And seeing you ladies and gentlemen, listening with compassion and understanding, with fairness and impartiality and without prejudice, with open-mindedness instead of one-mindedness, as been an inspiration to us all. The frantic, maddening turmoil in Fred Taylor's mind may one day calm down, knowing that this trial has taken place as it has.

Regardless of the outcome, he will always be indebted to you for the trial, because it has provided a kind of therapy or salve to his pain which nothing else could provide; for here is a sensitive and honest man. What happened that night he does not know. He knows that Matilda died, and every time this realization comes to him he dies a little inside, as any of us would on losing someone close to us.

"Let us turn to the issue of proof and try to clear up our thinking on the lines of responsibility. Who is to make the proof? The District Attorney has that burden at the beginning of the trial and all during the trial. The burden of proof never shifts. It is always upon the District Attorney, and he must prove each and every essential element of the crime beyond all reasonable doubt. What are the essential elements? First of all, an essential element in any crime is criminal intent. If that is not proven, there is no crime. An act alone does not constitute a crime. The court tells you that a crime consists of an act coupled with intent. If the intent is not proven there is no crime whatsoever, regardless of what happened.

"Civilization has long since abandoned the notion that when somebody dies, somebody else must pay. Rather, ours is a system that defines a crime by giving it certain elements and places the burden upon the accuser to prove all of these elements. If the accuser cannot do that, the charge fails. The district attorney talks about our defense as if to place the burden on us to prove something. The fact is that under the law we do not have to prove a thing, and if our defense merely raises a reasonable doubt as to any one of the essential elements of the crime, then the people's case must fall.

"I do not have to remind you of the oath you took to follow the law and the evidence. I knew you would do that when Fred Taylor and I accepted you as our jurors in this case where everything is at stake for him, unlike some of the other participants to whom it is just another trial. But I do feel justified in emphasizing what the law is—that nobody can be guilty of murder, or any crime, without intent to do the act—and that is the philosophy behind this insanity plea, provided by law.

"Now let us talk about presumptions, because the court uses these in guiding you by his instructions of law. First of all, there is a presumption of innocence, and this remains with the defendant throughout the trial unless the District Attorney overcomes the presumption by proof beyond a reasonable doubt of each and every one of the essential elements.

"Let us next look to the presumption of sanity. It is given the same name, but here quite a different rule prevails. First of all, anybody, whether charged with a crime or not, is presumed to be sane. But as you see from the court's instructions, this presumption is overcome when any, even slight, evidence of insanity is brought into the trial, in which case the burden then rests upon the District Attorney to prove the sanity of the defendant and to prove it beyond all reasonable doubt. Has he done that for you? Has he sustained his burden on that point?

"The state doctor informed you that he took a life history of the defendant during his forty-minute examination and, because he found no evidence of insanity, he then rendered the opinion that the defendant was sane. Did he consider the part of the law stating that an irresistible impulse is insanity under the criminal code? Did he think about that? Did he examine it and try to determine whether this was the case? You heard his answers to my questions along that line on cross examination. They could only be described as evasive. The only implication you could attach to his testimony is that, even though he is employed as a state psychiatrist, he chooses not to follow the law as set out by the legislature. He chooses to set himself out as one above the law. He chooses to render the verdict in this case rather than aid you in rendering it. He just doesn't believe in irresistible impulse, and I submit that from his testimony and his manner and demeanor on this witness stand, we can validly say that in no case, regardless of the circumstances, would he find a defendant insane under the irresistible impulse language of our statute.

"Our psychiatrist, on the other hand, has carefully considered the word and the law of the state, and has seen that it was his duty to conform to it, and to examine the defendant in the light of the irresistible impulse rule. Unlike our state doctor, he has seen his duty as an expert witness, not to act as an advocate, not to write in his own personal notion of what the law should or should not be, and try to influence you with it. And after he had applied his highly trained mind to the task of ascertaining all anyone possibly could about the defendant and about the case, he then reached the solemn conclusion and opinion which he honestly and forthrightly presented here to you—that the defendant was suffering under an irresistible impulse when this terrible occurrence took place. Did he hedge, hem, and haw on cross examination? No. He answered the questions forthrightly and stood by his clear, reasoned opinion.

"I submit that the only evidence in this case is that the defendant did not know what he was doing when Matilda Taylor met her death. Dr. Barnaby examined the defendant not in the same way as he was examined by the detective or in the same way he was examined here under pressure of this public trial, but he examined him in a skillful, professional, face-to-face conference where, if ever the facts would come out, if ever fakery was going on, it would necessarily be exposed. Do you believe that Fred Taylor here, a laborer, could fool Dr. Barnaby? Our doctor has the confidence in his own skill—based, I might say, on ample justification—to know that he can flush out a faker in five minutes if the person actually is a faker. Our friend from the state hospital does not have this confidence, perhaps also with some justification.

"Fred Taylor fled in terror. Ladies and Gentlemen, you have the insight to know why that happened. You and I know that he was not scheming at that moment as the District Attorney so blithely contends. If he were the cold-blooded schemer we have heard about here, what would he have done? He would have disposed of that body. He would then have made up intricate excuses to the neighbors, stating that his wife had gone out of town or something of the sort. Fred didn't even have the presence of mind to get out of town himself. He was dizzy and confused, consumed with remorse, and when he was picked up by the police, it was an immense relief, and he showed this by the honest and straightforward manner in which he told everything to them. You heard the officers say that he was cooperative, that he gave no resistance, that he did not try to cover up or hide a thing. Did he act like a Dillinger and try to shoot it out with the cops? Did he kill for money or malice? Is he in the class of fiends you think of when the term 'murderer' comes to your mind? No. He is a pitiful human being involved in a tragic mistake.

"The district attorney says we are going to try to malign Mrs. Taylor. We would not do that under any circumstances. We have more respect for the dead than to try to tell you about some supposed unfaithfulness or unworthiness. But as you and I know, domestic matters always have two sides, and remember that this was a domestic matter, not a case of a robber and murderer shooting down people for money. We feel it necessary to point out one thing as to this domestic argument: Who had the weapon? Did Fred Taylor have the weapon? No. Matilda had the weapon, a heavy pair of scissors capable of inflicting great bodily harm or death. And you are instructed that self-defense is a lawful activity. Consider your instruction on involuntary manslaughter. This, Ladies and Gentlemen, is why the district attorney was shouting so much about the word 'malice'—because that instruction tells you that a killing as a result of a lawful activity, such as defending oneself, done in an unlawful manner is involuntary manslaughter, and nothing else.

"The instruction then states that a killing with malice, however, is murder. And that is why we have all of this loud noise using the word 'malice,' although there is not one scintilla of evidence about malice. The District Attorney knows that sooner or later in your deliberations you are going to come to this instruction and may very well decide that it applies. He then wants a bell to ring in your mind based on his repeated use of that word malice, which, he assumes, will then make you discard that instruction and go to some higher degree of homicide. But what the District Attorney says is not evidence, and you are so instructed by the court. The only source of evidence is from the witness stand given by people here sworn to tell the truth. And ask yourself this: Did you hear any witness in this case use that word 'malice'? No. Only the district attorney has used it in an attempt to supplant the evidence with his own words.

"Self defense, then, is a lawful activity. Your determination upon the lawfulness of the manner in which it was carried out would determine the applicability of this instruction.

"But, ladies and gentlemen, I am not going to attempt to substitute my thinking for yours. You are the ones to render the verdict. That you will do it in good conscience and after fair deliberation, considering the fact that you have an entire man's future in your hands, is beyond any question in my mind.

"Freddy Taylor and I again thank you. You have been most patient with my tedious delivery here. I should inform you that the

District Attorney has the last word. Why? Because he has the burden of proof. He had it at the beginning of the trial, and he still has it, and therefore, I can only speak once in this final argument, whereas, he can get up to rebut what I have said. If he should say something that I may have forgotten about—and because of this rule, we are required to sit quietly and just listen—I have confidence that you will then try to consider what our comeback would be as if we had said it. Thank you again."

The District Attorney then rises for his rebuttal argument:

"My friends, and I do think of you as my friends by now, as we have been through this lengthy trial together and are about to complete it. My honorable opponent may have placed a misconception in your minds as to the purpose of this rebuttal argument. It is a rebuttal argument, and it means just that. I am limited to talking about things he talked about and, therefore, I cannot bring up things that he did not think of.

"I am always a little astounded to hear the type of argument given here—and he only made one point in his argument—and that was when he said that no witness used the word 'malice,' and therefore, there was no evidence of malice in the trial. This, if I may say, is an insult to your intelligence.

"In the first place, no witness would be allowed to use the word 'malice' because that would be a conclusion on his part, which is not permitted. A witness can only tell what he saw, heard, or did. A witness cannot give you his interpretation of what happened, because interpretations of what happened are all left to you, the jury. Can you imagine the court allowing a police officer, or somebody else, to get up here on the witness stand and say 'he killed his wife with malice because she was being unfaithful?' Counsel for the defense would rise so fast out of his seat that you would be astounded at his agility, and he would object so strenuously that the judge would be inclined to declare a mistrial and call the whole thing quits. Yet he turns around here on his closing argument and says that because no witness said what they would never in the world be allowed to say, therefore, there was no evidence of malice.

"That is exactly like saying that because the Japanese didn't say 'war' before they started dropping bombs on Pearl Harbor, they, therefore, were not making war. And I didn't notice our country waiting around to hear them say it. They didn't have to say it. Their actions said it for them. And Fred Taylor didn't have to say 'malice and murder.' His actions said it for him. But look what he did say. He did say they were 'arguing.' Well, what does that connote? That is a contest of words in anger, with malice. Then followed the act. The horrible, brutal physical manifestation of his malice which had, by his own admission, been previously expressed in words.

"I feel justified in assuming that you agree with me that the tale of the scissors is out. I think it's significant to note, also, that they just said 'scissors.' They didn't tell you anything about the manner in which she was supposedly using these scissors, whether they were open or closed, in which hand she was holding them or anything else that would necessarily have been brought out very clearly, if it had been a true story.

"Who transformed the exchange of angry words into a heinous act of physical violence? The defendant just thought he would win this argument once and for all, which he did. And I submit to you again that he is now—with cool, detached, scheming calculation—trying to complete the circle of his triumph, which necessarily would include a triumph in court. And anything less than the proper verdict in this case—first degree murder—would, indeed, be a triumph for him.

"We hear impassioned statements about the defendant's remorse, although we haven't seen it. We have just heard about it. Well, wouldn't we like to hear about Matilda's remorse at having ever seen this man who was to take her as his wife and then eventually kill her?

"And we hear that because a psychiatrist, employed by the state, does not agree with the defense interpretation, he is then, necessarily, being dishonest with you, and is not following the law. Well, isn't that interesting? By this line of reasoning, if you don't agree with me, you are then not only mistaken but you are also dishonest.

"I hasten to point out also that it is Fred Taylor, the wife killer, on trial and not Dillinger or anybody else. Are we supposed to have a double standard whereby people who kill their wives are less the murderer than people who kill anybody else? No. I think wives are entitled to live just as much as anybody. And I submit that there is an added element of hatefulness in this because I recall something about 'love, honor and obey' in the marriage vows. Nine-tenths of what we heard from the defense concerned how sorry they all are that it happened. I think it would be more accurate to say that Fred Taylor is sorry he is faced with a first degree murder conviction. This is understandable, but it does not change the facts. The only logical deduction from all of this evidence is that he stood at that window and saw something going on that he thought was improper; he then resolved to kill his wife, and did so a few minutes later—in the most extreme and brutal manner imaginable.

"One doesn't strangle the life out of another human being, squeezing so hard that it breaks bones in the neck, by mistake. You might make a mistake in driving your car and, unfortunately, kill somebody. But people just don't get strangled to death by mistake. That is indeed a unique theory.

"I don't know why you and I should have to rack our brains to find some justification for Fred Taylor's actions. But just as exercise, I have tried to do so, and I have tried my best to utilize the sterling words of my opponent in seeking out anything at all, even the slightest indication of validity to any of these claims which might appeal to any one or more of you members of the jury. This is part of my job, because if there is such a thing, I have to examine it and see whether or not we are doing the wrong thing here by prosecuting this man. We are sworn to protect the innocent as well as prosecute the guilty."

The defense attorney hastily rises and states: "I object, your honor; this is improper comment. Counsel implies that no innocent person is ever prosecuted because of his alleged oath—which is just not so. It's for the jury to decide . . ."

The judge: "All right, gentlemen, that's enough. The defense objection is sustained. Limit yourself to this case, counsel."

The prosecutor continues: "Very well, your honor. I would think, for instance, that if he had slapped her instead of strangling her to death there might have been some justification because physical violence, vile as it is, still is less vile if used with some degree of humanity and restraint. But I beseech you not to misconstrue your duty here because we happen to have a democratic system where the defendant is first presumed innocent and a burden of proof happens to be on the District Attorney. The instructions do not say that you cannot do justice. They tell you that you *can* and *must* do justice. Given the facts, you must avenge foul murder. These rules don't mean that we can't prove crimes when we have the facts. On the contrary, we do have the facts in this case, and we have proven the crime.

"I ask you to consider the two sides of this domestic case, as my learned opponent would have you categorize it. The one party is now in the grave cruelly murdered, unable to defend herself, unable to give her version, her lips muted by the defendant's own act. On the other side, we have the defendant here in court trying to write this off as a petty case.

"I submit that it would be entirely justifiable and proper for you ladies and gentlemen to imagine Matilda Taylor here on this witness stand telling you that Fred Taylor announced that he was going out to play poker that night, and that she, faced with an evening alone, wanted to go to a dance. She went to a dance and did nothing wrong. She was offered a ride home, and she took it. She did nothing wrong in connection with that ride home. And then, when she walked into her house, not realizing that she was walking into her own casket, she found not a husband but a vicious murderer making violent and false accusations against her, and who, before she had any chance to defend herself or to escape, there snuffed out her life in one atrocious act.

"The defendant's lawyer seems to say that what Mr. Taylor wants most is to cleanse himself from the guilt of this thing. Well, there is nothing more cleansing than justice, and I submit that if he got any less than that he wouldn't feel clean. Justice is what you owe to him, to yourself, to this court, and to the people of this state—and this is what we ask, nothing more, nothing less.

"Thank you."

After the arguments of counsel, the judge then swears the bailiffs and places the jury in their custody. He discharges the extra jurors and informs the jury that they should first choose a foreman and, when they have reached a verdict, to so advise by pressing a buzzer.

When the jury arrives at a verdict, they ring the bailiff and he calls the judge and the attorneys, as well as the sheriff's officer who is holding the defendant in custody. If these individuals are not in immediate attendance in the court room, as they might not be if the jury had been out for several hours, the jury will have to wait a half-hour or so while they come down. The jury is then brought into court where the judge, the defendant and the attorneys are all present. This a dramatic moment in any trial. Fred Taylor sits staring straight ahead, his insides tied in a thousand knots. Anything less than the death penalty would satisfy him. The lawyers, and even the judge, feel the pent-up emotion of a hard-fought battle about to be resolved. The verdict could be anything, and they know it. They have been through too many trials to think they could guess the outcome. Carl Decker carries the signed verdict tightly gripped in his hand. He finds himself compelled to look at the defendant once more, hoping to see something to give him a final confirmation of the correctness of what they are doing. The other jurors do the same, and they see what they want to see. Their verdict is as follows:

"We, the jury, find the defendant, Fred Taylor, was sane at the time of the alleged offense.

"We, the jury, find the defendant Fred Taylor, guilty of voluntary manslaughter."

The penalty for this degree of homicide is one to eight years in the state penitentiary. The jury does not know this until they read it in the newspaper story regarding their verdict.

After the jury has filed out of the court room, tired and all wanting to get home, the defense attorney rises and asks the judge for a period of from ten to twenty days within which to file a motion for a new trial. The judge grants him this time. The defense attorney also asks the judge to set a bond in a reasonable amount because the verdict was not first degree murder, and voluntary manslaughter would be a bailable offense under the law.

The judge considers himself then well enough informed to set a bond since he has just heard all of the evidence in the case, including information as to the defendant's past convictions, but he asks the District Attorney for his position on this subject.

The District Attorney states that the defendant's criminal record includes one or two minor offenses in addition to the burglary conviction that was brought out during the trial, but it does not appear to contain any information regarding an escape or a failure to appear in court when ordered. The District Attorney concedes that because of the verdict a reasonable bail would be proper.

The judge sets bail in the sum of $5,000, but he points out at the same time that the defendant has been utilizing the services of a court-appointed lawyer, paid by the state, and asks the defense attorney how the defendant intends to make this bond. The defense attorney states that he does not know the answer to that question at present, and it may very well be that the defendant will not be able to make it because he does not have sufficient property to put up or enough money to pay a commercial bondsman at the rate of 10% of the face amount of the bond. He concedes to the court that because of this circumstance asking for bail may very well be an empty gesture, but he felt that his client was entitled to have a figure set.

In the motion for a new trial, which is presented to the court and to the District Attorney in written form, the defense attorney asserts certain errors that he feels have been committed during the trial. In this case, he does not pursue the motion with great energy, but rather presents it merely to preserve the record, to complete his responsibility to the client, and to give the judge an opportunity to reconsider any rulings made during the trial which the judge himself may feel had been in error.

The reason why the motion is not strongly urged is this: Should the motion be granted, then the defendant would be tried again, and it might be that another jury would consider the case more serious and find him guilty of murder. The attorney presents the motion, stating to the court that he wishes to waive any oral argument in the court. The court denies the motion and asks the defendant whether or not he desires to apply for probation. The defense attorney states that they would. Whereupon the judge says:

"Very well, we will have a report made up by the investigation department of our probation office and the defendant will return into court one month from today for either granting of probation or sentencing."

The probation office is an arm of the court. It comprises a number of specialists in probation work who not only investigate cases very thoroughly after the defendant has either been found guilty by a jury or has pleaded guilty but, when people are granted probation, they supervise them very closely. Probation is an almost universal practice under American criminal law. It has many advantages in that it allows the court to try to redeem convicted criminals under close supervision rather than send them to the state penitentiary where their upkeep will be very expensive, and where the surroundings could very well do more harm than good for them and for society. Probation is designed only for convicts who are not considered dangerous in any way and whose entire life would indicate that they would respond to this type of treatment and become worthwhile citizens. Probation is most helpful and appropriate in the case of a young offender whose transgressions may be attributed to his youth, and who needs some special care and supervision in order to learn how to get along with society.

Fred Taylor's probation report consists of approximately ten long typewritten pages compiled by a specialist who writes to all of his former employers and to his friends and family members, and interviews people who knew him in order to create a complete picture as to this person. The courts are sometimes criticized, by sociologists particularly, for concentrating all of their efforts on the ascertainment of guilt or innocence. The sociologists claim that this issue is only a minor part of the entire picture as to any criminal or his offense. In the probation program, the courts do exactly what the sociologists think they should. Under our legal system, where everyone is presumed innocent until proven guilty, the court has no power over the defendant to investigate his life or his character or anything else until that moment when he either pleads guilty or is found guilty of an offense. It is only then that the court is enabled to help him, and the court does so through its probation department.

It is understood that should probation be denied, then the investigative material in the report will also be used in determining what sentence to give. The court has a broad discretion as to sentence—in this case one to eight years, and the court gives a minimum and maximum sentence within those two figures. The minimum is the base sentence that the defendant will serve in the penitentiary. Under the formula set out in the statutes of the state, his actual time of confinement will be considerably less than the minimum if he earns all the good behavior points possible by his conduct at the penitentiary. On the return date for the probation report, Fred Taylor is again brought into court and his case is called.

The judge informs Fred and his attorney that he has examined the report and that probation is denied. He then asks if they have any statement to make before sentencing.

The lawyer makes a plea in Fred's behalf, stating he does not feel that Fred is a dangerous individual, that this was an unfortunate domestic situation, and Fred never intended to kill, as the jury found, and so he should get leniency.

The judge then asks Fred if he has anything to say. Fred says that he feels his lawyer had said everything that could be said.

The judge then says, "It is the judgement and sentence of this court that you be taken by the sheriff to the county jail and thence to the state penitentiary there to serve a term of 5 to 7 years."

The lawyer says: "Your Honor, the defendant has been in jail now for 8½ months. I wonder if that might be taken into consideration in the sentencing."

The judge says: "Well, part of that time he was in the hospital being examined under an insanity plea."

Lawyer: "That is correct, your Honor, but we just wanted to point out that he had been confined for some length of time."

Judge: "I am aware of that, and I did take that into consideration in my sentence."

Lawyer: "Very well, your Honor, and thank you."

Fred will serve approximately three years under this sentence, if he conducts himself in an exemplary manner at the state penitentiary. When he is released, he will be on parole for an additional four years to complete the seven-year maximum sentence given. Parole is very much like probation. The parolees are under constant supervision by the state parole department, although they are out in the world making their way. The parole department seeks to help them find jobs, adjust to society, and stay away from criminal activities and associates.

Thus ends the trial of Fred Taylor and the jury service of Carl Decker and his friends. Often when jurors have served on a capital case where they have been confined for several days, the judge will order that they be excused from further involuntary jury service. The jury burden is spread so thin over the populace that the court can well afford to do this.

One of the basic things we have tried to show in this trial story is how living facts become a part of a judicial proceeding to produce a judicial result. This might be compared to putting various substances together in a test tube and watching what happens. Here the three basic elements are facts, law, and the power of human reason. Mix them together and shake well. The result—justice.

All states, in fact all civilized countries of the world, have degrees of culpability in homicide based upon the factors of intent, premeditation, malice, deliberation, and provocation. Also, insanity as a defense is known throughout the civilized world. All jurisdictions have their own way of defining these things. However, the idea is basically the same everywhere, with distinctions based on the use of different terminology. No one has yet managed to simplify homicide and, so long as justice is a consideration, they never will.

Chapter Six

SUPREME LAW OF THE LAND

Elvin Gard and Rollie Riggins were good family men with a bond of friendship based on mutual love of the outdoors. Last summer they had hit on Siwassee Lake, and had talked about it all winter. A three-day weekend was too good to waste in town. It was quite a drive to Siwassee Lake, but they took off one weekend in Elvin's pick-up truck, fully outfitted with boat and fishing gear, and brought along Rollie's two boys, Brad, 12, and Rex, 10.

It was early in the season, and from all appearances not another soul had been at the lake yet that year. They parked their truck and as they tramped up to the lake the first day Rollie noticed that the sign was down. Apparently, it had somehow come loose from its post and was lying in the wet grass by the side of the road. The sign was a board put up by the State Game Department. Engraved into the wood deep were the words "Siwassee Lake" and an arrow.

When they came back to the camp after the first day's fishing, they noticed a station wagon parked about fifty feet away from their truck. The driver turned out to be one Carl Stiger, whom they had not met before but they struck up a fisherman's acquaintance.

Elvin had helped out the Game Department over in another part of the state as a volunteer, checking game through during the hunting season. On the way back to the car the thought occurred to him that he should pick up that sign and take it down to the warden's cabin ten miles down the road, on the way home, so that

Supreme Law of the Land • 91

they would be aware it was down and could have it repaired. He slid the sign under the front seat of the pick-up truck.

Just as they were finishing lunch and getting ready to fold up the tent and pack for home, Officer Keith Mills, State Deputy Game Warden, arrived on the scene. He was friendly and courteous and went through the usual procedure of asking to see their licenses and their fish, which he very carefully counted to see that they were not over the limit. While the warden was there, Carl Stiger came tramping back from the lake with his catch for the morning.

By this time Carl had moved his station wagon over to within about eight feet of the pick-up, and the two parties had shared a meal or two together. Deputy Warden Mills also asked to see Carl's license and his fish. Carl showed him the fish in his creel and in the top of his ice chest. They counted out to just the legal limit for possession.

Carl was a rough-talking individual, and somehow the warden felt he should look further. He asked Carl to empty out his station wagon so that a more thorough search could be made. Carl complied, and it wasn't long until the warden found another very small ice chest covered with a sleeping bag. In the chest were eight excess fish.

At this point, Game Warden Mills began to feel that he was being duped by some law breakers. He said, "What else have you guys been stealing around here?" and he fumed over to the pick-up truck, grabbed open the cab door and started looking intently all through the belongings of Elvin Gard and Rollie Riggins. He soon came across the sign under the front seat and his temper rose to boiling. "I should have known I would come onto a bunch of thieves," he said. "Just picking up a little souvenir, is that right? Something for your den!"

After various threats to "take the whole bunch to jail," Warden Mills finally settled on issuing a penalty assessment against Carl Stiger and giving Elvin and Rollie what they thought was a mere warning. "I'll talk to the chief about this," he said, as he drove off in his jeep with the sign.

Two weeks later, to the complete surprise of Rollie Riggins, a police officer arrived at his home and informed him that he had a warrant for his arrest charging petit larceny out of the county where the lake was located. He was informed that he would have to come down to the police building and remain in jail until the morning, when he could make bond.

Neither Rollie Riggins nor Elvin Gard had ever been charged with any type of crime before in their lives. The shocking thing to Rollie was to have his two boys, Brad and Rex, see their father's honesty questioned in this way. Neither of them had ever met Carl Stiger before he came to the lake that weekend, and they had no knowledge of or participation with him in overfishing his limit.

What does all this have to do with the United States Constitution? A great deal, as we shall see.

The case is filed in the lowliest court of the land, a Justice of the Peace Court; the charge is the pettiest of crimes: "Stealing a sign, property of the State, of the value of $7.00." Rollie hires a lawyer to defend him.

The case is small but the issues are profound. Each of us alive in America today has inherited a great background of development, economic, technological, and political, but the greatest of all our blessings, the most worthy of protection and perhaps the hardest won of all, are our personal liberties as guaranteed by the Constitution. These did not come to us by gift from above. They were won by endeavor. They are the result of centuries of application of the best thought of man, enforced by bloodshed. Nor will our freedoms be maintained without effort. They are subject to being lost at any time.

The lawyer finds that, fortunately, the case involving Rollie Riggins and Elvin Gard is filed in the court of a legally trained Justice of the Peace. The lawyer files a motion to suppress evidence, asserting that neither the allegedly stolen sign, nor any testimony about it, can be admitted into evidence, because it was discovered by the officer as the result of illegal search and seizure of the personal effects of the defendants.

When the Justice of the Peace assumed his office, he took a solemn oath in which he vowed to uphold the laws and the Constitution of the State and of the United States. This minor judge is a judicial officer of the state. And the states, when they bound themselves together in union, each promised to uphold the Constitution of the United States. The Constitution of the United

States, in addition to establishing the framework of that government, guarantees personal rights to all of the citizens of all of the member states. So if the Justice of the Peace is to follow his oath, then the United States Constitution lives in his courtroom just as surely as it lives in the lofty chambers of the United States Supreme Court.

The lawyer's brief in support of his motion to suppress use of the sign as evidence in the case contains a number of citations of United States Supreme Court opinions and opinions of state Supreme Courts throughout the land. It contains a reference to the Fourth Amendment of the Federal Constitution and utilizes the language of judges in explaining when and under what circumstances a search of the private effects of a citizen is illegal and when evidence so obtained must be suppressed in a prosecution.

But rather than go through a musty brief, let us call our discussion "People, Places and Principle." The people and places change but the principle crops up over and over again.

Deputy Warden Keith Mills was doing his job, and he thought he was doing it well, but little did he know how intimately involved his actions were with some of the most significant events in the history of man.

"The freedom of one's house," spoke James Otis, "should be as secure as a prince in his castle." It was February 24, 1761, and Otis, a brilliant young lawyer and patriot, was using England's despised writs of assistance as a whipping post for revolutionary ferment. "The liberty of every man is in the hands of every petty officer," he said.

Otis spoke for five hours before a colonial court sitting in the Council Chamber of Boston's old town house. The Crown had petitioned to renew the writs, which were blanket warrants allowing customsmen to search and seize private property at will in aid of tax collection. Otis represented some of the sixty-three merchants who were in the audience opposing the writs. "Slavery, villainy . . . a tyrant's device!" he shouted. He showed that the writs were obtainable on "bare suspicion without oath," and that they were negotiable, passing freely from one officer to another, and once granted would "live forever."

"Every man prompted by revenge, ill humor, or wantonness to

inspect the inside of his neighbor's house may get a writ of assistance. They are used by petty officers moved by malice as much as zeal for law," he proclaimed. Otis lost his case, but John Adams, who heard him speak, afterward wrote: "A flame of fire . . . then and there the child independence was born." Men were moved to take up arms.

Events such as this ultimately caused the enactment of provisions such as these: "The right of the people to be secure in their persons, houses, papers, and effects against unreasonable searches and seizures shall not be violated; and no warrant shall issue, but upon probable cause, supported by oath or affirmation, and particularly describing the place to be searched, and the person or things to be seized." (The Fourth Amendment); "No person shall be compelled in any criminal case, to be a witness against himself; nor be deprived of life, liberty, or property, without due process of law." (The Fifth Amendment); "Nor shall any state deprive any person of life, liberty, or property without due process of law." (The Fourteenth Amendment)

On May 23, 1957, seven police officers raided the home of Miss Dollree Mapp in Cleveland, Ohio. An informer had accused her of harboring a bombing suspect and some policy paraphernalia. On advice of her attorney she demanded to see a valid search warrant, whereupon an officer waved a paper before her face. She snatched the paper and thrust it into her bosom. The officers then forcibly recovered this from her person. They seized her, twisted her hand until it pained her, and, because she was belligerent, handcuffed her to a bedpost. While she was thus held, a prisoner in her own bedroom, the officers ransacked her home from top to bottom. They didn't find what they were looking for, but instead, while rummaging through her drawers, closets, and suitcases, they came across four little pamphlets, a couple of photographs and a little pencil doodle—all alleged to be pornographic. She claimed no knowledge of these things, that "they must have belonged to a recent lodger, a man who left and went to New York."

She was convicted of a crime for knowing possession of "obscene, lewd, and lascivious" items and was sentenced to jail. Her lawyer appealed to the Ohio Supreme Court and lost. The Ohio Court held that even though there probably was no valid warrant and the search may have been unreasonable, offending a sense of justice, still, the question of police methods should not be confused with the issue of guilt or innocence of the accused. Evidence, however obtained, may be used in court to prove someone guilty of a crime.

The historical idea of a search warrant is to strip law officers of discretion in dealing with a citizen's rights. Instead of taking the law entirely into his own hands, cutting a swath of abuse throughout society, he must, whenever possible, go before a judicial officer of some sort (a justice of the peace will do) and show, under oath, that "probable cause" exists for the police action contemplated. If so, a warrant will be prepared not only allowing him to make the search but ordering him to do so. Both the action of the officer and of the magistrate is always subject to a higher judicial review. An independent judiciary thus controls the "petty officers moved by malice" at the bottom and the tyrants moved by hate and lust for power, at the top.

The question is how shall this control be accomplished: by allowing aggrieved citizens to sue officers who have abused their rights or by refusing to let the jury see any evidence improperly obtained? A majority of the states have rejected the latter approach, declining, as Justice Benjamin Cardoza once put it for the State of New York, to let "the criminal go free because the constable has blundered."

"The criminal goes free, if he must, but it is the law that sets him free," spoke the United States Supreme Court on June 19, 1961, in an historic ruling. "We hold that all evidence obtained by searches and seizures in violation of the Constitution is, by that same authority, inadmissible in state court . . . such evidence shall not be used at all. The security of one's privacy against arbitrary intrusion by the police is implicit in the concept of ordered liberty and as such enforceable against the states through the due process clause. Other remedies have completely failed to secure compliance with the constitutional provisions."

The Court likens this freedom to the Fifth Amendment right against self-incrimination, as having "the same constitutional purpose—to maintain inviolate large areas of personal privacy."

Prior to this decision in *State of Ohio v. Dollree Mapp*, the United States Supreme Court had not required states to exclude the evidence illegally obtained.

Armed with the Dollree Mapp decision, the lawyer for Rollie

Riggins and Elvin Gard points out that the search of Elvin Gard's automobile was made without a warrant and without any prior knowledge or probable cause on the part of Deputy Game Warden Keith Mills to believe that the defendants had committed the alleged crime of petit larceny, or any crime. A careful review of the facts would indicate that the warden was, immediately prior to jerking open the door of the pick-up truck, entertaining thoughts of guilt by association. He was, in his own unguarded discretion, indicting the defendant because an apparent companion, Carl Stiger, had violated the law. But the law has long since deprived him of the right to infringe upon the privacy of citizens in circumstances such as these.

On hearing the lawyer's argument for suppression of the evidence, the law-trained Justice of the Peace grants the motion to suppress with this comment:

"I think it is a close question. There is a difference between searching one's home without a warrant and searching a car. A car is ambulatory. It can go from place to place and it may be impossible for an officer to obtain a warrant to search. To obtain a warrant, an officer must come before a judge, take an oath to tell the truth, and give evidence which will satisfy the judge that there is probable or reasonable cause to believe that some specified stolen goods or other item or items which may be relevant to some proper law enforcement function are at a particular place. Now, of course, an arrest may be made without a warrant and a search accompanying such arrest will be legal if the arrest was legal. The Constitution does not state that every search and every arrest without a warrant is illegal. It states that the people will be protected from unreasonable searches and seizures of their private papers and property. The question then becomes: What is unreasonable?

"If an officer has actual knowledge that a felony has been committed, whether or not this knowledge is based on hearsay, then he is justified in making an arrest and in conducting a reasonable search in connection therewith. Or if a misdemeanor is committed in his presence, then he may arrest and he may conduct a search.

"Since Deputy Game Warden Keith Mills is here in the courtroom, I would dearly like to be able to give him some reliable guidance for his conduct in situations such as this. This is most difficult, because each case must be considered on its own individual merits. It may be strange that this is so when one is speaking of a constitutional issue, but perhaps the first rule in this field of law is gentlemanliness. The gentleman is reasonable. Even though he is doing something or saying something contrary to the interests of a person in his presence, he is being reasonable about it. He has his emotions under control. He does not show force until force is shown to him or until force becomes necessary. He does not swear and stomp and fume. He has a detached and an objective attitude.

"Things are often difficult to define. It depends upon the circumstances in each case. This becomes particularly difficult when you have this 'association' problem. Every law man knows that a good way to find crooks is to go among the crooks. Birds of a feather fly together. In fact, some of our laws in this state recognize this principle. For example, our parole and probation laws prohibit a probationer or a parolee from associating with known criminals, yet a person can be, to all appearances, associated with a lawbreaker and yet be entirely innocent. This presents a real dilemma.

"Another point is this: The law gives way to strict rules by allowing a search in connection with a lawful arrest. No arrest was made in this case, from the evidence I have heard here in support of this motion. Apparently the officer left the scene, leaving the defendants with the impression that a chewing out in front of one of the men's young boys would satisfy the state. I am not prepared to say, and I do not have to rule, what the result would have been had there been an actual arrest. However, there was not an arrest, and therefore the rule that a search in connection with a lawful arrest is legal cannot apply. I must, therefore, grant the motion to suppress this evidence and as a result, the case itself will have to be dismissed and the defendants totally acquitted of the charge.

"Now, Mr. Mills, I am afraid that I have not given you much guidance. If there is any doubt in your mind about the legality of a search, you must take it upon yourself to first go get a warrant. The law may seem to be unsympathetic to the exigencies of law enforcement. We are well aware of these, and yet we would rather see guilty people go free than give up our constitutional protection."

This case shows a fortunate circumstance: a petty crime, if indeed any was committed, upstanding citizens in a rare role for them as defendants, and a legally trained Justice of the Peace. The Constitution does not always have so facile a route. Many of our minor judicial offices are held by individuals with no qualifications —by training, background, intelligence, or otherwise—to interpret the law and to determine what is reasonable or what is not in enforcement of the law. Additionally, many of our Justice of the Peace Courts are endowed with an invidious fee system which makes a finding of guilty necessary in every case in order to collect "costs" of four or five dollars. The court may be minor and the offense petty, but there is no such thing as an unimportant case. When the Constitution is involved, and it usually is, the case is always important, not only to the parties but also to the country and to the cause of liberty for mankind.

But this is not the only strain against the Constitution. Another one is the occurrence of hard facts. Say, for example, that a dead body had been found in the cab of that pick-up truck—or a stolen gun or a bomb or a cache of narcotics. The facts of an arrest and search control, and not the heinousness of the crime committed or a type of contraband recovered. The Supreme Court has said, "We have had frequent occasions to point out that a search is not made legal by what it turns up. In law, it is good or bad when it begins and does not change character from its success." Yet the legality of an arrest may depend upon subtle distinctions which an officer must understand, not only on the beat but while undergoing tough cross-examination in court.

The protection against illegal searches and seizures is only one of the several essential personal liberties and protections guaranteed by our Constitution. Others are freedom of speech, press, assembly, and religion, the right against self-incrimination, the right to a trial by jury, the right to reasonable bail in a criminal case, the right to keep and bear arms, the right to protection of due process of law and the equal protection of the laws. In actual practice all of these things are subject to multiple, quizzical, and continuing problems in practical application. And this will always be so.

The personal guarantees and liberties of our Constitution were hammered out on an anvil of human misery. They are what distinguish ours from other major systems in the world. They can and should be preserved in spite of all costs and difficulties.

Chapter Seven

THERE OUGHT TO BE A LAW

Where the Law Comes from and How Lawyers Find It

The famous industrialist and inventor, Charles F. Kettering, used to preach that all things may be understood if broken down into their individual components. And so it is with law.

We will illustrate how a lawyer works with a particular problem. Silas Sharp, a widower for ten years, eighty-five years old, had been senile for approximately five years. Since senility is a regressive disease, he became slowly worse as the months and years passed by. Even though he possessed approximately one million dollars, having made his money in real estate and other business enterprises, he lived in one of the hotels which he owned, an old building in one of the poorer sections of town.

On many occasions, his lawyer had advised him to make a will or create a trust, which he refused to do. He had no children, and his only relatives were some distant cousins and one niece who was also rather elderly, but was, under the laws of the state where he lived, his sole heir at law. And heir at law is a person in a family lineage who, under the statutes of the state, will inherit from a deceased individual if the person dies intestate or without a will.

The niece and the cousins lived at a distance in other parts of the country, and Silas was alone in the world with his money until one Betsy Cross, a middle-aged lady, came into his life. This resulted in two legally significant occurrences: (1) the execution of a Will by

Silas Sharp; and (2) the marriage of Silas Sharp to Betsy Cross. The Will left the bulk of the estate to Betsy Cross, "or to her children if she should not survive me," but left a number of specific gifts to others, including the niece, a church, a fraternity to which Silas had belonged, and ten or twelve devoted friends of Silas'. These bequests ranged from five to fifty thousand dollars each and totalled about two hundred thousand dollars. Thus, his wife Betsy would be eligible to receive about eight hundred thousand dollars by the Will.

Two fundamental rules of law (in the state in which he was resident) became involved in these events: (1) When there are no children, a widow will receive the entire estate of a deceased man when he dies; and (2) When a person makes a Will and thereafter marries, the act of marriage automatically revokes and cancels the Will.

The connubial bliss of Betsy and Silas was of comparatively short duration. Silas had, in his last few years, taken to shopping around among lawyers, and although his lifelong lawyer was too kindhearted and considerate to have him adjudicated as a mental incompetent, one of the other lawyers he consulted was not so sentimental, since he realized that Silas was not really competent to handle his own affairs and that his property should be placed in the hands of a Conservator to prevent its dissipation, for which situation a law is provided.

Therefore the lawyer presented a petition to the County Court to have Silas Sharp adjudicated and his property placed in the hands of a bank as Conservator. The Bank then chose this lawyer to represent the bank in the estate. Having learned of the alleged marriage, the lawyer requested the Court for leave to bring an action to annul the marriage on the grounds of mental incompetency. This action to annul was filed in another court, and several months afterwards, a lengthy trial took place. The evidence was overwhelming that Silas Sharp did not have the mental capacity knowingly to enter into a marriage, and the jury so found. The Court decreed that the marriage be annulled.

The attorneys representing Betsy then appealed this case to the State Supreme Court, contending that numerous errors were made by the trial judge on questions of evidence and procedure.

During the time this appeal was pending in the Supreme Court,

Silas Sharp went to his reward. Nevertheless, the Supreme Court, approximately four months after his death, handed down a lengthy written opinion, wherein they directed that a new trial must be held because of numerous errors in the first trial of the case.

Faced with another long trial, and with a very serious legal question as to whether or not a marriage can be annulled after one of the parties to it is dead, the attorneys for either side entered into an agreement whereby the niece would receive one-half of the estate and Betsy would receive one-half. Both of these ladies were getting on in years and the amount under this agreement, was, for all practical purposes, just as valuable to them as would be the entire estate.

Something was overlooked, the various legacies which had been provided in the Will. At the time when Silas Sharp died, Betsy was in an anomalous position, in that a jury had ordered her marriage annulled; the case had been appealed to the Supreme Court, but she had no way of knowing whether the annulment would be upheld as valid and final or not. She, therefore, took out the will and lodged it in the Probate Court, asking that it be admitted to probate and that its terms be used as the guide for the distribution of Silas Sharp's fortune. Betsy Cross was in a trap. The people named in the Will had become her adversaries regarding the alleged marriage.

Few legal principles, standing alone, are difficult to understand. But when many legal factors converge into a problem, the skill and the learning of a lawyer is required. The lawyer does not have all available legal knowledge at his finger tips, but he knows where to look for the answer to questions and he understands how different principles and rulings may work together. Thus he is able to say what the controlling rule of law may be as to any particular fact situation.

First we study the annulment statute. In it we see that a marriage ceremonialized by an incompetent may be annulled in court, if it can be proven that the individual did not have the capacity to know what he was doing, when the marriage took place. But we see that the only people who can bring an action for annulment are the parties themselves to the marriage. One of the parties having died, who is to further pursue the claim for annulment? We see that here there is a possibility that no marriage can be annulled after one party has died, no matter how strong the evidence might be that it was an invalid marriage. But such a rule would be grossly unjust here because the marriage not only involves the status of the parties to it, it involves important property rights of other people who are also entitled to their day in court.

We know that when statutes are drafted by the legislature, they cannot possibly be made to cover every conceivable fact situation and are not intended to do so. That is why we have courts, and one of the most important functions of any court is to interpret a statute as it may apply to a particular case. This is called "statutory construction," an important legal art for both judges and lawyers. We cannot always just look to the bare statutory words. If we did this, many injustices would result. The words "annulment actions shall be brought by the parties to the marriage" would stop us cold. Instead, we must look to the entire act and notice the general intent behind it. We must look to other statutes on related subjects. Often we go into legislative history, that is, we compare the old and the new acts to see how and why it was changed. Sometimes, we will take speeches, committee reports or comments made by legislators when the bill was under consideration and use these to determine the legislative intent. We argue that equity and justice requires a certain interpretation. In all these things, we are not trying to change what the legislature has said, but rather, seek to find the true meaning and intent of the statute as applied to the fact situation at hand.

We might argue that the purpose behind the provision in the statute (viz only parties to the marriage can annul it) is to avoid an attack on a marriage by a mother-in-law, or the town crank, or somebody who should not rightfully have the standing to object. In this case, the marriage having been once attacked in court by the husband, through his Conservator, the philosophy and reasoning behind this provision of the statute would not apply. Furthermore, we consult another section of the statutes and see that the legislature has provided legal actions will survive the death of one of the parties thereto, and that the legal representative of the estate of a party can either continue a suit, start a suit or be sued for some cause of action which arose during the lifetime of the deceased.

Here the legislature has stated a public policy which would apply in this case. We will, therefore, argue that an annulment action under these facts does survive the death of one of the litigants.

After we have studied the applicable provisions in the statute books, we then turn to some other law books. These books contain all the printed opinions written by the Supreme Court of the State since it was admitted to the Union, which number many volumes.

Our search through the State Supreme Court opinions is to find a case which is so similar to the one we are considering that the rule stated for that case will necessarily control. The difficulty is it is seldom the luck of the lawyer to find a case which is 100% controlling of the controversy with which he happens to be concerned. The best he can do, in most instances, is to find a case similar in important respects.

In the case of Silas Sharp's annulment, we have an additional problem, and that is that the legislature has seen fit to change the annulment statute, which was done just two years prior. This means that the annulment cases decided before the change would then be out-moded, and would not necessarily apply under the new law.

However, we find a case decided approximately fifteen years ago, which seems to apply to the matter at hand. This was a divorce case in which one of the parties died before the divorce became final, and the question was whether or not the divorce would become final even though the party had died. The heirs of the deceased party came into court to contend that the divorce should be finally granted so that they would receive the property in the estate rather than the widow who, since the man had died, wished to withdraw her action for divorce. The Court in that case said that ordinarily a divorce action will cease to exist when a party dies. However, where property rights are involved, there is an exception to this rule. This, as you see, makes a strong precedent for us.

We always look to the Supreme Court opinions of our own State first, because they are the strongest authority. However, it is permissible to bring in opinions of courts from other states, and a case decided in another state which is more completely in point with the controversy at hand than any case available in the home state will be persuasive.

We also look to some well known legal treatises in which

practically all fields and questions of law are discussed in general terms. We may be disappointed to find that, even though this work may cover 70 large volumes, it does not necessarily fully discuss our particular problem. We will find that it covers situations very close to what we have, but skirts around our issue so that we are still left without distinct, definite and conclusive authority. The treatise is written to give both sides of the question, and for this we are often grateful because we would not be happy to find a rule which is, at least according to the writer, directly contrary to the contention which we must make in order to prevail in court for our client.

In a treatise we find the following statement: "As a general rule, an annulment action will die with the death of one of the parties to the marriage and the marriage will thereafter be held to have been valid for all purposes. However, in the case of a marriage alleged to be invalid because of the mental incompetency of one of the parties thereto, it has been held that other parties having a property interest in the status of the deceased may contend that the marriage was invalid and should be annulled, regardless of the death."

In a footnote, we find a case from another State Supreme Court, and a short paragraph setting out the facts of that case and the rule of law. This appears to be closely in line with the facts of our case, so we immediately go to the shelf and find this case. We read it in full in order to see what legal reasoning was utilized.

We find that a man of considerable wealth, age 84, was joined in holy matrimony with a lady aged 50, who had been his housekeeper for a period of three weeks prior to the marriage; that the trial for annulment was commenced and that during the trial the gentleman was asked: "Do you know where you are?" He replied, that in his opinion, he was in the Fourth National Bank Building, whereas in reality he was in the courthouse. When asked why, he said, "I guess to swap real estate"; whereas he was actually at his annulment trial. And it was also shown by the record that during this trial, his "bride" came up to him, put her arms around his neck, and kissed him on the cheek, and that shortly thereafter he was heard to say: "Who was that?" The poor gentleman died during the process of the trial, before the matter was ever presented to the jury.

The question, then, became whether the action for annulment died with him, in which event the marriage would ever after be considered valid. His heirs contended that the annulment action should continue, otherwise they would be excluded from taking any of his property, and his "bride" of short duration would take it all. In this case, by a sister state, the Court held that under these circumstances, the annulment action did not die with the man, and that the heirs could continue the action in court.

Inasmuch as we have some persuasive authority that the marriage could still be annulled, our next problem is to decide where, that is, in what court. Should we attempt to contend in the Probate Court that the marriage was a nullity, or should we, the named beneficiaries and legatees under the will, attempt to reopen the matter in the other court where the annulment was first commenced, contending that the agreement to dismiss this action was not made with our consent and was against our interest?

This leads us to an entirely different but, in this instance, related question of law; that is, whether we have a right to go into the court where the annulment action was started, and if so, how and in what capacity. We were not a party to that action; we did not appear in it; and until Silas Sharp died and this will turned up, we had no idea that we had any interest in the action. We read about it in the newspapers and took a casual interest, but had not the slightest notion that it would ever become so important to us.

We then look to the Rules of Civil Procedure and we see that there is a provision allowing intervention in court by a party who has not either sued or been sued in the case. This provision allows somebody who, because of a particular circumstance has a vital interest in the outcome, to file for intervention in a case and thereby, by his own act, become a party.

But another problem is present, which now takes us back to the annulment statute where, as you recall, it is provided that only the party to an allegedly illegal marriage can pursue the action to annul it. We anticipate that the opposition would argue very forcibly that intervention would not be allowed in an annulment case because of this provision and that if the action were held to survive the death, only the personal representative of the deceased could pursue the action in court.

The Conservator of Mr. Sharp started the action while he was still alive. After he died, the same bank was appointed as Administrator for his estate. Their contention would be that only they, as Administrator, could pursue the action which thereby presents another dilemma.

This leads us to a search of the law regarding the duty and responsibility of the Administrator of an estate. We find a case decided by our Supreme Court approximately twenty years ago, where a will was presented for probate and a certain individual was named as Executor or Administrator of the estate. This Executor was represented by an attorney in the probate proceedings. A woman presented herself at the hearing and claimed that the deceased approximately six months prior to his death, had orally agreed with her to will her a large sum of money in consideration for past household services which she had allegedly rendered to him. The lawyer representing the Administrator rose in court and objected strenuously to this woman's contention.

When the Supreme Court of the State received this case, they said that the lawyer had misconstrued the responsibility of the Administrator, stating that the Administrator is merely a stakeholder of the funds and property of the estate, and that he should not take sides between the different claimants to the property, but should apply his energies only to preserving the property and not allowing it to be dissipated by imprudent investments or unbusinesslike practices. The Court said that it is the responsibility of the Probate Court alone to decide which of the claimants is correct and the Administrator should not involve himself in disputes between different claimants.

Now, what did the Administrator do in our case? It entered into an agreement with Betsy Cross without including a consideration for the legatees under this will; therefore, there might be a way to bring this to the attention of the Probate Court in a petition requesting that a Special Administrator be appointed to reopen the annulment action in the other court.

Our next action is to examine the problem of reopening any action in court. The policy of the law is to give any aggrieved party his day in court, but once he has had his say, to make the judgment final and not subject to any further litigation. However, this is not and could not be a hard and fast rule without exception; otherwise many injustices would result, as witnessed by the very case we are considering.

We look again to the rules of civil procedure and see that a particular provision states that for good cause a court may reopen and change its judgment at any time within six months from its date of entry. While scanning through the rules of civil procedure we also noticed that the time for appeal of any judgment by a lower court to the Supreme Court of the State is three months. This leads us quickly to recheck the date when the annulment action was dismissed to see whether we are within this three months period. We see that it occurred approximately two months prior to the time when we are doing our study, and here is another opportunity for relief.

But the idea of appealing the case is not without its own peculiar problems, the first of which is the requirement in the rules that before any appeal can be made to the Supreme Court, a motion must be filed in the trial court asking the judge to reconsider and reopen his decision, and this motion for a new trial must be filed within ten days from the time of judgment. The ten-day period has long since passed. The philosophy behind this provision is readily apparent: that before a party can burden the Supreme Court with the problem, he should give the trial judge one last chance to go his way. Would the petition to reopen the case, as allowed under the other rule, be considered a motion for new trial so as to preserve the right to appeal? This is an uncertain question and we search without any success in the law books of our state for a definitive answer to it.

During all these research efforts, a haunting spectre lurks in the back of our mind, the fact that even if we should succeed, through long and tedious effort, in seeing the marriage finally annulled, we would still face the problem of proving that the will was valid. One definite requirement is that the maker of a will have the mental competency to make it when he signs his name, and the judge of the Probate Court must be satisfied on this issue before he allows it into his court. All of our efforts, then, might result in the exclusion of Betsy Cross from her rights as widow of Mr. Sharp, but would then result in all of the property going to the niece because she is the sole heir at law and if there is no marriage and if there is no valid will, the niece will receive all of the property and we will be excluded. We are walking on a tightrope. We have to contend that Silas Sharp was mentally incompetent when he was married, and then we are placed in the position of reversing our position and contending that he was competent to make a will when he made it seven months prior to the alleged marriage.

We know that reputable doctors will testify as expert witnesses that senility is a regressive disease, and that often seniles have lucid moments. Whether or not this illuminating intelligence will ever convince a court or a jury that Silas Sharp was competent, and knew what he was doing when he made this will, is a serious question, but we cannot let this difficulty deter our course through the books. Betsy Cross has, it appears at the moment, obtained some advocates on her side in upholding the validity of the will.

After some thought on this situation, we realize that we are siding with an unappealing and unsympathetic individual, and that when, and if, the facts of the association of Betsy Cross and Silas Sharp are revealed in the Probate Court, everyone will be surprised and antagonistic to her. Our next step, therefore, is to see if there is any legal way to disassociate ourselves with her cause and still, at the same time, see that the will is recognized as valid.

We study the will over again and a part providing that "any legatee or beneficiary, who attacks the will or obstructs its smooth administration through the courts, will take nothing thereunder," takes on a new and an intriguing light. Betsy Cross has attacked the will and has obstructed its smooth administration through the courts by the fact of contending that this marriage exists, because, if it does exist, the will cannot be admitted into court. Here is another string in our bow which we resolve valiantly to utilize. This has particular appeal because we, as everyone else, would like to see Betsy Cross frustrated in her designs. Upon further research, however, we find that to achieve this is not without difficulty.

We look to a treatise and find that this type of provision in a will appears to be quite common, and that generally the courts uphold the provision as valid and enforceable because the person who makes the will has full power to dispose of his property as he desires, and if he wants to give a certain amount to an individual,

There Ought to be a Law • 109

that individual should not then be allowed with some unsubstantial objection to tie up the matter in court for years because of his dissatisfaction in not receiving more than he thought he was entitled to. But the courts generally go one step further and say that the party attacking the will is excluded from its terms only if the attack is made in bad faith. When the attack merely points out some fact which by operation of law has an effect upon the will, such as in this case pointing out that a marriage exists which revokes the will, it is usually not considered bad faith, and would not exclude the legatee so advising the court.

Thus we are led to another possibility, and that is that Betsy Cross might be excluded from taking any part of the residue of the estate after the specific bequests are fulfilled. We would argue that at the time the will was made, she was exerting duress, coercion, or undue influence upon Silas Sharp. Whether we could really prove this we do not know. We are merely considering the possibility for purposes of legal analysis. Upon making further study of this point, we find that another tightrope must be walked, in that under some of the decisions if duress and undue influence is shown to have been applied by the principal beneficiary, then the entire will falls. But this is not necessarily so, and each case must be decided on its own merits from the facts and circumstances surrounding the signing of the will.

Prior to filing the petition in court, we reach the lawyers for Betsy Cross and the lawyer representing the Administrator of the estate of Silas Sharp. We tell them what we have decided as to the many legal points involved and argue that they should agree to pay us our legacies without any action in court. In this case we find that our research and study has indeed been worth the effort. Since we are asking only a small percentage of the total estate, since the estate is of a size in which the inheritance taxes will be large, since both the niece of Silas Sharp and Betsy Cross are elderly women, since they would still be receiving a bonanza even after we are paid off, and since the case involves so many issues and so many possibilities whereby we could and would tie it up in the courts for a period of years, keeping them from getting their money during that time, after some negotiation, they finally agree to settle and to pay us our legacies without any further argument in court.

This case is explained here in detail to give you an idea of how a lawyer handles a problem. He must be creative and must keep an open mind and search diligently through the law books for all angles of the matter before him. It also shows quite vividly that a lawyer does not work with absolutes. You will recall that practically every question presented had two sides, and that none of them indicated a sure and definite result. This is a part of the fascination of law. It is also why matters are presented to court, because there are often things upon which not only reasonable jurors but upon which reasonable lawyers might differ about the law.

Happily, however, this matter was settled without further and protracted litigation. Settlement of cases is very common. The lawyers find from experience that it is better to settle and to go on to the next problem than to cling to a position which may waste their time and the time of the court to such an extent that it would be a disservice to their client.

The case never reached a trial, and no one will ever know for certain how it would fare in court, but this is just as well. It is not the lawyer's purpose to use his client's problem in order to create rules of law. Rather, it is his responsibility to serve his client by obtaining a satisfactory result. The courts will always have an ample supply of controversies upon which to promulgate rules of law and lawyers strive to avoid litigation whenever they can, rather than to promote it.

We have seen how law applies in a particular case. Now let us examine the origin of law and outline the patterns of authority.

All law is first derived from the power of reasoning and the conscience of mankind. As ancient as society itself, law necessarily took form when the first two people existed on the earth. Any naturalist can tell you that there are laws and customs in the animal world. All laws derive from necessity and without necessity there would be no law.

Necessity in America means the public welfare and justice for the individual. It does not mean the furtherance in power of particular men. In a very real sense, we have a government of laws and not of men, which distinguishes us from totalitarian regimes.

While it is true the Constitution of the United States is the supreme law of the land, it does not purport to govern all things. It is supreme only as to that which it does specifically cover, and all the rest of governmental power and responsibility is left to the states or to the people themselves.

Basically, the Constitution governs the structure of the United States government itself, the nature of the union of the states, and several fundamental rights which are guaranteed directly to the people. Each state is a sovereign government limited only by its union with the other states. Cities, counties, and towns are governmental units within the state. They are not sovereign governments and are always subject to the power and authority of the state. They are given authority to govern purely local matters but they are never allowed to break away from the state and pass laws contrary to the state constitution or laws.

All levels of government in America have executive, judicial, and legislative branches. All of the different levels and divisions of government are bound together in a vast and complex network of laws. None is completely independent of the others. For this reason the lowliest judicial officer—perhaps the Police Magistrate in a small town—is required to take an oath to uphold the charter of the town where he presides, the local ordinances, the laws and constitution of his state, and the laws and the Constitution of the United States, because all of these sources of law must be taken into consideration if he is to properly conduct his office. In fact any judge—whether state, federal, or municipal—must uphold all of these laws.

Legislatures make laws by passing statutes. Courts make laws by passing upon specific disputes. It is for the legislature to set out comprehensive rules governing various activities in society. The courts do not have this function. Rather, they rule only to the extent that is necessary to determine the controversy presented and will go no further. The legislature can overrule and change rules of law made by courts, but courts cannot change legislative rules except in cases where the legislature has done something contrary to the constitution, in which event it is the duty of the court to invalidate the legislation.

Courts decide what the law is as to a particular case. This is not the duty of the jury, or of the lawyers, or of anybody else. The lawyers merely decide what they feel a court would decide. When the legislature has spoken by statute on a particular point involved in a case, then the court is bound by that ruling of the legislature so long as the legislature was acting properly according to the constitution. But the legislature could not possibly decide in advance what the controlling law would be as to every conceivable controversy; therefore, the court must lay down its own rules of law and must interpret and construe the acts of the legislature in light of the fact situation at hand. The legislature cannot make retroactive laws and cannot decide specific disputes as the court does. Legislation must apply equally to all and cannot discriminate between people.

When the legislature passes an act, it is making law for the future and stating that from this point forward this will be the law. On the other hand, court-made law is retroactive in operation, that is, the court says, in effect, "This has always been the law and we now recognize it and put it down in black and white." Law from many sources must be brought together in order to determine what the outcome will be or should be in a case.

In the case of Silas Sharp we looked to the court-made law of our own state, some court-made law of a sister state, the statutes of our state, and the Rules of Civil Procedure promulgated by the Supreme Court and approved by the legislature of our state. We also looked to some learned treatises on law which may appeal to a court and be adopted by it as the law. It is not uncommon to see all of the sources of law directly involved in a single controversy.

Laws from whatever source may be classified in two broad categories: substantive and procedural. In the case of Silas Sharp, we were rapidly stepping back and forth between the two. We were concerned with procedure when we were trying to determine how to pursue our rights, in which court and what parties should do what. We were concerned with substantive law when we tried to determine what our rights actually were as legatees or beneficiaries under the will of Silas Sharp. Since we did not actually get to trial, we were not closely concerned with the law of evidence. However, in any trial the court and the attorneys must constantly concern themselves with the rules established over the years as to what evidence will be allowed in court and what will be excluded. The law of evidence is governed partially by statute and partially by case law and also by rules laid down for procedure by the Supreme Court of the state.

When we briefly discussed "statutory construction" as a legal technique, we saw that the goal and purpose of the endeavor was to find out, as near as humanly possible, what the legislature really intended to say about our particular case. The handling of court-made law poses similar problems. Here, our goal is the same—to determine what the law really is as to our case, not to make new law or twist the law to make it what we would like it to be. This technique, or art as some might call it, involves two fundamental processes: (1) distinguishing between holding and dictum and (2) synthesis of cases.

If you find something rather refreshingly different about some lawyers you know personally, it may be their particular approach to serious discussion of any type. It is probably this ability to sift the wheat from the chaff and to draw seemingly unrelated subjects into meaningful juxtaposition with each other, which gives them their distinction.

The holding is the wheat, the kernel or the nub of a case. Dictum is the chaff. Often an appeal judge will branch off into a general discussion when writing his opinion on a case. He will make statements that are not really necessary or pertinent to the controversy before him. He will philosophize. For example, if the issue in a case is whether or not the jury should be allowed to see a confession of the accused, which he signed after having been held in jail incognito for ten days, and after having been hit on the head with a blackjack, instead of merely stating that under these circumstances the confession should not be used, which is the real holding of the case, the court digresses on a lengthy dissertation complete with historical references to the "rack and screw" and generalized admonitions against "tainted" confessions of any type. This opinion of the court is then printed up in the books and is thus given the dignity and status of written law.

Shortly thereafter, a patently guilty criminal comes to trial. Having nothing else to go on, the accused's lawyer argues that the confession was "tainted" because the accused was alone in the room with four law officers at the time it was given. The trial court gives weight to the holding in the prior case, but not to the pages and pages of dicta, which was not really necessary to the determination of the issues. He rules that the confession can be used because even though it may have been "tainted," it was not extracted by a blackjack and ten days of solitary confinement.

Synthesis of cases is a sophisticated technique based upon logic. Its purpose is to enable lawyers to find out what the law really is in a given fact situation even though there may be no case in point. Any conceivable set of facts could lend itself to this technique. But just to illustrate, let us say that Henry Spear bought a new house. One night, eight months later as he was walking out to his incinerator to burn the trash, he fell into a hole and broke his leg. It appeared that the builder had not adequately packed the dirt-fill over a sewer line excavation so that, after a time of erosion, the loose fill caved in and caused a hole.

Henry's attorney thinks someone was negligent and should pay for his client's injury. But there are no cases directly in point. This may be surprising as you would think that sometime, somewhere an accident like Henry's would have occurred. It probably did, but this does not mean that the case would necessarily become a part of the recorded law. Perhaps the party didn't sue, or if he did maybe the case was settled and did not go to trial; or if it went to trial perhaps it did not reach the appeal stage. Only appeal cases appear in the law books. At any rate, Henry's lawyer can find no case exactly in point. So what does he do?

The lawyer looks to other cases, and through a process of logic comes up with an interpretation of the law for Henry Spear's case. He finds a case in which no personal injuries were involved but a builder was sued and held liable for damage to a lawn because of the cave-in of a water line excavation. He finds another case in which a roof had fallen in and the builder had to pay for the personal injuries resulting. He ties these cases together and builds an argument that his client can recover for personal injuries caused by "hidden defects" in the builder's work. This is a very simplified example, but it is the type of thing that lawyers must do every day in working with the law.

This chapter surely points up the necessity of professional counsel, advice and represenatation. A matter which may appear simple on its face is far from simple when all of its ramifications through the legal system are considered. Think, for example, how much injustice and difficulty and turmoil could have been avoided if Silas Sharp had, during his many lucid years of life, taken the advice of his lawyer and written a will and planned his property in a way to protect it from the perils of life.

Chapter Eight

TELL IT TO THE JUDGE

More people go to traffic court than all other courts combined. Included in the word "court" is a concept of justice and this presupposes a free intelligence, that is, a judge who has some learning and the ability to know the difference between justice and injustice plus a decent amount of dignity and freedom to do what his intelligence tells him is right. This requires that the judge be free from economic or other entanglements which motivate him away from justice. If you do not have a free, independent, dignified, intelligent judiciary, there is no justice in the administration of law.

The fact is that at least one-half of the so-called traffic courts in this country are not true courts. Fortunately, these account for far less than half of the traffic cases. The courts in our cities are very often excellently staffed and run. But the point is that everything we are talking about here is totally moot if your case happens to come up before the chicken farmer who has gotten himself elected Justice of the Peace. Many of these so-called Justices are on an incentive system to find guilty everyone who comes before them. Obviously an innocent person cannot be charged court costs so, realistically, there is no such thing as an innocent accused.

Even without the vicious fee system, an untrained judge is often worse than no judge at all. There are exceptions to this, of course. Once in a while you will find an excellent non-lawyer judge, but this does not make it right. The trouble is that in smaller communities the minor judgeships do not pay enough to hire a lawyer for the post. And one thing is certain: You cannot hire a lawyer and expect

Tell it to the Judge • 117

him to do you any good in any true sense before the "drumhead" Justice of the Peace (taken from the military summary court martial in the field, conducted around a drumhead used as a table.) This is like hiring a jet pilot to drive your car. He may be able to do it all right but no better than you could do it yourself. Of course, many lawyers in these smaller communities play along with the game on a purely personal basis; they know the judge and the judge likes them, and is always impressed with what they have to say quite without regard to what it happens to be, or the judge can, of course, appeal your case to a higher court and even set you up with a jury trial. But who, may we ask, if he gets tagged by a speed trap while going through a small town, will bother to do all that?

But suppose we happen to be someplace where the courts are real and the issues are genuine. Here we have some very interesting issues. The elements are the same as in any other court. There are facts, there is law and there is the super law, the constitution.

Probably the first thing anyone wants to know about traffic court is: "When I get nabbed, where am I? Can I beat the rap or do I just give up?" The answer is if you are right, and you ought to win, then you can win.

A traffic court is not just a special type of contraption devised to torment the citizens. It is a court like any other court, and it is a criminal court. In any criminal court the State meets the citizen and the citizen meets the State. Whenever this happens, the terms and conditions of the confrontation constitute the most vital issues known to man.

Traffic charges are offenses against the State. They are misdemeanors in that they do not involve possible imprisonment in the penitentiary. But the terms "crime" and "misdemeanor" are actually synonymous. Remember that a town or city is an arm of the State, and when it defines an offense and imposes a penalty it is the State acting. Any offense against the government is a crime, from a parking ticket right on up through the ranks to murder.

The constitution is your best protection against an unjust conviction in traffic court because there are a lot of requirements in your behalf that filter down to the individual. One of these requirements is that you be informed of the charge against you. This is accomplished with the traffic officer's ticket. A traffic ticket may be just a ticket to most people but actually it is a pretty special type of legal instrument. It is a summons and complaint. It advises you of the following: (1) the name of the court you are in; (2) the date and time you must appear; (3) the nature of the charge against you; and (4) what will happen to you if you do not appear in court as directed.

As a matter of fact, the officer should arrest you and take you to jail where you would be held until formal complaint could be made to the court by the prosecuting office, and only after that could you make bond and promise the judge that you will be back at the time when you are supposed to return. In order to save the officer all this trouble and, to say the least, to save yourself embarrassment and inconvenience, you sign the ticket, in which you agree to accept service of the summons and complaint, and you are at that moment let out on "personal recognizance" bond. This means that rather than put up money and property, your word is your bond that you will show up in court as required.

You should read that ticket over pretty carefully. Does it really tell you what you are charged with? A failure in this simple constitutional requirement is one of the slipshod little errors that government frequently falls into. And the constitution is concerned about this for two vital reasons: (1) it wants to make sure that the officer really has a bona fide charge that can be put down in writing and (2) it wants to make sure that you know in advance exactly why you are in trouble so that you can defend yourself against some specific charge. It is very frustrating for a person to go into court thinking he has a red light violation only at the last minute to find out that it was the speeding three blocks back for which he is being charged.

Police officers sometimes memorize the various traffic offenses and the ordinance section numbers applying to them. They are then inclined simply to put down the ordinance numbers on their tickets. So you get a ticket and you are charged with 511.3-2(1), 511.6-3(4)(a), 512.16-1. What this is, you do not know. Is this a legal summons? No. You must be informed in English what the charge is all about. So if the ticket does not specifically tell you with what you are charged and against what you are going to have to defend yourself in court, this places you at a distinct disadvantage before you ever get to trial, something the constitution will not abide.

Say you are charged with going 40 miles per hour in a 30 miles per hour zone, and you think you may have been going a little over the speed limit, perhaps 35 miles per hour, but you definitely do not agree with the officer that you were going 40. The officer bases part of his information as to your speed on his radar equipment mounted in his patrol car. What do you do? Well, you can plead guilty and the judge will listen to your statement as a mitigating circumstance in the case, that you are sure you were not going over 35 miles an hour. It would be preferable to discuss the matter with the officer in court prior to making your plea. If he would join in your statement of 35 miles per hour just as a matter of compromise and fairness, then this would be an accomplishment having two important aspects for you. (1) It would cause the judge to impose a lesser fine or penalty on you, and (2) it would save your driving record.

You should think of your driving record with the State licensing bureau as an important part of your assets. For good and obvious reasons, most states have established an efficient and strict method of keeping driving records. Often a point system is used. By this, certain offenses such as failure to observe a stop sign, improper passing, drunk driving or careless driving are allotted a certain number of points. If you plead guilty or are found guilty of any of these offenses, then the Court is required to submit the information to the central record bureau of the State. When this happens, those points or demerits are permanently on your record, a situation you cannot change.

Why is it important to subtract five miles an hour from that speeding charge? You may find that the State allots a certain number of points to a speeding conviction where your speed is five miles over the legal posted speed limit and perhaps twice this number of points if you were going ten miles per hour over the speed limit.

Now let us say in your speeding case the officer will not listen to reason so you have to go to trial. Does this mean that you are going to have to take the witness stand, swear to tell the truth, and then lie, say "No, I wasn't speeding at all."? No. You don't have to take the witness stand at all unless you choose to do so, but if you choose to do so, then you had better tell the truth. First of all, however, the State has to prove its case and it has to prove it beyond a reasonable doubt. In establishing your speed, the officer gives an opinion. This is similar to his qualifying as an expert witness on this particular subject, and he backs his information with the results of his radar reading. Does this mean that the officer has to be a radar expert? No.

At the end of the People's case, your attorney moves for a judgment of acquittal or a directed verdict of not guilty, stating, "The People haven't proven their case at all, let alone beyond a reasonable doubt, as is required. They rely on the testimony of an officer who admits he doesn't know anything about the radar machine he was using and who admits that his personal observation as to speed may be inaccurate. That machine could be inaccurate for any one of a number of reasons, and unless you have someone who can state they know all about it, enough to be sure it was working correctly, you can't convict somebody on testimony about the operation of the machine."

The Judge says, "The motion for judgment of acquittal is denied. It is not necessary that an officer be a radar expert in order to present testimony about the results of a radar test, any more than it would be necessary for a person to know and understand the inner workings of a clock in order to be able to testify what time it was. The same rule pertains to radar testimony in court. It is up to the jury whether they choose to believe it or not."

Other mechanical and scientific devices used in traffic enforcement, particularly in drunk driving cases, are blood tests, breatholizers, and moving pictures. Drunk driving is obviously an immense hazard of the road. Strangely enough, though, it is a very difficult type of case for the prosecution to prove. This may be due in part to the tendency of a certain number of jurors to think, "There, but for the grace of God, go I." In any case, jurors are notoriously lenient in drunk driving cases. Perhaps this is because, of course, the defendant comes to court sober and looks so guileless that the testimony of his condition on the night of the crime seems unconvincing. Therefore, in order to pin down the proof and preserve the evidence for reconstruction in court, blood tests are often made. How does this work? Well, first of all, you should know that it is a voluntary proposition. If you refuse to submit to a blood test, you cannot be forced and then have the test used in court.

But say you submit to the blood test. Here a small amount of blood is taken from your veins and is subjected to scientific laboratory specific gravity test, which precisely determines how much alcohol there is in your blood. One thing about which the investigating officers and the police laboratory technicians must be very careful is building the chain of custody element of the proof. It must be very clearly established that your blood sample was the one tested, and was not confused with some other blood sample of another person in the laboratory. If there is a "break in the chain,"—in other words, if the vial with your blood in it was unmarked even for a brief period of time it could have, not that it did, but it could have lost its identity and have been mistaken for another blood sample—in which event it cannot be used in court.

If the chain of evidence is clearly established and the laboratory technician testifies, "I found this blood to contain .15 percentiles of alcohol by volume.", what does this mean to the jury? Unless they are given some guidance, it means nothing. But they are given guidance in the form of a written instruction which sets out the language of a statute of the State.

> "Ladies and gentlemen of the jury: You are instructed that a person having .05% or less of alcohol in his blood by volume is presumed to be capable of driving; that no legal presumption attaches either of capability to drive or incapability to drive if a person has more than .05% but less than .15% of alcohol in his blood by volume; that if a person has .15% of alcohol in his blood by volume, or more, he is presumed to be incapable of driving."

There are important things to understand about this statutory instruction. First of all, relating the amount of alcohol in the blood to a person's inability to drive has been established by a series of tests producing statistical averages. The tests are merely an aid and guideline for the jury and are not conclusive. They do have validity because of the characteristics of alcohol. One thing known is that when consumed, alcohol almost immediately spreads itself evenly throughout the body through the bloodstream, and it dissipates itself or burns up at a fairly even rate. The blood must be extracted as soon as possible after the arrest, but the test is still valid even if an hour or more elapses. And assuming, of course, that the individual does not consume any alcohol while he is in custody, the presumption would be that his blood alcohol content was higher an hour earlier because the body will burn up alcohol at the rate of about one ounce per hour.

The reason why blood tests can be used only as a guide is that people vary markedly in their capacity to "hold" liquor. A frequent drinker will build up an immunity to alcohol so that a much greater volume is required to affect his judgment, reaction time, and his general ability to control himself. A youthful or inexperienced drinker can be rendered incapable of driving by intake of just a small amount of alcohol. The only definite thing about the test is that the alcohol content quite reliably shows how much has been consumed.

The breatholizer, a machine which performs the same function as the blood test, has the advantage of being quicker, simpler, and less offensive to the accused, and it relies on the scientific fact that alcohol spreads itself quite evenly over all body fluids and gases. The defendant breathes into a balloon; his breath is captured and tested for alcoholic content. This is interpolated into blood content, and the evidence is used in the same way that blood test evidence would be used. Just as with the radar machine, the officer or the technician administering the breatholizer test need not necessarily know and understand all of the inner workings of the machine. However, the test is usually administered by a technician who can qualify as an expert on the workings of the machine and who can explain its function if called upon to do so. A person may also refuse a breatholizer test, just as he may refuse a blood test.

As stated, these scientific procedures are only tools to aid the proof. The real proof comes from testimony of people who observed the defendant's driving or manner and demeanor shortly after the arrest. Also, a high percentage of drunk driving charges come after an accident has occurred and the facts of the accident may, of course, be considered by the jury bearing upon the issue of drunkenness. Most law enforcement agencies have worked out a check list for the information of the arresting officer. He goes down the sheet and checks, "Eyes: Bleary, red, clear. Speech: Slurred, thick, normal. Breath: Strong odor of alcohol, slight odor, not noticeable," and so forth.

But the most devastating proof of all is obtained by motion pictures, and these are most effective if a sound track is used. The subject is asked to do two or three simple things before the camera in a lighted studio. He is asked to walk a clearly painted line on the floor; he is asked to stoop over and pick up a coin dropped on the floor; and he is asked to put his hand on his head. Consent is not a prerequisite to this test or its use in court. The movies are often shown to the defendant before the trial and it is remarkable how often the defendant chooses to plead guilty rather than go through the embarrassment of having the movie shown before a jury.

In most states, one drunk driving conviction is enough to revoke a person's license, and many urge that a jail term be mandatory. Because of these tough laws, a truly amazing number of tactics are thought up to defend a drunk driving case. "I was just tired, working too hard; the doctor had me on drugs; I had a piece of dirt in my eye and was rubbing—that's why they look so bloodshot; I had been swimming in a pool with a lot of chlorine in it"; etc., etc.

Many people get themselves in trouble in traffic court because they are unused to court procedures and think that being overly humble and fair to the other fellow will stand them in good stead. This is dangerous, because the officer is going to say, without equivocation, "I saw him go through the red light." If your rejoinder is, "I thought I had the green light" or "I must have had the green light because I always stop if it's red" or something equally indefinite, then your testimony is going to take the back seat. Therefore, be as forceful, definite, and confident as you can in asserting your version of the facts.

The law requires that a person involved in an accident remain at the scene and give a report to the investigating officer. Should you fail to do this, you may be charged with "Leaving the scene" or "Hit-run" which is a serious additional charge. These laws have been held to be constitutional, even though a person has a right against self-incrimination. You can refuse to make a statement to the officer, but you cannot legally refuse to remain at the scene until the officer arrives.

Some states have compulsory auto liability insurance laws; others have a barn door sort of an arrangement whereby a person who gets in an accident involving damage to person or property must immediately show that he has liability insurance coverage or he must put up a bond to cover any possible damages assessed against him in the case. If he cannot do this, then his license is immediately revoked. By this the State sees that the barn door is closed after the horse has run away. For incomprehensible reasons, the compulsory insurance approach is opposed by the insurance industry, although it certainly is the only correct solution.

Tough, but fair and just, traffic law enforcement is vital to all of us, and considering the huge volume of cases in a nation on wheels, the courts do a remarkably good job. But the most remarkable thing of all is to realize that every step in the court process—from your first encounter with the officer to your right to bond, the burden of proof on the State, your right against self-incrimination, clear on to the question of whether or not your right to drive will be maintained—is clearly governed by the United States Constitution. And the fact that the Constitution, devised long before motor vehicular traffic was ever dreamed of, can and does function so well on this subject is about the most astounding thing in the world. How can this be? It seems impossible. The reason is this: The Constitution adheres to fundamentals and states them in general rather than specific terms.

Chapter Nine

REDRESSING THE WOUND

1—The Accident

Ralph and Mary Olson had passed many milestones in their fourteen years of married life. Four years before, Ralph began his own consulting engineering firm and had met with success. Just six months ago, they had moved into a new house, and the crowning jewel of their opulence was a brand new, gleaming white station wagon.

This spring seemed to be the most promising of all. Ralph had his office in a one-story building on a busy thoroughfare in the industrial section of town. He had some things to do this Saturday morning and thought it would be a good time to take the car by the garage for its one-thousand-mile check-up. As promised when he bought the car, he was provided with a shag-boy service to drive the car back to the garage from his office. Ralph had never met Rick Ronner before, but he seemed to be a mature enough lad. He was extremely accommodating and appeared to enjoy his work, particularly the opportunity to drive new cars.

During the morning, Mary called at the office and mentioned that their daughter Susie, aged thirteen, was starring in a ballet recital that afternoon, and asked Ralph to drop by to see her dance. Ralph pointed out that this would cut into his business because he had planned to work straight through until 1:00 o'clock. He suggested it would save time for Mary to call the garage and have the shag boy pick her up with the children at the house and then come by the office. Afterwards they would drop the shag boy off at his destination and then the family would go on to the ballet school together.

Mary phoned and spoke to the garage foreman, explaining the situation. While Mary was still on the 'phone, the foreman called to Rick and explained that he would have to do a little extra driving and probably wouldn't be through as soon as he thought he might, but if he wanted to do so he could drive the car by the Olson home, as Mary had requested, and could go on from there. Rick called across the garage and said that it would be a little farther than going by Ralph's office but he wouldn't mind it at all, since they would probably take him very near his home.

Rick then drove the new station wagon to the Olson home and rang the doorbell. Mary had not expected quite such prompt service and asked Rick to come in and sit down. They would go in about ten minutes—after the children were ready. Rick was very accommodating about this, and when the group was ready, they walked out of the home and began to get into the car. Mary, who expected to do the driving, asked Rick on the way down the walk to the car where he wanted to go. Rick said, "Oh, that's all right, wherever you're going. I can get off just practically anywhere," and, rather to the surprise of Mary, Rick walked around to the driver's side of the car and got in just as though he were a hired chauffeur.

As they drove off, Mary asked Rick where he wanted to be dropped off, explaining that she would be glad to take him there on the way to the office if that was what he wanted to do. Rick said, "Oh, I don't care. I'll just take you by the office and then we can go from there." Since Mary wanted to put the finishing touches to Susie's hair, she and Susie got in the back seat together with Karen Walters, the twelve-year-old next-door neighbor girl.

Shortly thereafter they came to Ralph's office and, rather than pulling off to the side where the cars usually parked, Rick pulled up in front of the building, with the right front door of the car very close to the front door of Ralph's office. Ralph came out and noticed with some surprise that the shag boy was at the wheel of the car. As the car was temporarily parked it made it rather difficult for Ralph to come around in the face of traffic and enter the driver's seat. The whole positioning of the car at that moment seemed to be designed for Ralph to take his place as a front-seat passenger.

About five blocks from Ralph's office, Rick turned east onto a thoroughfare with two lanes of traffic going in each direction. This street was controlled by stop signs on the side streets and traffic signals every four or five blocks as the street intersected other busy thoroughfares. One of the controlled cross streets was a one-way street north. At this particular intersection, the local telephone company happened to have a large truck parked at the southwest corner with a workman on a boom, and the truck obscured the traffic signal on the southwest corner. There was another traffic light signal on the northeast corner of the intersection, which was plainly visible to Rick. Rick was driving at only between twenty and twenty-five miles an hour. But he did not notice the signal visible to him on the northeast corner when it turned to caution as he was about fifty feet back from the intersection. The telephone company truck and a building obscured his vision of cars which might be coming north on this one-way street.

Ralph noticed the caution light and assumed that Rick also saw it and was going to stop, but Rick didn't. The light turned red when Rick was about twenty feet from the intersection, and Ralph quickly cautioned Rick to stop. Rick reacted with his right foot, but became flustered and instead of hitting the brake, he pushed the accelerator, and the car sailed on through.

At that moment, Alfred Stihart was driving alone in his automobile in the northbound one-way street. Not seeing the Olson automobile because of the telephone company truck, he proceeded through the intersection on the green light and smashed into the new station wagon.

Neither car was speeding. Stihart was going between twenty-five and thirty miles per hour on this thirty-mile-an-hour street, hitting the green lights. He applied his brakes very briefly before the impact, but not soon enough to slow him down to any appreciable degree. The Olson automobile was violently thrust diagonally across the street into the traffic light signal pole on the northeast corner, knocking the pole down. The right front door of the car flew open and Ralph was violently flung out onto the pavement. Later it was found that he had suffered a concussion and chest injuries. Karen Walters was thrown violently forward inside the car and also had a concussion. Susie was flung out of the car through the right rear door which was thrown open, and was run over by Stihart's car. Mary was badly shaken, but not injured. Stihart's car ended up on its side, but he was uninjured. Neither was Rick hurt.

On the way to the hospital in the ambulance little Susie Olson died. Ralph Olson was on the critical list for a period of days, but recovered sufficiently to leave the hospital in six weeks' time. Karen Walters suffered facial injuries requiring extensive plastic surgery. And Mary receives much aid and comfort from her friends and family, but she is too distraught to think clearly for herself or to make decisions. As a matter of fact, her family doctor becomes gravely disturbed about her mental state and refers her to a psychiatrist for diagnosis and treatment. The psychiatrist determines that she is suffering under traumatic neurosis, a serious disturbance of the psychological functions of the nervous system due to the horrible shock she has been through. After a brief period of experimentation with tranquilizing drugs, the psychiatrist prescribes a period of hospitalization and a series of narcosis interviews designed to aid the patient to integrate with reality. Mary stays in the hospital for five weeks. The therapy meets with some success, but Mary remains under psychiatric care for an indefinite period.

The police officer who was called to the scene made a thorough study of the accident. He took the names and addresses of witnesses, made a diagram showing the positioning of the automobiles as they had come to rest, and determined the point of impact by observing debris on the street where the cars had collided.

During the activity immediately after the accident, Rick stood near the scene, crying and shaken. When questioned by the police officer, he admitted that he probably went through the red light, as he did not see what color the light was when he entered the intersection. Stihart stated assuredly that he had entered the intersection on the green light.

This type of tragedy is by no means uncommon, and it presents resounding and complicated human, moral, legal, and financial problems, going to the very roots of our economic and political system, and involving our values of human life.

This accident has many aspects, as we shall see. All of them involve important issues of justice and responsibility. At least in theory, the law ignores nothing about this occurrence. A civil wrong was committed, unquestionably innocent in intent but grave in consequences. The law seeks to right the wrong in its every aspect in the only way it can—through just and appropriate compensation for the wrongs assessed against the wrong-doer. Not one scrap of fender metal wrongfully bent escapes the law's concern. And in seeking justice for the wronged, the wrongdoer in a civil tort case is also given his fair and full day in court.

The events leading up to this accident could certainly not be called unpredictable. Much stranger things can and do happen every hour everywhere. Let us examine the multifold nooks and crannies where the law leads us in its quest for justice in this apparently simple case.

2—Preparation for Trial

Rick reports the accident to his employer about an hour after it occurred, and in turn the garage notifies its insurance company. It undertakes an investigation of the accident, and the insurance adjuster first goes to the police building and obtains a copy of the accident report which had been made out by the traffic officer. From that he learns the names and addresses of the various parties involved and sets out to interrogate them.

He first questions Rick at length, writing down the story as given to him. He then asks Rick to read the document, to make corrections where it is not complete or true, and to sign it. The adjuster then seeks to approach Mary, but is advised by her brother that she cannot speak to him, because she is too ill to consult with anyone. The adjuster attempts to see Ralph in the hospital but finds him unable to receive visitors, so he then goes to see Mr. Stihart, similarly taking down his version of the accident in a detailed written form and asking him to read the document, make any necessary corrections, and sign it.

The adjuster also determines from the accident report, and from speaking with Rick, that the officer on the scene had handed Rick a summons to appear in traffic court on charges of running through a red light, reckless and careless driving. He states that if Rick has not already hired a lawyer for this case, he will consult with his company as to whether they will supply a lawyer for his defense. Rick agrees to do whatever his employer says, and the garage owner for his part, determines to go along with whatever the insurance company advises, as they are paying the bill.

While the adjuster is still completing his investigation, he reaches the insurance lawyer for advice as to how to handle the traffic case, outlining the general facts and circumstances that he has discovered up to that time. The lawyer states that the central issue of the case appears not to be the liability of Rick in running through the red light and negligently causing the accident, but rather whether or not the garage will have to stand behind their employee. He perceives that there may be a distinct conflict of interest between Rick and his employer and advises that although he, the lawyer, will attend the hearing, the boy should get a lawyer of his own or take whatever action he may wish in the traffic case. The lawyer knows that if the traffic case goes to trial, and if Rick is found guilty of one or more of the charges against him, this fact would not be admissible or controlling to any extent as to the damage suit coming up. He knows, too, that if Rick pleads guilty to the charges, his guilty plea might be admissible as evidence in the damage trials later; but from all of the information given to him, there appears to be no dispute as to Rick's guilt, and this will not be the central issue in the damage cases anyway.

In the meantime, the insurance company for Ralph and Mary is notified of the accident. The adjuster for this company undertakes a similar investigation of all of the facts and circumstances of the accident, studying the police report and interviewing all of the witnesses. The adjusters advise their companies that there appears to be no possibility of an out-of-court settlement inasmuch as the Olsons are both unable to consult with them.

Several days after the accident, Mary's brother decides that a lawyer should be consulted. This attorney also obtains a copy of the police report and undertakes his investigation of the accident with the cooperation of Mary's brother. The lawyer finds out that Rick is still working at the garage in his capacity as shag boy. However, in an interview, Rick tells him that he is planning to join the Navy as soon as he can. This lawyer also attends the traffic court hearing where Rick pleads guilty and is fined for running the red light and careless driving. The Assistant City Attorney assigned to prosecute the case dismisses the reckless driving charge.

The Olsons' lawyer calls in Mary's brother and advises that the boy should be served with a legal paper very promptly as he may be leaving the jurisdiction of the court. If he does leave before he is served with a summons, there might be difficulty in getting service of process on him. The lawyer explains that the real target of the lawsuit would have to be the garage. The boy apparently has no personal liability insurance coverage for this occurrence; and in comparison to the opportunity to collect against the liability insurance policy kept up by the garage, going against the boy for satisfaction of the large amounts which may be involved would be a worthless pursuit for his clients.

However, in full protection of the clients, and due to the difficult questions that he sees in attaching liability to the garage, he feels it to be highly important also to sue the boy in order to place him personally under the jurisdiction of the court. The lawyer perceives a rather unique but distinctly possible result, and that would be that the injured parties in the Olson automobile, including Ralph, might obtain satisfaction for their injuries from Ralph's own insurance company, but this would be possible only if Rick were sued and found liable for the injuries.

The Olsons' lawyer then drafts the summons and complaint for three separate lawsuits. One is a claim in behalf of Ralph and Mary against the garage and against Rick for the wrongful death of their daughter Susie. Another is the claim of Ralph for his injuries and his loss because of Mary's injury, and the third case is the claim on behalf of Mary for her injury received—a traumatic neurosis—plus her loss due to Ralph's injury. The lawyer realizes that all of these three cases might be consolidated into a single lawsuit; however, he feels that distinct and different elements attend each case and chooses to separate them in different complaints. At a later time a court may order that all three of the cases be tried at one time. However, he will oppose this action, seeking to have them tried separately.

The parents of Karen Walters are approached by the adjuster for the garage insurance company. He seeks to determine whether they would be willing to settle the case for a sum sufficient to pay for the medical expenses involved and for the difficulty, grief, and inconvenience they feel Karen has suffered. However, having previously consulted the lawyer and realizing that there is some question as to the garage's liability for any of these injuries, the adjuster is not in a position to offer a substantial settlement. For this reason, he is unable to reach agreement with Karen's parents, and after a period of time they decide to consult their lawyer.

Upon learning the facts of the case, this lawyer explains that he often seeks to negotiate the settlement of a case prior to any legal action; however, he would advise immediate filing of this lawsuit due to the uncertainty of where the liability will ultimately lie and due to the possibility that the driver, Rick, may be leaving for the service within the near future.

All of these lawsuits contain difficult and puzzling legal questions. Let us first consider the case of Karen Walters. She is a minor and cannot pursue the claim in her own behalf, being considered incapable of sufficiently aiding her lawyer in conducting the lawsuit and being responsible for it, she therefore pursues the claim through her parents. Any recovery belonging to her would be held in a guardianship trust until she comes of age. The title of the lawsuit reads:

> KAREN A. WALTERS, by her father and next friend, RUFUS G. WALTERS,
>
> Plaintiff,
>
> VS.
>
> RICK RONNER, CRAIG JONES AUTO SALES AND SERVICE, INC., a corporation, and RALPH E. OLSON,
>
> Defendants.

In drafting this complaint, the lawyer is immediately presented with a difficult problem—that Karen Walters was a nonpaying guest in the Olson automobile. She had received the ride in the car as a simple gratuity from the Olsons. The statutes of the state provide that a nonpaying guest of an automobile owner or operator shall have no cause of action for injuries received as the result of the negligence of the owner or operator, with the exception that should the driver be guilty of willful, wanton, or gross negligence, or should the injuries be caused by drunkenness of the driver, then such passenger would have an action for his or her injuries.

The philosophy of the so-called "Guest Statute" on the books in many of our states is to prevent connived or "friendly" lawsuits between passengers and insured automobile operators, the thought being that the driver might admit he was just a little negligent so that his friend could recover damages from the insurance company.

This law also rests on the general proposition that a guest, who has gratuitously accepted a ride in an automobile, should not then be able successfully to sue his benefactor. Karen's lawyer notes that there has been a great deal of discussion in the legislative halls, and in some recent court opinions passed down in the state, regarding the constitutional validity of this provision and the soundness of the rationale behind it. It is a harsh measure in that the entire body of tort law seeks to open an avenue for redress whenever a negligent injury occurs, but the lawyer notes that in the most recent case decided by the State Supreme Court this law withstood the attack. The claimant in that case argued strongly before the high court that this was a deprival of due process of law, that the constitutions of the state and of the United States provide that no person shall be deprived of life or property without due process of law and that the courts shall be open to all parties for redress of wrong. This statute, it was claimed, flies in the face of these guarantees and deprives an injured party of a remedy.

The Supreme Court of the state noted, however, that the legislature is the elected representative body of the state empowered to make laws, and that this is a law which they in their wisdom chose to make, that it has some reasonable basis, and therefore it must be enforced. Should it be changed, the proper body to change it would be the legislature and not the courts.

In his analysis, Karen's lawyer faces the major problem of all the cases, which is as follows:

Rick Ronner was negligent, and he is personally responsible for the accident. He was guilty of a tort, a civil wrong. However, he is not the one to whom the injured parties can reliably look for financial recompense for their loss. They must, rather, look to the insured parties. And who are they? They are the garage owners and Ralph Olson.

The law provides that a principal is liable for the torts of his agent; or, in other terms, a master is liable for the torts of his servant; or, to put the same concept in still other language, an employer is liable for torts of his employee. All of these different titles refer to and designate the same principle of law, and in order for a principal to have an agent it is not necessary that there be any formal contract of employment or be any real employment in the usual sense of the word. Yet if there is employment, in order for the rule of law to apply, the agent must be within the course and scope of his employment at the time of the accident. This is the crux of these lawsuits. But here two different rules of agency law clash against each other.

An employee who is engaged in some pursuit generally within the scope of his employment, whether or not in response to specific orders to do the particular act he was performing at the time of the accident, will be held to be within the scope of his employment. Yet another principle of agency law is that the driver of an automobile wherein the owner of that vehicle is riding is at that time the agent of the owner. Ordinarily an agent cannot serve two masters at the same time. Therefore, the question is: Who was Rick Ronner serving at the time the accident occurred? Was he the agent or servant of Ralph Olson, or was he the employee, agent, and servant of the garage?

If he were the garage's servant at that time, then the Guest Statute would not apply. Karen was not the guest of Rick nor of the garage; she was not invited into the car by them; and she was not given any gratuity by them. The general principles of negligence law would apply, and they state that whenever there is a wrong done by any person resulting in injuries, then the person so wronged will have a case against the wrongdoer. Yet if the other principle of agency law applied (that the driver of an automobile is the agent of the owner who is riding therein), then the same defense Ralph would have, had he been driving and caused the accident, would go to his agent Rick, and Karen would then be excluded from any recovery. Nevertheless, Karen's lawyer, realizing that Ralph might very well be held to be the principal of Rick, joins Ralph as a defendant in the lawsuit, taking his chances as to how the Guest Statute might affect his case.

As to a third party a principal stands in the shoes of his agent, and vice versa. A defense which one has will also belong to the other. But there are exceptions to this, not only in general agency law, but also, in this case, by the wording of the Guest Statute, which, as we have seen, allows a guest to recover if the owner or operator is guilty of "willful, wanton, or gross" negligence. It is said that an agent's negligence is "imputed" to his principal. However, willful and wanton negligence is not imputed unless the principal actually encourages or participates in the willful and wanton act. If the driver were guilty of the higher degree of negligence, this would solve Karen's problem. Not only could she obtain judgment against Rick, but she could then recover against Ralph's insurance company because of the definition of "insured" in Ralph's policy, as follows: "'Insured' includes the named insured and also includes any person using the automobile with his permission."

Was Rick guilty of willful, wanton, or gross negligence in running through the red light? Karen's lawyer doubts that the circumstances would support this finding, but nevertheless he charges this in the hope that a judge might feel that reasonable minds could differ on this subject, and allow the jury to determine the degree of negligence involved. This claim in no way endangers the claim of simple negligence, nor does it preclude the possibility of Karen's recovering against the garage.

Now let us consider some of the agitated thought processes of the Olsons' lawyer. He is concerned with liability, proof of damages, and recovery of damages for his clients. What are the damages? It is still uncertain what Ralph's personal loss will ultimately be; the medical expenses are not yet completed, and there may be a large loss of earnings in the future. Mary's personal damages are even more uncertain. Even Susie's death poses many quizzical problems as to the actual amount of damages recoverable. The only sum now ascertainable with certainty is the loss of the car, and this will be soon paid for by Ralph's insurance company, with $50 deducted, and with the proviso that the company can go against the garage, if in fact the garage is liable for the accident, or, in any case, against Rick, for reimbursement of the amount that it paid out for loss of the car.

But the lawyer first approaches the liability problem. He

examines the facts carefully because if there is even the slightest chance that the driver of the other car, Mr. Stihart, was negligent, then he should also be included as a defendant in the case. The lawyer notes that Rick pleaded guilty in the traffic court and has never denied that he ran a red light. With this, the lawyer dismisses the idea of suing Stihart. He is not concerned about Mr. Stihart's claim for the damage to his automobile because either the Olsons' or the garage's liability insurance coverage for property damage will take care of it.

He then directs his thoughts to the telephone company truck which was parked on the corner. He does not immediately decide in his own mind whether the men in charge of the truck were acting illegally or negligently in the manner and place where it was at that time. Rather, for his analysis, he assumes that at least simple negligence could be proven against the telephone company. Simple negligence is the mere failure to do what a reasonable and prudent person would under the circumstances for the protection of life and property of others. Parking a truck at a busy intersection in midday, obscuring the view of a traffic signal light and of cars approaching each other on busy thoroughfares, would probably constitute simple negligence. Yet there is another element to every lawsuit charging negligence, and that is proximate cause.

A party may be negligent, or even grossly negligent, in his actions, and yet if what he does is not a proximate cause of the injuries received by the plaintiff, then he is not liable. Two or more defendants can be negligent at the same time, and can jointly share responsibility for any accident. Yet the actions of each must be a proximate cause of the damaging occurrence—not just a cause, but a proximate cause. It could certainly be argued that the truck was a cause of the accident, and some might even say that it was *the* cause. The lawyer was not present when Rick talked to his employer and then went home to face his parents after the accident, but he could just hear the boy say, "Well, there was this big telephone company truck right there at the corner, and I couldn't see the light or the other car coming. If it wasn't for that darned truck, the accident would never have happened."

The lawyer concedes in Rick's thinking that, but for the truck, the accident might not have occurred, yet he realizes that the "but for" test is not the complete definition of proximate cause, only a small part of it. Proximate cause of an accident is that which, in a natural and continuous sequence, unbroken by any efficient intervening cause, produces the injury, and without which the result would not have happened.

It is clear to the lawyer that Rick's careless driving was an "efficient intervening cause" of the accident, and the negligence of the truck was not "in a natural and continuous sequence" with what happened. He decided that the causal connection is not sufficient to sue the telephone company, its agents or employees. The truck's positioning in no way excuses Rick, because there are trucks either parked or going down streets at all times, and often by their size they obscure the view of traffic signal lights, and that is why lights are provided on two corners, visible from both directions, instead of just one. The truck was a cause, perhaps, but not a proximate cause of the accident, there being an intervening cause and no real foreseeability that parking the truck there would result in the accident which did occur.

The lawyer then directs himself to the overriding problem of agency law. The key to this is the term "scope of employment," which is discussed in volumes upon volumes of cases, and each case seems to be decided on the particular merits and equities of its own facts, offering only general and inconclusive guidelines as to the probable ruling in this case. The problem is of immense importance to each of the Olsons' three cases, and if it cannot be established that Rick was within the scope of his employment with the garage, then the Olsons might not recover at all. Of course, they could always get a judgment against Rick, but the only practical way to win the lawsuit would be to find some insurance coverage, as it would be a tedious and perhaps fruitless pursuit to try to collect personally from Rick.

We have already seen that the "definition of insured" in Ralph's insurance policy includes any person driving the automobile with permission of the named insured. The next question is: Can the named insured himself and his family become the beneficiaries under the policy? The Olsons' lawyer would have to argue that they could recover for their injuries under their own insurance policy. But just as the "scope of employment" problem is fraught with uncertainty, so is this problem an unknown quantity. In addition, there is the question of policy limits. At a later time during the lawsuit the plaintiffs' lawyers will be able to discover the policy limits of the garage insurance, but they have no question in their minds that the limit of coverage is probably very high—perhaps $300,000 for the injury of any one person for which the garage may become legally liable or $1,000,000 total for damages occurring in any one accident. Ralph's policy is not quite so adequate, providing a $10,000 limit of liability for each person injured and a $20,000 total limit for each accident. The $20,000 would not compensate Ralph and Mary for all of their damages. They feel that the one case for Susie's death should bring them the maximum amount $25,000 recoverable by statute in the state in which they live. The difference in coverage available here makes it all the more essential to the Olsons that the garage be held liable.

Each of the four complaints filed contains the essential element of the lawsuit: a description of the time and place of the event and the relationship of the parties involved, a general description of the accident, and a claim as to the damages suffered. In addition, the pleader will claim interest on the judgment, the court costs (that is, the filing fee and other suit costs), and a general claim for "such other relief as the court may deem proper." The claim for damages will include what is sometimes referred to as "specials." These are the actual expenses which the aggrieved party has been put to because of the negligence of the defendant: hospital bills, doctor bills, automobile repair bills, travel expenses, telephone calls attributable to the accident, and so on. Then there are the general damages. These are the claims for pain and suffering, loss of earnings, disfigurement, loss of consortium claimed by one spouse because of the injury to the other, and all other types of loss, past, present and future, which may be attributed to the accident.

Ordinarily, the plaintiff's attorney will set a figure in the complaint as to the total amount of damages claimed. But since this is merely an allegation by one side of the lawsuit, subject to later proof and to the opinion of an impartial body, the jury, it has no controlling effect whatsoever on the outcome. Usually the figure is pegged very high—sometimes as much as six to eight times the amount which the pleader actually hopes and expects to recover.

All of the four lawsuits are filed with fair promptness after the accident, due to uncertainty as to Rick Ronner's whereabouts. The lawyers do not know what the total damages will be. Therefore, they explain the damages in very general language and also state in the complaint that damages may be incurred in the future (that is after the complaint is filed) in an unknown amount. Under modern procedures, a person is given liberal leave to revise his complaint to conform to the proof as presented at the time of the trial.

But the pleader must keep one thing carefully in mind, which is that even though under our law every possible harm to the victim which is in any way capable of being given a dollar value may be claimed, there is only one lawsuit for each person for each accident. In Ralph's case, for example, the trial might take place one year after the accident occurred. At that time he may very well still be suffering some ailments arising out of his injury, and it will be an unknown factor how long this trouble will continue and how much of a decrease in overall lifetime earnings he will suffer because of it. It is entirely possible that he might have to go into a hospital for a corrective operation arising directly or indirectly out of his injury, perhaps five, ten years in the future. Yet, once the case is decided and he is given a verdict for his damages, he is excluded from any further action. Under no circumstances could a case be reopened to claim additional damages. For this reason, it is essential that the complaint take the gloomiest possible view of the injuries and that the jury be impressed that this is a one-shot proposition for the injured party.

The damages recoverable for simple negligence are compensable damages, that is, damages designed to compensate the injured party for all of his loss. But willful, wanton or gross negligence may entitle the plaintiff to "exemplary" or "punitive" damages. These damages are in addition to compensatory damages and are assessed against the defendant by way of penalty for his extreme wrong. Punitive damages are often sought but seldom obtained. They are an entirely separate and distinct element of damages and quite often are not covered by a liability insurance policy. In other words, the insurance company insures the policyholder against compensable damages but leaves him personally liable for any punitive damages which may be assessed against him.

Exemplary damages are not recoverable at all unless some compensatory damages are made out by the proof. Likewise, the punitive damages must bear a reasonable relationship to the compensatory damages allowed. In other words, a person could not collect $1,000 in punitive damages for a claim which justified compensatory damages only in the sum of $100. Generally speaking, if it is a $100 case, then $100 in addition is all that could be assessed against the defendant for punitive damages, regardless of the nature of his offense.

Frequently, as we have seen in this case, a single act will constitute a public offense and also a private tort. Traffic offenses, although they are termed misdemeanors, are crimes against the state. The degree of proof in a traffic case, or any criminal case, petty or grand, is quite different from the degree of proof required in a civil case. The criminal and the civil case are in no way interrelated. The result in one case is not binding on the court trying the other case. The parties are entirely different. In the criminal case the state makes the charge, and because the criminal sanction and power of the state, or of one of its political divisions, such as a city or a town, is being imposed upon the accused, the proof must be beyond a reasonable doubt. In a civil case, on the other hand, the plaintiff need merely prove his case by a preponderance of the evidence.

The jury in a criminal case must have an abiding conviction of the truth of the charge against the defendant. In a civil case, the jury is called upon to rule with the side which produces the mere weight of evidence. The burden of proof is upon the plaintiff in a civil case, but his burden is satisfied by proof which might fall far short of the abiding conviction test. He need only convince the jury that his version of the transaction is slightly more convincing than the defendant's version. And there is no right against self-incrimination in a civil case. As a matter of fact, a defendant may be called for cross-examination at the outset and may be required to explain away his actions.

If Rick Ronner were actually guilty of willful, wanton and gross negligence, he could be charged with criminal homicide in causing Susie Olson's death. This would of course be a more serious criminal charge than the traffic case, but the fact that he was not so charged by the public authorities does not preclude the charge in the civil cases.

The insurance companies are not made party defendants. This would be improper under the law and under the insurance contract. The liability insurance contracts constitute a promise on the part of the insurance company to pay whatever damages the insured may become legally obligated to pay and a promise to defend a policyholder if he is sued. The insurance company stands in the shoes of the insured and is entitled to urge any defense available. But the law will not even allow the word "insurance" to be mentioned at the trial, it being considered that a jury would be inclined to render damages against an insurance company regardless of proof, but not against an individual or a small business.

And yet these four cases are a battle of the insurance companies from the outset. It is no surprise to the garage insurance lawyer when he receives the cases in his office. The company forwards the summons and complaint to him and also their investigation files, a copy of the policy involved, and all the pertinent information which their personnel have gathered about the case. One of the first actions the lawyer takes is to order Rick Ronner in for a deposition.

The Olsons' lawyer and also Karen's lawyer have taken the precaution of forwarding copies of the summons and complaint to Ralph's insurance company, along with an accompanying letter stating their theory that Rick Ronner was an insured under Ralph's policy in that he was driving the car with the permission of Ralph and that the injuries received might be ultimately assessed against that company. The lawyer for the Olsons' insurance company takes on defense of Rick, along with the garage insurance lawyer. This is done despite the obvious conflict between the two companies.

By the time Rick Ronner's deposition is taken, he has a fair idea of the issues involved in the case. However, neither he nor the Olsons have a sophisticated knowledge of the law pertaining to scope of employment, and Rick, full of remorse and feeling very repentant

142 • SO YOU'RE GOING TO COURT

for the tragedy, desires only to tell the truth. Present at Rick's deposition, in addition to Rick, are the two insurance lawyers and the Olsons' lawyer. Rick is placed under oath by the certified shorthand reporter. The garage insurance lawyer, having called the deposition, begins the questioning. As we have already seen, a deposition may cover many points which would not necessarily be considered admissible in court as relevant, competent and material evidence. The questioning begins as follows:

Q. State your name and address, please.
A. Rick Ronner, 1843 South Jersey Court.
Q. Your age?
A. Eighteen.
Q. Your occupation?
A. I've been employed as a shag-boy at Craig Jones Garage.
Q. How long have you worked there?
A. Since last September—about seven months.
Q. Do you work there full time?
A. I do now, but I started out part-time.
Q. What do you get paid?
A. $50.00 per week.

("Plus all the cars I can wreck," the lawyer thinks to himself, but due to the seriousness of the occasion he restrains himself from uttering this remark.)

Q. You weren't getting paid by the Olsons, were you?
A. Well, indirectly, I guess, because they were customers.
Q. No, but I mean you weren't on their payroll?
A. No, I was on the garage payroll. That was my job. That's the way I made my living.

The Olson insurance lawyer also questions Rick, in an effort to establish that he was, although perhaps not acting in accordance with a specific and direct order of his employer, generally acting within the scope of his employment with the garage; that he was doing the very thing which the garage hired him to do, and was not doing anything directly contrary to the orders of his employer.

After Rick's deposition is taken, and within the twenty days allowed by the Rules of Civil Procedure to answer the complaint,

Redressing the Wound • 143

both the insurance lawyers file their answers in court, serving copies on the plaintiffs' lawyers. In the answer by the garage, the lawyer makes a general denial that the garage is in any way responsible for the accident; also he denies the claim as to damages, putting the plaintiffs on strict proof as to those.

The Olson insurance lawyer appearing in behalf of Rick admits that Rick was in the scope of his employment with the garage at the time of the accident and denies the allegations as to negligence and as to damages.

Both the defense lawyers also file motions to consolidate the three Olson cases for trial at one time before the same judge and jury. They also seek to join and consolidate the Karen Walters case in the same trial, claiming that similar issues are involved in each case, and that it would be more convenient and appropriate to try them all at one time. The plaintiffs' lawyers object very strenuously to consolidation for trial, claiming that entirely distinct and different elements attach to each case and that they should each be given their individual day in court.

A hearing is held before the judge on the motions to consolidate. The motion to consolidate Karen Walters' case with the Olsons' cases is denied. However, the three Olson cases are consolidated in one trial, over the objection of the Olsons' lawyer.

The cases are then set for trial several months later. Ordinarily a plaintiff desires as early a trial date as possible. However, the Olsons' lawyer, in this instance, does not mind the passage of almost a year until the trial date because he feels that he will be in a better position to know what the actual damages are at that time, and will be better prepared, inasmuch as it will become apparent through the mere passage of time just how permanent the injuries received by Ralph and Mary are. None of the lawyers has much control over the court docket, it being governed by the number of cases on file, and there is always a delay in getting a trial setting.

The two defense lawyers file motions requesting specific information as to the alleged personal injuries of Ralph and Mary, and demanding medical examination by a physician of their choice. These motions are granted by the court, and as soon as Ralph and Mary are able, they go to doctors for the insurance companies, to be examined. After this is completed and the medical reports are supplied to all of the lawyers involved, and when it becomes apparent that both Ralph and Mary are able to have their depositions taken, they are noticed in by the insurance lawyers for this purpose. This examination also zeroes in on the scope of employment issue. Ralph being questioned by the garage insurance lawyer, in part, as follows:

Q. The shag boy had completed his job with the garage when he got the car in the hands of your wife, isn't that correct?
A. No, that is not correct.
Q. Why do you say it's not correct?
A. Well, I can't define the limits of his job with the garage, but I was given to understand that we were to get the boy either back to the garage or to his house, or wherever he wanted to go that day, and that was part of the arrangement with the garage that I paid for when I bought the car.

The Olsons' own lawyer makes the following points:
Q. When did you first see this boy?
A. To my knowledge, the first time I ever saw this boy was about 9:00 o'clock on that morning, Saturday, May 18th.
Q. Did you ever have an opportunity to check out his competency for the job he fulfilled?
A. No, I didn't.
Q. Did you even know whether he had the proper chauffeur's license for this job?
A. No, I didn't. That was the garage's responsibility. I left that all up to them. I was relying on them.
Q. Why did you let this boy drive?
A. I let the boy drive because he had been hired by and presented to me as an employee of a supposedly responsible business organization. I was counting on their reliability when I bought the car from them and I was still counting on it when I was letting their employee drive my car, and I understood that it was a part of the shag-boy deal that the boy was to be returned somewhere and then the shag-boy deal with the garage would be completed when he was returned to wherever he was going.
Q. Now, even though the garage was closed, to be closed at 12:30,

they agreed to deliver the car to you at 1:00 o'clock, didn't they?
A. Yes, they surely did.
Q. Were you ever given to understand that all of their service would end, bluntly end, at 12:30 P.M. on Saturday, May 18?
A. No, I was given to understand the exact opposite, that it would continue until I got the car and I got the shag boy wherever he was going.

The depositions also go extensively into the question of damages, which is a very large subject in this case, having a number of distinct elements. Even though the depositions constitute testimony under oath, they are not a substitute for the trial, and all of the questions asked in the depositions which are considered by the judge to be relevant, material and competent questions, are repeated at the trial. The purpose of the depositions is for the different sides to know beforehand what the substance of the testimony is going to be, so that they can adequately prepare and so evaluate the case for possible settlement.

3—The Trial Begins

The trial of the Olsons' case is set to begin on April 12 of the following year. By this time Ralph is heavily in debt although he has been able to return to his business and is beginning to build it up again to some extent. Mary is not the same as she was before, her difficulty being a combination of her own psychiatric troubles, financial worries, and the continuing grief at the loss of Susie. Rick has joined the Navy, and is back in town in uniform.

The case opens with a conference in chambers in regard to claim for $50,000 for wrongful death of Susie Olson, which is twice the amount set by the wrongful death statute. A claim for $20,000 in addition thereto has also been made for exemplary damages. The defense attorneys have moved to dismiss the claim for damages over and above the statutory limit, and they have asserted that punitive damages be included in the $25,000 statutory limit and additional damages on this ground over that limit may not be allowed. The Olsons' lawyer asserts that this statute is unconstitutional, claiming that he can prove actual damages in excess of $25,000 and that he should be entitled to all he can prove; that the legislature is not authorized to limit the amount of damages recoverable because of the provisions in both the state and federal constitutions stating that one shall not be deprived of life, liberty or property without due process of law.

This demand over the statutory limit is made by the lawyer with the knowledge that the case might later be appealed to the Supreme Court of the state by one side or the other, and he desires to make a plea before that high body on this constitutional issue, believing sincerely that he has a worthy argument. Before any claim or argument of any kind can be made before the appeal court, it must be first asserted before the trial court, otherwise the high court will not even entertain it. Generally speaking, the high court will consider nothing in the first instance. They are a court of review, and only review matters which the lower court has been given an opportunity to determine.

The judge listens patiently to the arguments, then rules that the statute is constitutional and valid, that the Olsons are entitled to claim only the statutory limit of $25,000. He also rules that if any punitive damages are awarded, they must also come within the $25,000 limitation, so that the total damages assessable for Susie Olson's death could be no more than $25,000. He issues his ruling on this subject with the comment that without statutory permission there might not be any claim whatsoever for wrongful death, observing that years ago, back in the common law of England, there was no claim for wrongful death; it did not exist. Allowing a claim is something the legislature did not have to do, but chose to do, and they, being the lawmaking body of the state, are entitled to set a reasonable limitation on it.

The judge also questions the argument that the constitutional right to life, liberty and property involves a right to monetary compensation for wrongful death of a loved one, not agreeing with the Olsons' lawyer that this necessarily follows. It is also pointed out that damages for wrongful death, if any, must be the pecuniary loss which can be made out by proof on behalf of the parents of the dead girl, and that the jury will be instructed that they will not be allowed to give damages merely for the pain, suffering and grief at the loss of the daughter.

Redressing the Wound • 147

The defense attorneys contend very earnestly that although there is no greater tragedy than the loss of a child in this way, the concept of monetary damages in law should not be subverted into a vale of tears. Monetary damages do not allay the grief suffered and they are not designed to do so. Rather, they are merely designed to compensate for monetary loss, and they will contend before the jury in all earnestness that there is no monetary loss in the death of a thirteen-year-old girl—on the contrary, there may very well be a monetary advantage—and they assert strongly to the judge that even the statutory limit of $25,000 will be impossible for the plaintiff to prove on this claim, let alone the excess amount which is being sought. The judge at this time does not decide what the damages are, or whether any punitive damages will be allowed at all, because these matters rely on the proof which will be presented.

Proof of injuries and all they entail—the pain and suffering, inability to enjoy life and to work, and the expenses incurred for doctor bills and drugs—may be made through testimony of the injured party himself, as well as medical testimony. Generally speaking, any mode of proof is proper so long as it conforms to the rules of evidence. As we have seen, these rules are safeguards against falsity or fabrication. There are no particular requirements as to the order in which witnesses must be called. The order of proof is left up to the discretion of the attorney, whose job it is to get the message across.

The rules of evidence give little guidance as to what to prove or how to prove it. Rather they are rules of limitation. They state what cannot be done. Hearsay, speculation, opinions of nonexperts, and like departures from reliability are prevented by the rules of evidence. Most attorneys utilize a check sheet where they list all the different points of their lawsuit which they must at one time or another in some way bring out by the testimony. If an attorney should forget some important point, he would then be faced with a loss at the end of the case. For this reason, attorneys give long thought before they state the words, "I rest my case."

Several diverse elements of a lawsuit may have to be established by a single witness, and oftentimes medical witnesses or other very much occupied experts are taken "out of order" and then excused so as to conserve their time. For these reasons, presentation of testimony is not and cannot be an orderly one, two, three by the numbers proposition. The sworn presentation is often a hodge-podge and it is difficult for the jurors to sort out which parts apply to the different elements of proof. This is why no lawsuit could be properly complete without both the opening statement and the final summations of the lawyers. In these, the lawyer's job, in addition to arguing for his contentions, is to reconstruct the lawsuit into an orderly, simple, and understandable whole.

The testimony in the Olson cases consumes two and one-half days of court time during which many points are covered. Applying to Ralph's case alone, there is extensive medical testimony establishing his permanent disability in chest pain, shortness of breath, fatigue, and continuing periodic headaches. Ralph also testifies as to these, as to the drug expenses and the cut-down in productivity he has suffered. He testifies at length establishing all the financial details of his business: the hours he worked, the type of work he performed, and his prospects for further profits had the injury not occurred. On this point, his accountant also comes in to testify. The accountant and Ralph in concert establish the facts and figures of his business and of his past and prospective professional life, which are then related to the diminution in earning prospects caused by the disability.

Among the expert witnesses is an actuary, who states that his job is to study normal life expectancies of persons of certain age and occupational brackets for insurance underwriting. Since the jury must assign a present dollar value to all of the prospective losses involved in the lawsuit, and since this is similar to what the actuary does in determining premium rates, the testimony is most helpful to the jury in the Olson cases. For example, the actuary states that a man thirty-eight years of age has a life expectancy of thirty-four years. It having been established by other testimony (subject to whether or not the jury believes it) that Ralph is going to suffer an average of $200 per month less in earnings for the rest of his life, than he would have received had the injuries not occurred, the actuary then multiplies $200 per month, $2,400 per year, by thirty-four years, and comes up with a sum of $81,600 just for the one element of Ralph's damages—loss of prospective earnings. This figure is then reduced to its "present dollar value" of $63,396.00 by taking into account the interest (3%) earning power of money.

In a very real sense, the task of a plaintiff's attorney is to conceive, create, and paint a complete multi-dimensional picture of the accident, the injuries, the liabilities, and the damages. Damages for personal injury rest on the idea that a person is entitled to be a "whole man." Subject to the normal restrictions, confinements, and responsibilities of life, a person is entitled to its full and complete enjoyment—the right to walk, to talk, and to move about free from pain; the right to read and to think, to run and to jump, to engage in sports or not, as he may choose, to earn money, to guide his own destiny as his talents, energies, and inclinations may dictate. As one great trial lawyer once put it, to "walk in his bare feet on the damp, green grass, kissed by the morning dew."

If a person's full and free opportunity to do any of these things has been limited or taken away by the tort-feasor, then he is entitled to remuneration. Much veteran benefit legislation, which by the way is as old as war itself and by no means confined to the U.S.A., rests on this fundamental theory. The right to breathe air, to be alive, to be a person, shall not be taken away; and if it is due to the wrong of another, monetary compensation shall be substituted therefor. Why compensation? (1) Because there are no other means to eliminate wrong and (2) Because the compensation itself may enable one to hire doctors, to take trips, to seek proper care, and, in general, to alleviate the results of the wrongdoer's act.

The attorney for the plaintiffs starts out with an empty canvas. On it he applies, stroke by stroke, a total picture of his lawsuit. In his opening statement he sketches in the general outline. In his presentation of testimony, he fills in the different colors, the dimensions, the details. He shows the past, the present, and the future. He shows the total man, the total woman, or the total child, and the many parts that every person is, has been, and will be: the father, the husband, the breadwinner, the lover, the recreational person, the aspirational person, the spiritual, the material, the psychological, the physical, the mental, the emotional—and the interrelationship of all of these parts.

But the central theme of his work is to show in brilliant and unmistakable delineation the contrast between what is and what might have been had the accident not occurred. This has three parts: (1) the person and all he was before the accident occurred—his education, health, marriage, occupation, financial status, hopes, and his dreams—all that he was; (2) his prospects for continuing and improving what he was and for how long; (3) what the defendant has done to those prospects—what has happened to the financial status, to the dreams, to the hopes, to the health, to the occupational prospects, to the person as a whole.

In his final summation to the jury, the attorney for the plaintiffs fills in, enriches, and enlivens the canvas—makes it appear as a glowing message-packed work of art, unmistakable in message, meaning, and significance. No part of the canvas can be left unfilled. No element of damages or liability or material proof of any type can be left unsaid. Nothing may be taken for granted. If gaps are left, they will be filled in by the adversary. The boxer who drops his guard, even momentarily, may find the void filled with winged leather. This is what is meant by burden of proof—the burden of putting on the case, of painting the picture. This belongs to the plaintiff.

The defense attorney also paints a picture, and he is not averse to crossing up the plaintiffs' efforts whenever he gets a chance. In fact, this is his purpose. The defense must keep the plaintiff honest; must prevent him from exaggerating, from putting more emphasis on things than they deserve, from painting contrasts more brilliant than life. The defense attorney paints another picture, another version, another interpretation of the accident: "This is all very tragic," he admits, "but we didn't do it; or if we did do it, we didn't mean to do it. We are not so bad as they say we are. Damage compensation is not designed to make a person whole. The Lord himself can't do that. Accidents happen all the time. No one is perfect. People are prone to err. This lawsuit should not be utilized as a tool to make the plaintiffs rich. The idea of compensation is only to help folks out a little bit, to pay a few doctor bills—not to penalize or impoverish anyone, not to give anyone a windfall. Time heals all wounds. You can't project these things thirty years in the future. The human body heals and the human mind does, too. Money won't solve this problem. It might aggravate it. Things are never as grim as a skilled advocate can make them out to be."

One might think the case of wrongful death could be proven merely by establishing that Susie Olson was the daughter of the plaintiffs, and she died in the accident. However, this is only a small part of the proof required. Under the law, the fact of a death, wrongfully caused, does not necessarily entitle anyone to damages in any amount. Damages for death must be proven just as any other element of damages, and only the amount proved can be allowed. Also, the party or parties claiming the damages must show that they are the ones entitled to such damages. Generally speaking, the people who would be heirs, if the deceased left an estate, are the ones entitled to claim damages for death. This would be the parents of a deceased child, the husband or wife of a deceased spouse, and so on. The amount of damages to be awarded is a fact question for the jury and not a legal question; however, the judge will not allow the jury to award damages unless there is some proof to substantiate the award.

The judge cannot tell the jury what to believe or what not to believe or, within certain limitations, how much to award in damages. Just as in other fact questions, the test is reasonableness. The judge will allow the jury to do anything which reasonable men might do under the circumstances but he will prevent them from doing what unreasonable, impassioned, prejudiced, or ill-informed people might do. The only legal basis of damages in Susie Olson's case is monetary loss to her parents, Ralph and Mary, resulting from her death.

On his opening statement, the Olsons' lawyer waxed eloquent in claiming that the ultimate lifetime "joy and benefit" Ralph and Mary would have received from Susie would far exceed the $25,000 allowable. "Benefit" is a reasonably accurate legal statement; "joy" is not. Yet innumerable things may be shown on a death claim. First, the Olsons' lawyer establishes the age of Susie and of both Ralph and Mary. Their life expectancy is then established by a statutory mortality table set down by the legislature on the basis of reliable expectancy studies. Since Susie's life expectancy exceeds her parents', the period of time during which service and benefit might have been received by the plaintiffs is their life expectancy, not hers. Some courts will cut off the period at the date when the deceased minor child would have become twenty-one, the theory being that after her majority, the child has no duty to serve. Other cases state that the test is not whether there is a duty but rather whether there is a reasonable expectancy that the services would be performed, and which do not limit it to the minority of the child. It matters not if the child is too young to have been of any service prior to her death. The test is what she later probably would have performed, and for how long, if she had lived.

Both the health of the deceased child and of the parents are relevant. The injured condition of Ralph and Mary might lead a reasonable jury to conclude that Susie, had she lived, would be of more service to her parents than the child of completely healthy parents. Both Ralph and Mary testify at length about Susie's intelligence, kindliness, tractability, obedience, helpfulness; her character and morals, her industry, generosity, and inclination toward economy and thrift. They also testify as to the type of services she has already performed, such as washing dishes, baby sitting, and helping around the house. Her friendliness and affection are pointed out.

In most states there is a statutory duty of solvent adult children to support their indigent parents. Even though this line of thought would project the proof many years into the future, conceiving a situation in which Susie is an adult and Ralph and Mary are elderly and unable to support themselves financially, it is still proper for the jury to consider this. But there is another side to it, which is that the costs and expenses of rearing, educating, and clothing the child must be offset against the claimed benefits.

The damage elements of loss of consortium are similar to the death claim. Until recently this claim belonged only to the husband. Now many states have enacted laws which also allow the wife to have this cause of action when her husband is injured. The older cases seem to be based on a theory which places the wife in a servile capacity and the husband was given the claim because the wife was no longer able to act as effectively "as a servant for him." Modern theory places the sexes more on a par, thus the new legisla-

Redressing the Wound • 153

tion. The loss of consortium claim is often difficult to put across to a jury. The verdicts tend to be minimal, especially when they are combined with general compensatory damage claims, such as in this case.

Sometimes a judge will have the jury sign a separate monetary verdict on this claim, and at other times he will combine it with the overall claim, instructing the jury on the subject and asking it to come up with a total figure covering all claims and not requiring them to delineate how much they may be allowing for loss of consortium, although this claim is entirely separate and distinct. Sometimes lawsuits are filed with loss of consortium being the sole element of damage. On this point, both Ralph and Mary testify at length to establish the respective wifely and husbandly services performed by the spouse prior to the accident and the inability of each to fulfill as well afterwards.

When the testimony is completed for both sides, the defense attorneys make several motions to the court. This takes place in chambers, out of the presence of the jury, and is accompanied by extensive legal arguments. These motions are:

1. A motion to dismiss the case claiming damages for wrongful death of Susie Olson for the reason that the damages in this type of case are by law limited to the "net pecuniary loss" of the parents and no such loss has been shown; or in the alternative, should the judge deny the motion to dismiss the claim for wrongful death, then the defense attorneys ask that the jury be instructed that they can return only nominal damages in the sum of $1.00.

2. A motion to dismiss the claim for exemplary or punitive damages, there being no proof that the defendant was guilty of willful, wanton, or gross negligence.

3. A motion to dismiss the entire claim of Mary Olson versus the defendant because no injury or damages have been shown.

4. A motion to dismiss all of the cases for the reason that the plaintiffs have failed to join an indispensable party, the telephone company.

5. A motion to dismiss all of the cases made on behalf of the garage inasmuch as the evidence shows "as a matter of law" that the defendant Rick Ronner was not acting within the scope and course of his employment.

6. A motion to dismiss Ralph Olson's case on the grounds that he was guilty of contributory negligence, claiming that his own personal negligence in failure to control his own automobile in which he was present contributed to the accident and excludes him from any recovery.

7. A motion to dismiss all three cases on the ground that both Ralph and Mary were owners of the automobile and were contributorily negligent in not controlling it while riding therein.

The Olsons' lawyer counters with three motions:

1. A motion for a directed verdict on the question of Rick Ronner's negligence and his liability for the accident, asking that the cases be submitted to the jury on the question of damages alone.

2. A motion for a directed verdict finding the garage liable for Rick Ronner's actions.

3. A motion to dismiss the claim of contributory negligence.

Whereas the burden to prove the case is on the plaintiffs, the burden is on the defendants to support their legal motions with authorities and argument. After the motions are made, the defense attorneys then present their legal reasons and arguments. The Olsons' lawyer answers these arguments to the judge. Then the defense attorneys rebut the Olsons' argument. These motions and arguments are made orally. The court reporter records the motions but not the arguments. These legal matters consume a half day of court time, all out of the presence of the jury. During this time the jury is excused and ordered to reappear at a certain hour. After the arguments are completed, the judge delivers his ruling, which is recorded by the court stenographer but not heard by the jury.

4—The Judge's Ruling

"Thank you, gentlemen, for a very scholarly presentation. The court is now ready to present its findings of fact and of law and its opinions and conclusions as to each of the matters presented. This is being recorded as part of the trial record, because if I should be mistaken in any of these matters you gentlemen may wish to seek review in the Supreme Court, and you are entitled to have my reasoning on record.

"First of all, there is the motion to dismiss all of these cases because the plaintiff has failed to join the telephone company as a party defendant. There is testimony that the telephone company had a large truck parked at the corner which obscured the traffic signal. The defense contends vociferously that the telephone company is a joint tort-feasor in this action and that the fact that it was not sued precludes any final disposition of this case, in other words, stating that the telephone company was not only a proper or a possible party but an indispensable party.

"Generally speaking, an indispensable party is one who by the facts and circumstances of the case is so involved and intertwined with the controversy that no disposition could be made without that party's being named. The plaintiff has an obligation to sue all indispensable parties and, if he does not, then he must fail as to the parties he has sued. But the plaintiff is not required to sue everybody whom he conceivably might sue. And if the defense feels that they can transfer the responsibility for the claims made against them upon some party not named, they then have the opportunity under our rules of civil procedure to bring that party in as a third party defendant, but neither are they obliged to do so. Under the testimony in this case, the court feels that the telephone company might very well have been sued and perhaps they should have been.

"But while they may have been a proper party, the court feels that they were not in any sense an indispensable party; and since the defense has not exercised its prerogative to bring them in as a party, the court feels that the defense cannot then take advantage of the plaintiffs' failure to join. Thus, the court will deny the motion to dismiss for failure to join an indispensable party.

"Next, we have the motion to dismiss the case of Ralph Olson on the ground that he was guilty of contributory negligence. In this, counsel for defendants rely on general law stating that an owner riding in his own automobile has the duty and obligation to control it and is responsible for what happens. Now, in this state, we have the strict contributory negligence rule, stating that if the plaintiff in any way contributed to the happening of the accident through his own negligence he will then be excluded from any recovery. Many other states have what they term a comparative negligence rule stating, for example, that if the defendant was largely responsible for the accident and the plaintiff was responsible only in small part, then the jury will be asked to make an evaluation as to how much of the blame applies to each and should mitigate or adjust the damages accordingly. But we do not have that rule. Contributory negligence in even a slight degree, if it was a proximate contributing cause of the accident, will exclude the plaintiff.

"As the court views the proposition making an owner responsible for the negligence of his driver, it applies only to other people outside of the automobile and not to the situation where the owner himself is injured. The court is not ruling at this time whether or not the driver, Mr. Ronner, was an agent of Ralph Olson. That will be a decision for the jury; the court views that as a disputed question of fact upon which reasonable minds might differ under the law. But whichever way that goes, there is nothing in the law stating that a principal cannot recover from his agent for negligent injury caused to him.

"Was Ralph Olson negligent? It cannot be said that allowing this young man to drive his car in and of itself was a negligent act, nor can it be said that the fact that the driver went through a red light shows negligence on the part of the owner in the car. What more Mr. Olson could have done as a reasonable and prudent person does not appear. The court feels that it is conclusive that neither Mr. nor Mrs. Olson was guilty of any negligence and will thus grant the plaintiffs' motion to dismiss the contributory negligence claim. There is no evidence of negligence on their part and the court cannot allow the jury even to consider this.

"Now we have the motion to dismiss the wrongful death case. This case certainly cannot be dismissed. There is proof here of a loss. This is countered by proof of expenses in rearing the child. Intermingled in the proof on any case of this type are unmistakable factors which the jury is not supposed to consider under the law— the natural bereavement and grief which any jury must necessarily share with the aggrieved parents. The law is probably very unrealistic in setting the damages at monetary loss. One can hardly conceive a preachment more likely to be ignored than the court's instruction on this point. Yet, the jury could reasonably find considerable monetary damages here and they must be allowed to do so, if they so choose.

"Now the court will address itself to the case of Mary Olson v. the defendants: Very frankly, gentlemen, this claim has caused much concern in the court's mind. The court admires the resourcefulness of counsel for the plaintiff, but what concerns the court here is that three different claims are being made for practically the same thing. This woman suffered the shock of seeing her daughter killed and her husband injured. She has a lawsuit claiming damages for the death of her daughter. She has another lawsuit claiming damages for the loss of services and consortium of her husband due to his injury, and she has a third claim for her own injury. Yet she did not receive an injury as we usually conceive it. She suffered the death of a daughter and the injury of a husband. Compounding of claims in this way gives the court great pause. Counsel for plaintiffs has skillfully placed each of these three claims in its own legal and medical pocket, and as he presents them they are each distinguishable one from another. Yet will the jury see these distinctions? Or is this merely telling them, in effect, that they can grant no more than $25,000 in damages for the girl's death, but for Mrs. Olson they can add another large sum because she suffered such grief that a psychiatrist had to be consulted?

"To the court's knowledge, this is a case of first impression in this state, which is remarkable when one considers how often the situation must have occurred. The court does not know, nor has it been advised, of a previous case in which a person receiving no physical impact or trauma of any type has recovered for 'injury.' And yet the court is impressed with the proof presented by the plaintiff. The court is also impressed with the lack of proof rebutting the testimony of Dr. Blase. The law must not reject a proposition merely because it is novel; therefore, the court concludes that the jury must be allowed to pass on this point. The motion to dismiss will be denied.

"Now the court will dispose of the motions pertaining to the negligence of the driver. In all three of these cases, we have a claim of willful, wanton or gross negligence and a demand for punitive damages. The evidence is that the driver failed to heed a traffic signal. Few derelictions of the road are fraught with more danger than this, as the tragic consequences here dramatically show. But what is willful, wanton or gross negligence? First, why do we use three words together? Why would not one suffice to describe the concept? Willful connotes a conscious exercise of the will in wrongdoing; not necessarily an intent that tragedy should follow, but an intent to do an act so neglectful of duty that tragedy might well occur. Mere inadvertence in driving, even inattention to a traffic signal, if not done in a gross and defiant way showing an invidious aggression of mind, would not to the Court's thinking constitute willful negligence. But these words are used in the disjunctive, not the conjunctive. Wanton connotes criminality and abandon, an anti-social bent amounting to intentional neglect. In the Court's mind, the testimony would not support this finding. The word 'gross' means extreme neglect, encompassing acts which may not be wicked, mischievous, pernicious, malevolent, evil or depraved, but merely extreme and serious by their nature. As reasonable people, the jury might so find as to the actions of the defendant, Ronner, in this case. The Court will deny the defense motion to dismiss the claim for punitive damages and will present this matter to the jury under proper instructions.

"The plaintiffs have asked the Court to submit these cases to the jury on the question of damages alone with the direction that they find that the defendant Ronner negligently caused the accident. The Court feels that a reasonable jury could not find otherwise and will grant the motion for a directed verdict as to the negligence of Mr. Ronner, and his responsibility for the accident, the amount of the damages to be assessed being left to the jury's sound discretion.

"And now we have the question of scope and course of employment. The attorney representing the garage has moved the court for a directed verdict dismissing the garage from any liability in these cases. This question has also been of great concern to the court. The doctrine of respondeat superior holds that an employer shall stand responsible for the torts of his employees. This venerable doctrine has gained validity with the passage of time. In our highly organized society, a one-man business is comparatively rare. Sales and service organizations function by and through their employees. It would be sad indeed for the cause of justice if a business could demand payment for the proper and desired services of its employees and then deny responsibility for their improper or neglectful actions. The prospect of suffering damages for negligent injury to person or property is and must be one of the many risks of doing business. Equity has long placed the responsibility on the superior, where it belongs.

"Yet this doctrine is also tempered by limitations. An employer does not own an employee. Every employment contract has its time and scope. There are certain hours of employment and there are certain functions and duties. A line is drawn between when the employee is on or off the job. An employee by day cannot then see his employer charged for his indiscretions of the night. But this is too easy an example. We have a much closer case here. Will the law draw hard and fast lines based on time and place? No. This would often be unjust. An employee can be on the very premises where his job takes him, and within the hours of his working day, and yet if he departs, even momentarily, onto a frolic of his own, engaging in some unauthorized or prohibited activity, he may well be without the scope and course of his employment, and his superior will not be required to respond for the damages he may cause. An example of this was given here in Court today where a lathe operator injured a customer while making a toy for his young child. Although he was 'on the job' the employer was not liable.

"The testimony in this case shows that the car was being driven on the way to a dance school. This surely had nothing to do with the business of Craig Jones' garage. There is no showing that the owner or the foreman or anyone connected with the defendant garage company except the shag boy himself had anything to do with the fact that he was driving the car for the Olsons at the moment the accident occurred. They did not authorize this specific act and there is a dispute in the testimony as to whether they ever authorized the boy to drive customers' automobiles after they had been delivered. Yet in order for the Court to say that the boy was outside of his employment 'as a matter of law' it would have to be said that there is no evidence worthy of belief, or if believed subject to any reasonable interpretation, placing him within the scope of his employment. This court cannot do.

"This young man was hired to drive customers' cars, and the jury could find that he was also allowed to drive customers' cars after the customers were in the car. The Court is not unmindful of the rule stating that the owner of an automobile appoints the driver his agent by becoming a passenger. The jury will be instructed on this and directed to make a factual conclusion under the law as to the question of agency.

"Now if you gentlemen have your instructions prepared, the Court will consider them."

5—*Instructions to the Jury*

With this rendering by the Court, the disputed issues of fact for the jury to determine have been boiled down to the following: (1) the liability of the garage; (2) the damages in each of the three cases; (3) whether or not Rick Ronner was guilty of 'gross' negligence and, if so, whether punitive damages should be assessed against him.

The Olsons' lawyer must urge responsibility of the garage and argue for maximum damages. The garage's lawyer must first urge non-responsibility of the garage and minimize the damages. Rick Ronner's lawyer (hired by the Olsons' insurance company) must urge that the garage share the blame and avoid punitive damages, if possible.

Some of the instructions given are as follows:

BURDEN OF PROOF

The burden of proof is upon the plaintiff to establish all the material allegations of his complaint by a preponderance of the evidence.

By "burden of proof" is meant the obligation resting upon the party or parties who assert a proposition to establish the same by a preponderance of the evidence.

By "preponderance of the evidence" is meant that evidence which is most convincing and satisfactory to you, and which you believe is a truthful account of the matters in controversy between the parties.

In order for you to reach a conclusion that the plaintiff in this case has proven his case by a preponderance of evidence, you must feel satisfied in your minds, after hearing and weighing all the evidence, that the evidence produced by the plaintiff in this case outweighs that produced by the defendant.

PREPONDERANCE OF EVIDENCE

You are instructed that the preponderance or weight of evidence does not depend wholly upon the number of witnesses testifying to a particular fact or state of facts, though the number of witnesses is to be regarded upon some circumstances. In determining upon which side the preponderance or weight of the evidence is, the jury should take into consideration the opportunities of the several witnesses for seeing and knowing the things about which they testify, their conduct and demeanor while testifying; their interest or lack of interest, if any, in the result of the suit; the probability or improbability of the truth of their several statements, in view of all the other evidence, facts and circumstances provided on the trial; and from all these circumstances determine upon which side is the weight or preponderance of the evidence.

DAMAGES

You are instructed that if you find the issues herein joined in favor of the Plaintiff, Ralph Olson, you will assess as his damages an amount which, in your considered best judgment, will reasonably and justly compensate him for his injuries.

In assessing such sum, you shall take into consideration the nature and extent of his injuries, the pain and suffering endured by him prior to the trial of this case, and the debts incurred and payments made for necessary medical, hospital and other expenses—all insofar as the above items have been established by the evidence.

You are further instructed that, if you find that the Plaintiff has established by a preponderance of the evidence that he will necessarily endure in the future pain and suffering resulting from said injuries, or that he has incurred any permanent injury or disability as a result of said injuries, or that he had lost any earnings prior to the trial of this case, or that his earning capacity and capability for the future has been impaired as a result of said injuries, then and in that event you may take into consideration those of the above items which have been so established by the evidence insofar as they have been so established.

You are further instructed that if you find by a preponderance of the evidence that Mary Olson has suffered injuries and that she is the wife of Ralph Olson and due to said injuries, if any, Ralph Olson has been deprived or will be deprived in the future of her services and consortium as his wife, then you shall assess damages for such loss as has been proven by a preponderance of the evidence.

In no event shall you bring in a verdict for more than $25,000. the amount sued for in the plaintiff, Ralph Olson's, complaint.

EXPECTANCY

You are instructed that pursuant to state law the plaintiff, Ralph Olson, has a life expectancy of 33.97 years, the plaintiff, Mary Olson, has a life expectancy of 35.78 years, and Susie Olson had a life expectancy of 56.80 years.

PRE-EXISTING CONDITION

If you believe from the evidence that the plaintiff, Mary Olson, had a pre-existing infirmity which was aggravated due to the negligence of the defendant, you will then assess damages against the defendant in such amounts as you may determine were proximately caused by said negligence.

EXPERTS

You have heard the testimony of witnesses who have given evidence and testified as experts, giving opinions. This class of testimony is proper and competent concerning matters involving special knowledge or skill, or experience upon some subject which is not within the realm of the ordinary experience of mankind and which requires special research and study to understand. The law allows those skilled in that special branch to express opinions and, upon a hypothetical state of facts stated to them, to say whether or

Redressing the Wound • 163

not, according to their experience and research, a fact may or may not exist. But nevertheless, while their opinions are allowed to be given, it is entirely within the province of the jury to say what weight shall be given to them. The jurors are not bound by the testimony of experts; their testimony is to be canvassed as that of any other witnesses; just as far as their testimony appeals to your judgment, convincing you of its truth, you should adopt it; but the mere fact that witnesses were called as experts and gave opinions upon a particular point, does not necessarily obligate the jury to accept their opinions as to what the facts are.

SYMPATHY

Jurors in the trial of a case, such as this one, are apt to allow their feelings of sympathy on the one side, or their feelings of prejudice on the other, to induce them to render a verdict which the law does not consider proper because such a verdict would be contrary to the law and contrary to the evidence.

Therefore, you are instructed that you should not be governed or influenced by sympathy for the plaintiff because he was injured in an accident, and you should not be governed or influenced by any prejudice or feeling either in favor of or against the plaintiff, or in favor of or against the defendants, but in arriving at your verdict in this case you should be governed solely by the evidence given from the witness stand and the instructions of the Court.

GENERAL INSTRUCTIONS

These instructions contain the law that will govern you in this case, and in determining the facts, you should consider only the evidence given upon trial. Evidence offered at the trial and rejected by the Court, and the evidence stricken from the record by order of the Court, should not be considered by you. The opening statements and arguments of counsel and the remarks of the Court and of counsel are not evidence.

The arguments, statements and objections made by counsel to the Court or to each other, and the rulings and orders made by the Court, and the remarks made by the Court during the trial and not directed to you, should not be considered by you in arriving at your verdict.

The Court did not, by any words uttered during the trial, and the Court does not by these instructions, give or intimate or wish to be understood by you as giving or intimating any opinions as to what has or has not been proven in this case, or as to what are or are not the facts in the case.

No single one of these instructions states all the law applicable to the case, but all of these instructions must be taken, read and considered together, as they are connected with and related to each other as a whole.

Separate damage instructions are given to Mary's case and as to the wrongful death case. Also the jury is instructed that if they find the garage responsible, they will assess the same sum for compensatory damages against the garage as they decided against Rick in each case, but will not assess any punitive damages against the garage.

6—*The Summations*

The Olsons' lawyer opens his summation as follows: "May it please the Court, and ladies and gentlemen of the jury, I don't think it is necessary for me to thank you, but certainly I think all of us appreciate your kind attention in listening to the evidence in this case.

"You know the most important aspect of any lawsuit is people. Here we have the Olson family spread before your eyes. We have the story of what was, and what most certainly would have been, if this tragedy had not occurred. And then we have what is.

"And we have Craig Jones & Company, a corporation, in the business of selling and servicing automobiles. There is nothing wrong with that. We are not attacking anybody. We are not attacking Rick Ronner. We are not trying to make him out as a criminal or anything of the sort. We are just here in the Court—your Court—trying to get justice. This Courthouse doesn't belong to the lawyers or the judge—sometimes I think we prance around here like we own the place, and I know how you must feel. You are strangers here, even though it is your own courthouse. But it is your justice that is going to come out of this case, your verdict, your ideas of what the ruin of a fine young family is worth. You have the chance here to say the right thing, and I know you will.

"Before we are through here, we are going to be using some human arithmetic. You can add things up just as well as I can; I am sure better. But maybe by working together we can be sure we don't forget anything. Most of us are lucky people; when God made us he didn't forget anything. He gave us ten fingers, ten toes, a head, a body, arms, legs and a soul.

"You know, once I wondered about talking about money in relation to human life. And then one Sunday I heard the preacher in church explain this for me and he settled that question in my mind once and for all. He was talking about the good missionary work of the church and said that God gave us money for a reason—so we could all be missionaries. By helping the good cause with our money, we could serve just as surely as the missionaries in the field. And, ladies and gentlemen, we have a means to serve justice in this case. Through dollars and cents.

"This case is not about who's wrong or who's right. That was decided before we ever got here, and after hearing the evidence, the Judge told you there was no question about liability. And then, of course, we have the corporation defendant. Now it is my job to collect the money in the case, not yours, and I don't want you worrying about that. But just apply a little logic. I don't want to get off on any technicalities. There are none in this case. It is only justice or injustice. But I just say this by way of explanation. You know in law a corporation is a person—it is a legal entity. It can sue and be sued. It has perpetual existence. It is created and then it exists. It has a name, a telephone number, and an address. But it doesn't walk and talk and think and breathe and see. And it doesn't drive automobiles, that is; it doesn't do these things itself. It does them through its employees and agents. And its President, Craig Jones, is an employee and agent of the corporation, just as Rick Ronner is. Now if Mr. Craig Jones had been driving a customer's car as an agent of the corporation, its President—one of its employees—who should take the blame for a wreck, the President or the corporation, or both? Obviously both. Why does he hold the job?

To serve. Who gets the benefit of his services? The corporation. And who is responsible if he makes a mistake? Of course, he is responsible individually and personally, but who else? The party who was going to benefit if he hadn't made the mistake. Now it is as simple as that, ladies and gentlemen. There was a benefit here. There was a customer-corporation relationship and a corporation always acts through an agent. It can't act otherwise. If this boy had done a good job of driving, there would have been one more customer that much happier with the service. But he didn't do a good job, and since the benefit would have inured to the corporation if he had, the responsibility has to go to it since he didn't. It's just business, and this kind of thing is a business risk, make no mistake about that.

"And remember that it was a business judgment made by Craig Jones and Company when they hired this young man to drive customers' cars. They determined that he was capable of representing the Company in that capacity. He was hired by them, paid a salary, and appointed to do this work day in and day out, just as Craig Jones was hired as President and appointed to do his work. If Craig Jones made a mistake, the company would pay, so if Rick Ronner makes one, the company most assuredly must also pay. Did Ralph Olson hire this boy, did he appoint him to anything, did he give him any status? Certainly not. There is only one reason why the boy was driving at that time, and that, however you look at it, relates back to the fact that he was a hired shag boy for the garage, and that Ralph Olson had taken his car in for a 1,000 mile check-up that morning. Those are corporation matters, that's corporation business, and that's why the accident happened.

"Do you know why corporations exist? I don't know if you jurors have traveled in Canada or in England, but you certainly have seen advertisements in our national magazines by British companies, and what do they place after the company name? The letters 'Ltd.' and what does this mean? It is an abbreviation for the word 'Limited.' Limited what? Limited liability, that's what. Now we use the letters 'Inc.' for incorporated, and what does this mean?—it means the same thing—limited liability. The company is a shield between the individuals operating it and the business. So we are not suing Craig Jones individually, we are just suing the business for a business debt.

"But this really isn't the important point of this lawsuit, and it would be a great mistake for you, under the law, to be concerned about where the money is going to come from to satisfy your verdict. Read your instructions on damages. It says 'you shall' award the damages made out by a preponderance of the evidence, and I know you will fulfill your duties in accordance with your oath as jurors, and will not consider matters outside the evidence.

"This is a citadel of justice. The court exists for justice. You are its agents. You are the missionaries of justice.

"Now let us turn to our human arithmetic. Ralph Olson is thirty-eight years of age. He has a life expectancy of thirty-four years. It has been a year since the accident. In that time he has incurred out-of-pocket medical expenses totaling nearly $3,000. Whereas he would have made $14,000 during that year, he made $6,000. There's $11,000 for the first figure we can place at the top of our column. He has suffered great physical pain and mental anguish; there's no dispute about that. The frightening experience of knowing his body was mangled, experiencing excruciating pain, the placing of a hollow needle in his chest, the escape of air, the entire chest opened by surgery, sutures placed in his inner organs.

"I know it's not a question of what amount of money you or I or he or any of us would take to go through that. We wouldn't do it for any price. Ten million dollars wouldn't move us. And I am just talking about the accident itself—the horrible blow, the lying in the street, the trip in the ambulance, the first days in the hospital. But I'm not going to try to give you a figure on that, or a figure on the pain, suffering and all the anguish of those six weeks in the hospital. That will be an unknown quantity, a sound judgment quantity. Fifty thousand dollars would not pay for it, but it would make it more just than it is now.

"But then let's go on down the line. Since he left the hospital, he has continued to suffer physical pain and suffering. Ten dollars a day might be an appropriate figure, but whether it is $5 or $3 or $20 a day, that is for you to decide. The point is, here is an element, a figure which must be entered in our column of human arithmetic. If it is $10 a day, for approximately three hundred days, that's $3,000 for pain and suffering since he got out of the hospital and up to the time of this trial. But the date of this trial has no significance as to

Ralph Olson's life of headaches and painful nerve reactions in the upper body. He had them yesterday, he has them today, and he will have them tomorrow and for the rest of his life. How many days are there in thirty-four years? Well, as I figure it, there are 12,410. Just allowing $2 a day for his future pain and suffering amounts to $24,820. You may want to make that $5 a day or $1 or $3. But in any case, it's an element which must be filled in our arithmetic column of human justice.

"Now let us consider loss of earnings. How many months are there in those thirty-four years? 408. We have a total loss, reduced to present dollar value, of $63,396, as you heard in the testimony. Now let us consider future medical expenses, drugs, the possibility of another operation, more and different and other pain and suffering necessitated and arising out of this accident. Remember, there is only one trip to the court house for Ralph Olson. If he has trouble in the future, he cannot come back for more compensation. This is it. How you will evaluate that is also something that I shall leave to your sound discretion. But there is another element in our column of human justice. It must be filled in. It cannot be left blank.

"Consider his wife, Mary. What is a good wife worth? A woman's work is never done, but now she cannot serve him as she has before. A substitute wife? What would it cost to hire such a person, if one could be hired? The myriad of tasks which Mrs. Olson cannot now perform so well, the laundry that will have to be sent out, the meals that will have to be bought outside, the transportation expenses—the gasoline, the time away from work, the poignancy at having less than a whole wife. Three dollars a day? I would say it would be more like $10. But if it is $3, there is $37,230 for this future loss. And what has the loss of consortium been during this year since the accident? It is reflected in his earnings and their decrease. Yes, we have already charged them for that, but it has reflected in a number of other things outside of the earnings—in the house, in expenses, the comfort, the service. Five dollars a day? I would say it would be more like $20, but if we peg it at $5 a day, there is $1,825 for past loss of consortium."

As he is talking, the attorney writes these figures on the blackboard, as follows:

$ 11,000.00	Past medical and loss of earnings
?	Pain and suffering—wreck and in hospital
3,000.00	Pain and suffering, past year
24,820.00	Future pain and suffering
63,396.00	Future loss of earnings
?	Future medical expenses
37,230.00	Future loss of consortium
1,825.00	Past loss of consortium
$141,271.00	

"And there we have roughly $141,000, with two large undetermined elements yet to be added—one, future medical and future pain and suffering from future complications, and, two, the gross pain and suffering of the accident and the days in the hospital. Twenty-six thousand for those? Just a figure I pulled out of the air; I feel almost ashamed to say it because of its conservatism. Remember, the figures are there for only one purpose—merely to show you how a formula might work. I am not trying to substitute my figures where yours should be."

(Similar calculations are presented as Mary Olson's damages and as to the damages for Susie Olson's death.)

"These figures that we have been talking about may seem high to you or they may seem low, depending upon how you look at it. And do you know that the valuation of something is a fascinating subject? It's not money we are talking about really; we are talking about values, and money is just a means we use to set values so that we can have something to put our finger on. God gave us money for this very purpose. That is to say, he gave us brain power to devise a system of money so that we can express ourselves as to the value of things and act accordingly, and so that we can express our will and our good works outside of our own bodies and beyond the stretch of our fingertips—like enabling missionaries to go where they are needed, or like erecting some beautiful building. If money is bad, then all the beautiful things that man has done and has created are bad because all of them took money. Money is the device whereby the thing was accomplished.

"You know, I was listening to the radio the other day about a race horse that sold for $468,000—a race horse, one horse, a creature with legs and a head and a body. And then I noted in a newspaper how a painting was valued at $2,300,000—just a painting, just a piece of canvas with some paint on it; a beautiful painting, of course, and an old one, but just a painting. So what is a human life worth? If a race horse is worth $468,000, and a painting is worth $2,300,000, what is a life worth? A man, a child, a woman, and more—what is a family worth? These are the questions you must ask yourself.

"Don't let my formula or any formula divert you from the important question. You know every price tag is an expression of human opinion as to value. An expression of justice, if you will. Give it a fair value and it reflects how much labor, talent, and material has been put into the item. You buy it for that and there is a just transaction. That's all we want here—a fair price tag; and if it isn't fair, then we won't have justice. You know these other gentlemen and I will probably try a lot of cases in our lifetimes; the judge will sit on another case next week, and another the week after that, and many hundreds of cases; and maybe even you jurors will sit on other cases; but there is only one case for the Olson family—and this is it. This is their day in court, and what you decide today will live forever in their memory. It will be with them for the rest of their lives. In a very real sense, it will be their lives. And if I'm not mistaken, it will be very much a part of your lives from here on out. This is a noble duty you have. I usually don't envy jurors at all, but in this case I think I do, for you hold a fine young American family in the cup of your hand. You can squeeze it, or you can love it and nurture it as it so needs; and I doubt if anything you might do in life could give you a better feeling. We thank you."

The lawyer for the garage rises and speaks:

"Ladies and gentlemen, I am touched by this deification of money. I'd always thought that money was something to pay bills with, and I have often heard it said that it's the root of all evil. I do know if money is going to have any value, there has to be a definite limitation on the amount of it floating around. The theory of compensation has always been to help people with doctor bills and pills, and to give them a little encouragement when they are down and out. And I just wonder what would happen to the value of the dollar if every time somebody made a mistake like going through a red light, tens of thousands of dollars would have to exchange hands. It's human to err, and it's human to help those who have had a setback; but it's not either human or economically sound to turn an accident into a means of becoming wealthy.

"I wonder when they toss around these figures in the hundreds of thousands of dollars by adding up things that have no validity whatsoever, or any reasonable relation to anything we know about in our life's experience, such as trying to project us twenty or thirty years into the future, ignoring the fact that human beings mend just by nature, just by the passage of time—I always wonder why it is that the United States Government pays only $10,000 when a soldier is killed. I know you appreciate the value of a dollar—you know how hard you have to work for it; and I know that just because you may be dealing with somebody else's money here, you won't treat it any differently than if it were coming out of your own pocket, your own sweat, your own worry and time and effort at earning that money. You must realize this—there is no dollar in this world but that somebody earned it. And if you had to earn the money, and if you were paying the bills in this connection, what would it be? Just put it on that basis—you're making out your own bill, because that's the only fair basis.

"I think it would be just fine if I could appoint somebody to make out my legal bills for me. Then they could say, 'I'm not paying it. It's no skin off my teeth. I might as well give it a real boost. This is my chance to be a real humanitarian with other people's money. Of course, I wouldn't do it with my own money; that's not my idea of justice. But when I've got other people's money to spend, I might as well gain a reputation for myself as the most generous God-serving contributor to the missionary fund of the church because nothing gives me a better feeling.'

"Ladies and gentlemen, let's talk about reality. Let's talk sense. You know, I was in a little store downtown the other day, and I saw one of those signs and this was one of the best I ever saw. It said, 'The worst days of my life are those when I wake up thinking I can get something for nothing.' You and I know there are folks all over this town who have headaches and nervous strain, and yet they go about their business probably as well or better than anyone. They don't cry and feel sorry for themselves. These things are a mental attitude as much as anything else. If you want to get on top of your troubles, if you want to meet the challenge in life with an honest day's work, you'll do it. If you don't, you won't. And the quickest way to make a person not want to work, not want to meet adversity in a realistic, healthy way is to have somebody come along with a big gift so then he thinks he doesn't have to work for a while. And then before he knows it, he's gotten out of touch and he's lost confidence with the competitive work-a-day world. And it builds. It's a vicious circle. 'Oh, I can't work; I can't do what I'm supposed to do; I was hurt.' And yet other people—you see them walking around the street, hobbling with one leg shorter than the other, using canes, stooped over—it doesn't stop them for a minute.

"But, ladies and gentlemen, that's not the crux of this lawsuit. You have been instructed that Rick Ronner is liable for this accident, and you have been instructed to assess such damages against him as you feel have been proven by a preponderance of the evidence. And then you have been instructed that the burden of proof is on the plaintiff to prove all of the elements of the lawsuit. Oh yes, they've tried to say that the garage is liable, but the facts speak for themselves and the law is that an owner riding in his own automobile is responsible for what happens in the driving of that automobile. We have heard a lot about the corporation. I can't see that Craig Jones & Company is any different than Ralph Olson in his engineering business. Let's just say that Ralph Olson hired an office boy; that he asked him to drive over somewhere to pick up some blueprints; that he met one of Ralph's customers standing on the corner holding a golf bag. The boy stopped and asked the man if he would like a ride. The man says 'Yes, sure, I'd like a ride,' and as the boy was taking the man to the golf course he had a wreck. Would Ralph Olson then have to pay some hundreds of thousands of dollars for that man's injuries? Does the fact that somebody is in business make them fair game for everything? Maybe the boy thought he was helping Ralph out by driving this man to the golf course. Does that make it an authorized act? Certainly not. This man took the risk. Ralph didn't take it. He had nothing to do with it.

"In relating back to our facts here, Ralph took the risk. This boy drove his car, and at any moment he could have asked to take over the wheel. He did not do so. He took the risk. He must have. He had to. Consciously, he took the risk. Did Craig Jones take the risk of driving Ralph Olson and his family to a dance school? Is the corporation liable just because it's a corporation? You know, ladies and gentlemen, there's one thing about justice that stands out above all others. It takes on its truest meaning when it is coupled with these words 'Equal justice for all.' It doesn't just say 'equal justice for people who got hurt in an accident'—it says 'for all.' That means equal justice for the defendant in this case as well as for the plaintiffs. Craig Jones is not now and never would try to get out of any just claim. But how can they be held responsible for something they had nothing to do with?

"Now, I know that you, the jurors, are full of sympathy for the Olsons, as I am, and I know you will follow your oath and you will give them some damages against the liable party, Rick Ronner, and I think counsel for the plaintiff has pinpointed better than I could the real area in this case where you might err, try as you may not to. It's the part that says you shall assess such damages as have been proven by a preponderance of the evidence, and the part that says you shall by your oath consider only the evidence and the law in this case; and I should like to paraphrase counsel and concur wholeheartedly in what he said. You are not to try to figure out how any damages are going to be collected, and if you try to do that, you are going to make a mistake because nobody has given you any information on that point. So if you get off on a tangent of thinking 'we had better stick the garage because that's where the money is,' you're not only mistaking the agency doctrine, because there are no facts here—none at all—that could place the responsibility on the garage; but you are violating your oath as jurors, which I know you will not do.

"I put you on your solemn honor, ladies and gentlemen; I ask you to take a good look at these facts. Now honestly, is the weight of evidence toward finding the garage responsible? Or is it the other way? Or is it a toss-up? If it is a toss-up, the garage is out. Why? Because the plaintiff has the burden of proof and they've got to sustain that burden. They've got to tip those scales. Now just imagine that you had this problem in your everyday life. You're being completely impartial about it, casting aside sympathy and talk about corporations and all of that. You've got no axe to grind. Wouldn't it, at the very least, be a coin-flipper of a problem? Well, you've got to realize that the defense has a two-headed coin because the burden is on the plaintiff. So if that would be your thinking, the toss is already decided before it is made—for the defendant.

"You know, another part of this business of 'equal justice' is embodied in these instructions of law—I mean the fact that they are given to you. They create a stability, an equality between cases—that is any other case with these same facts would have these same instructions. Why? Because this is the law as to these facts. If one jury in one case should ignore the instructions, and another jury in another case should honor their oath and follow the instructions, then you wouldn't have equal justice for all. It would be merely a lottery.

"Now I didn't cross examine that actuary fellow they brought in here because I didn't want to be using counsel's astronomical figures in calculating the present value of any particular sum of money! But you noticed he used a 3% figure on the earning capacity of the dollar. Well, the way things look nowadays, that interest earning capacity is much closer to 6%. And I think you can figure that out as well as any so-called actuary. You take a dollar today and it compounds itself into $2 in twelve years or so, and at the end of thirty-four years, it would be nearly $7. So if these astronomical figures are first drawn down to reality—to what you would award if you had to pay the bill, if you had to earn the money to pay it—and then divide it by seven, you would be more in line with realism on the damages on this case. But I say this merely for the benefit of Rick Ronner, the other defendant in this case—not for the garage. Because I know that, as honest, fair-minded people, sworn upon oath, you must determine that the garage is not liable at all. Thank you."

7—The Verdicts

After several hours of deliberation the jury returns the following verdicts:

IN THE DISTRICT COURT

MARY OLSON,

                Plaintiff,

vs.

RICK RONNER and CRAIG JONES AUTO SALES AND SERVICE, INC., a corporation,

                Defendants.

NO. 46542

TYPE OF ACTION: DAMAGE CLAIM FOR PERSONAL INJURIES AND LOSS OF CONSORTIUM

We, the Jury, find the issues herein joined for the defendants.

/s/ Harvey Eck
_____
Foreman

IN THE DISTRICT COURT

RALPH OLSON,

                Plaintiff,

vs.

RICK RONNER, et al.,

                Defendants.

NO. 46536

TYPE OF ACTION: DAMAGE CLAIM FOR PERSONAL INJURIES AND LOSS OF CONSORTIUM

We, the Jury, find the issues herein joined for the Plaintiff and against the defendant, Rick Ronner, and assess his actual damages at the sum of $50,000 and exemplary damages at the sum of -0- dollars.

/s/ Harvey Eck
_____
Foreman

IN THE DISTRICT COURT

RALPH OLSON,

              Plaintiff, | NO. 46536

vs.

RICK RONNER, et al., | TYPE OF ACTION: DAMAGE CLAIM FOR PERSONAL INJURY AND LOSS OF CONSORTIUM

           Defendants.

We, the Jury, find the issues herein joined for the plaintiff and against the defendant, Craig Jones Auto Sales and Service, Inc., a corporation, and assess his actual damages at the sum of $50,000.

                            /s/ Harvey Eck
                                            Foreman

IN THE DISTRICT COURT

RALPH OLSON and MARY OLSON,

            Plaintiffs, | NO. 46548

vs.

RICK RONNER, et al., | TYPE OF ACTION: DAMAGE CLAIM FOR WRONGFUL DEATH.

           Defendants.

We, the Jury, find the issues herein joined for the plaintiffs and against the defendant, Rick Ronner, and assess their actual damages at the sum of $12,500 and exemplary damages at the sum of -0- dollars.

                            /s/ Harvey Eck
                                            Foreman

IN THE DISTRICT COURT

RALPH OLSON and MARY OLSON,

                Plaintiffs,   NO. 46548

         vs.

RICK RONNER, et al.,

                TYPE OF ACTION:
                DAMAGE CLAIM FOR
                WRONGFUL DEATH

            Defendants.

We, the Jury, find the issues herein joined for the plaintiffs and against the defendant, Craig Jones Auto Sales and Service, Inc., a corporation, and assess their actual damages at the sum of $12,500.

                /s/ Harvey Eck
                                      Foreman

    The cases are solved. Now what are the results of these verdicts? Do they mean that Ralph can collect $50,000 twice, once from the garage and once from Rick? No. Rick and the garage are jointly and severally liable. Ralph is entitled to only one sum of $50,000 for his injuries, and Ralph and Mary together are entitled to collect a total of $12,500 for Susie's death. The plaintiffs may collect from either Rick or the garage, as they choose. But in this case there is no question as to who will pay, because Rick, having been found to be an agent of the garage, is an insured under the garage insurance policy.

    The Olsons do not collect their money immediately. Why? Due to the large sum of money involved and the close legal question of agency, the defense lawyer appeals the case to the State Supreme Court for review. This is an involved and lengthy procedure, taking eighteen months to complete; but the Supreme Court affirms the decision of the trial court, considering that the legal issues were resolved correctly, and stating that the factual issue as to the amount of damages awarded was apparently resolved by a fair and impartial jury in proper manner, and not subject to being upset, modified or changed by the Supreme Court, which concerns itself only with points of law, and does not review decisions as to disputed questions of fact.

Although the Olsons do not receive their money until the State Supreme Court appeal is final, it draws interest at the statutory rate of 6% from the date the complaint was first filed.

8—*The Karen Walters Case*

In another trial, Karen A. Walters wins a jury award of $3,500.00 for her injuries.

This chapter contains many significant lessons about the law—some large and some small, some subtle and some obvious—but none more fundamental than that two different juries, both acting within the law and within the realm of reason, are allowed to reach precisely opposite conclusions on the fact questions concerning (1) scope of employment, and (2) gross negligence.

The Walters jury found that Rick was Ralph's agent at the time of the accident and that he was guilty of gross negligence, avoiding the Guest Statute. Ralph's liability insurance pays the bill.

This case shows how the outset of a legal controversy is comparable to the striking of a tuning fork. The fork will first reverberate noisily, stirring up a disarray of sound waves; then the strength of its tines will gradually still the vibrations, calming them to a low hum, and then quiet. The law is a tine, flexible but strong. The judge administers the law by drawing the issues into a manageable scope, and then the jury stills the note with its verdict.

Chapter Ten

FOR BETTER OR FOR WORSE

The proud technological achievement of mankind is his ability to harness the volatile forces of nature. Man's individual atomic power is pride and nowhere is pride more involved than in the mating complex of human activities. Just as flame is controlled by respecting and confining it, humanity's pride must be respected and contained. Thus controlled, it becomes a potent power for good; on the loose, pride exacts a dreadful toll. Its essential thrust to divide and conquer, it engulfs everything in its path, and devours in the process the man or woman who harbors it without control.

We will take the case of Linda and Bob. Before their rather brief marriage which was followed by divorce, they were an attractive young pair. They met while still in their teens, healthy and full of spirit. As a single young man, things had been happening in Bob's life. He had the feeling that something would have to change very soon. Dissatisfied with living at home with his parents, he felt he was grown up enough to make a life for himself. He felt a real need of something. Defining it, Bob instinctively knew what he needed was someone to call his own.

At the same time strange things were happening in Linda's life. She mused that it used to be so perfect when she would meet her school friends, Sally and Mary. They would walk home from classes, stop to have a coke, and talk. It was lots of fun. Day by day, the friendships of the three girls became closer, and everything seemed to be so vital and secure when you had good friends. Then things seemed to change . . . the only topic they discussed which made any sense was—boys. The day they learned Karen Jackson had been married, Linda realized that things didn't look the same at all. She loved mother and dad, her brothers and sisters, the old backyard play area, even the family dog, Kraky, lovable old mutt. But suddenly Linda had a clearer self understanding than she had ever before known. This pleasant family, this comfortable home was no longer for her; it was obvious that this part of her life was going to end. She was going to have to leave them to build a life of her own, dependent on her own resources.

One evening as Bob and Linda sat beside each other in his car, it seemed as if they were surrounded by a magnetic wave which drew them together in a great harmony, making everything appear to be in perfect balance. Almost simultaneously the thought occurred to each of them that here seemed to be the answer to their longings and to their vague dissatisfaction, the desire to spread their wings and to leave the family nests. Nothing else was needed except being together, living and loving all of their happy days to come. The best thing about it was that they were both old enough— eighteen. Bob voiced it first. "I can't believe it, Linda, we're actually grown up! In one year, you're qualified to drive and to get married." In retrospect, all those juvenile years in the past now seemed to both of them like such a waste. "What we really need," Bob told Linda earnestly, "is each other. All it takes is two dollars."

Bob stifled with urgent kisses Linda's protests about a white dress, a church wedding, bridesmaids . . . with all of the tender ardor of his youthful years until everything was forgotten but the need of being married without a long waiting period. And so, Bob and Linda, who pledged their troth so impulsively, made their quick decision to marry sans benefit of clergy. They became one of the many young couples for whom the most serious undertaking in one's life was reduced to a simple matter. Sign here, blood tests, two dollars. There was no judge at the counter, no cross-examination, just a little old lady clerk. And then there was the Justice of the Peace out on the highway. The encounter was so brief, so perfunctory, that neither Linda nor Bob remembered what the man looked like thirty seconds after they walked out the door.

In a typical courthouse, the City Clerk's office can be just a few steps away from the divorce court. A lawyer will often find himself packing a briefcase full of legally worded vitriol for filing in court. As his papers are received, he can see young people like Bob and Linda standing in line at the marriage license counter. At that moment only the lawyer can appreciate the irony of the scene.

At least one in four marriages ends in divorce, and statistics from some areas show that one-half of all marriages fail. The state sets up that little clerk to issue marriage licenses because the state in a very real sense is a party to a marriage. Things happen in a marriage which escape the realm of the two little people sitting in a car parked in a romantic spot and feeling a physical attraction for each other. Children, property, and the state-conceived morality are involved. There is no such thing as a private marriage. Whether it be humble or grand, the state is a party in the sense that the rights and obligations of the contract are set by the state, and not alone by the parties, as in other contracts.

The Federal Constitution contains a provision that no state shall pass a law impairing the obligation of contract. In this the Constitution recognizes the necessity that people should be free to bind, or not to bind, themselves in contracts and should be free mutually to alter, amend or rescind agreements in the free exercise of their judgment and discretion. This is one of our most essential personal freedoms, lending responsibility and dignity to the individual by placing him in charge of his own destiny without interference from the state. Yet this provision is subject to many limitations—for example, a contract privately made between individuals for some illegal or immoral purpose will not be enforced by the state and the state can prohibit its enforcement, thus impairing the obligation of that contract. Similarly, although a contract of marriage will be enforced if both parties are legally eligible to marry, a private contract to break the marriage will not be enforced as such contract is illegal and immoral in the view of the state.

"I am going to divorce you," is a frightening pronouncement of one spouse to the other. Legally it is entirely incorrect. Marriage cannot be turned on and off at will. Only the state has the power to sever a marriage, and it does so on its own terms and conditions. This public nature of the union and the requirement of monogamy are the two major characteristics of marriage in our society, but these elements are not natural, universal or inherent in man since many societies accept polygamous marriages and, in Roman times, the marriage contract could be broken by the mere mutual assent of the parties. We consider this "collusion," and it is illegal. Throughout the world there are as many variations of acceptable marriage customs as the mind of man is capable of devising, with incest the one virtually universal prohibition.

The story of Bob and Linda could well describe the beginning of a happy and successful marriage, but this would require the faithful and continued mating of a number of rather delicately balanced pieces of mechanism; with such stringent requirements and close tolerances, there is an excellent chance that all will not continue to go well. And if love was once the mainspring, a breakdown elsewhere in the relationship can destroy the union.

There are two ways legally to end a marriage—annulment and divorce. The courts may also grant a legal separation or "separate maintenance," as it is sometimes called, but this does not dissolve the marriage. Annulment only applies where a marriage is either void at the outset or voidable, because of a variety of circumstances where either one or both of the parties to the marriage were not qualified to enter into the marriage contract, such as being under the legal age requirement for marriage, mentally incompetent and incapable of forming the intent to marry, or where the marriage was induced by fraud or duress or by use of drugs or extreme intoxication, or where one of the parites was already married, or where the marriage was incestuous, such as between a brother and sister.

If children are born of an invalid marriage, they are "legitimatized" by a state statute which simply provides that, for all purposes, the offspring shall be considered legitimate and not illegitimate children. Wherever it can, the law seeks to erase the stigma of illegitimacy.

Many states recognize "common law" marriage, and for good reason. This is a marriage consummated in fact, though without a formal ceremony of any kind. Such a marriage takes place where a man and woman, both eligible to marry, live together as man and wife and behave as marrieds in the community in which they live. If such a marriage takes place, then it is as binding as a ceremonialized union and can only be severed by divorce. The state thereby prevents people from enjoying the benefits without bearing the responsibilities simply because a mere formality is absent.

The common law rule also avoids the placing of undue emphasis on technical requirements of the ceremony. If the two persons have lived as man and wife, then any irregularity is erased. Otherwise, somebody might try to withdraw from the union because the preacher wasn't properly ordained, because some precise language wasn't used, or on another such technical basis. No specific time rule or requirement is connected with common law marriage, but the cohabitation must be of sufficient duration to indicate a mutual intent to marry and a desire to be thought of as man and wife.

Divorce can be granted upon proof of one or more of the grounds which will satisfy the state. Grounds for divorce vary among the states, but the one cause which is grounds in every state is adultery. Adultery is sexual intercourse by either spouse with a third person; direct evidence of the act is not required, rather a mere showing of an opportunity and the inclination will suffice. In New York State adultery is the only grounds for divorce.

Most other states name seven or eight grounds for divorce in addition to adultery, proof of any one of which is satisfactory. Mere "incompatibility" is rarely considered a sufficient ground, even though this word might serve to describe the real reason for divorce in most of the cases. The law seeks to discourage divorce and, at least in word, rejects all frivolous and unsubstantial reasons for it. Mere quarrels and disagreements will not suffice. Purposely, the law refuses to recognize the real essence of the breakup, which is usually caused by mental and emotional immaturity on the part of one party, or both, in a failure to balance desire with resources. The law also fails to recognize the possibility of a mistake. It will not suffice to say to the judge, "I don't know what came over me. I guess we all make mistakes, and I sure made one. I made the decision and married him, but I realized almost immediately that he wasn't for me. We tried to make a go of it, but it was just the original mistake which couldn't be corrected, and it will never work." Legally, this is meaningless.

At some time in the past, the word "cruelty" was introduced into divorce legislation as a grounds. Since then its true meaning has been stretched and distorted in all directions. Somehow even though cruelty, in its classic sense, should be the most odious of charges, it has proven to be the most widely used, particularly in noncontested cases. When cruelty came into the law as a grounds, the idea was that it be limited to physical acts, but ingenious advocates argued convincingly that cruelty can as well be committed by mental or psychological abuse, and "mental cruelty" has now been established as a cause. Many states require proof of "extreme and repeated acts of physical or mental cruelty." This requires a showing of systematic abuse, insults, and affronts, such as unjust accusations or belittling of the spouse in the presence of others. The word "repeated" has been interpreted to mean at least twice. Once won't do it, but two different acts on different occasions will.

Another ground for divorce is desertion without excuse, usually from one to three years, and it is interesting to note that some cases have held that desertion may take place even though the spouses are living under the same roof during the alleged period of desertion, if one spouse wrongfully refuses sexual intercourse for the period or sullenly refuses to communicate during all of the time specified. This has been construed to be desertion in fact, although actual physical absence was not the case. Conviction of a felony by one spouse is often grounds for divorce by the other; habitual drunkenness, incurable insanity, nonsupport of the wife and children, and sexual impotence are sometimes grounds.

If a divorce is being contested, there are various defenses which may be set up. One, of course, is nonproof of the grounds asserted. Other defenses are collusion, connivance, condonation, and recrimination. Collusion is not strictly a defense, as by its very nature, it would not be asserted by a defending party; however, it is grounds for the court to refuse to grant a divorce. As we have seen, collusion occurs when spouses agree that one will sue for the divorce and that the other will not object. If this is shown, the court cannot grant the divorce because it is against the law and against the public policy of the state to allow the parties to so agree. In actual practice, however, the courts do not raise the point of their own motion; and in truth, parties often do agree to this exact procedure, the court realizing that to refuse the divorce would merely complicate and prolong its business to no practical advantage.

An overriding characteristic of American divorce law discourages the heavy and stringent enforcement of the letter of the law, and this is that with fair ease and facility a couple or a party intent on divorce can go to another state and obtain a perfectly binding decree.

Connivance is a defense which arises when one spouse, suspecting the other of misconduct such as adultery, makes opportunities for the other to commit the illegal act. The suspecting spouse is deemed by such action to have consented to the misconduct of the other, and this is considered a fraud on the Court. Condonation is where one spouse has full knowledge of a cause for divorce and forgives it by continuing to cohabit. Recrimination is one of the most interesting yet idiotic of defenses, and it has been abandoned in many states. It says, in effect, that if both parties have grounds for divorce, then neither will get it.

Even though the law sounds tough, the actual administration makes it generally rather easy to obtain a divorce, particularly when the case is not contested. In effect, therefore, we have something very close to the rule in ancient Rome, where the parties could, by private agreement, dissolve their marriage, although one would never suspect this by reading the law. A divorce contest through the full process of the law is very rare indeed, and many lawyers will refuse to work on such a case because once the spouses have spread in public their venom against each other and before a jury of strangers, there is obviously no chance that there could thereafter be a marriage in any real sense, even if the defending party should win. Occasionally, though, some spouses will be so embittered against each other that one will contest a divorce and seek a decree in separate maintenance instead, thereby refusing to free the other spouse and preventing him from having the opportunity to remarry. Ordinarily, the reason for the separate maintenance provision is to provide redress to people who cannot become divorced due to moral or religious beliefs. Use of the law for the purpose described is not favored by lawyers and judges, and they will not be inclined to lend their services to the consummation of such a design.

In our society, in which freedom of choice and action is the keystone, one cannot force another to live in a state of connubial bliss if the will does not support it. The manner in which some divorce courts operate (relentlessly grinding out twenty to thirty cases a day), one might think that the whole form and substance of legal trappings could just as well be abandoned for some more efficient method of mass processing, and it is true that most divorces, perhaps 90%, would lend themselves to handling through a check sheet made out by an experienced clerk, in much the same way that one might apply for Social Security benefits. Yet the state won't give way to this summary approach but requires, at the very least, that the grounds be established under oath in a formal hearing before a judge.

Six years and three children after Bob and Linda first hopefully appeared before the Justice of the Peace and vowed themselves to wedded loyalty, their marriage approached disintegration. What has happened? Bob has not fulfilled Linda's dreams, she has not fulfilled his, and neither has fulfilled their individual dreams. Linda hurts Bob's pride by nagging him about his job and earnings, and Bob hurts his own pride by drinking and getting himself fired from jobs. Bob hurts Linda's pride by criticizing her friends, her family, and her homemaking, and Linda reacts by debasing her own pride through frequent sob scenes with her parents. Bob earns $400 per month as an automobile mechanic. Current installment bills, including the mortgage, come to a little over $300 per month so it is a great problem to find money for food, clothing and medical bills. Linda suspects Bob of running around with other women. She goes to a lawyer. He says that he can't go to court unless he has at least $150 in advance, and that his fee may be $300 or more, depending on how many court appearances he has to make, and whether there is a contest as to support money and division of property. Linda delves further into the depths of lost personal dignity and pride by borrowing the money from her father to start the court action. The visit to the lawyer occurred after Bob had struck her. This was the last straw. She could take everything but physical abuse. Hearing this, the lawyer asks if she thinks she should have an ex parte restraining order against Bob, ordering him to leave the house and not molest, communicate or interfere with her and the children, and she says that she most certainly does.

The divorce restraining order is one of the most brutal pieces of paper that has ever been devised. "Ex parte" means "by one side only," without hearing, consultation or representation of the other side. The restraining order is temporary, that is, until dissolved by further order of the court, and it is granted on the basis of sworn testimony given by the wife in court without the knowledge or the presence of the husband, stating that she is in fear for her life, her children and her property due to the actions of the husband. Some courts even grant restraining orders without personal sworn testimony in court, merely on the basis of an affidavit.

Linda's lawyer prepares a complaint in divorce charging extreme and repeated acts of physical and mental cruelty, asking that Linda be given custody of their three children who are minors, that the defendant be ordered to pay alimony and support and that an equitable division of the property of the parties be decreed by the court. Along with this is a motion for temporary orders, which means that until the final hearing, the Court should grant custody of the children to her, and asking that the defendant be required to pay a certain monthly sum for support, plus the wife's attorney's fee, and the costs of the action.

The theory of requiring the husband to pay the wife's attorney's fee is based on the fact that the husband is usually the employable member of the family, and if she were required to compensate her own attorney, then the husband would have an unfair advantage over her in that he could withhold the funds necessary for this purpose. Therefore, in order to place the parties in a position of equality before the Court, the husband is required to pay the wife's attorney as well as his own, unless the wife is capable of hiring her own attorney from her own resources. This provision does not free the wife from her primary obligation to pay her own attorney, but merely reimburses her for what she had paid, when and if the fee can be obtained from the husband through court process.

Attorneys will take some divorce cases without an initial retainer from the wife except to pay the docket fee and the service of process costs, if they think there is sufficient assurance that they will ultimately obtain their fee from the husband. But in the usual case, this is an impossible course of action for the attorney because one of the major reasons why the home is breaking up is due to the impossible financial straits of the parties who do not have enough money coming in and too much going out. Then when the home is divided into two separate entities, there are two rent bills instead of one, two food bills instead of one, and the financial tragicomedy becomes even more futile; so if the children are going hungry, the attorney is going to end up short, no matter what kind of court order he may obtain for his fee.

The court papers, including the restraining order, are served on husband Bob, and the typewritten originals are filed in court. So here we go. Bob consults his own lawyer, and ultimately the two lawyers get together and try to work out a settlement as to division of property, alimony and support. Neither party can afford to contest anything. Linda gets the house, the children and the furniture; Bob gets his clothes, the stereo set and most of the bills, plus a bill of $200 every month out of his $400 earnings for alimony and child support. The court is expedient enough to maintain an accounting office or "registry" for the making of these payments. Bob pays in, Linda draws out, and the court keeps its own record of these transactions. In this manner there is no question as to who paid and received what and when.

The Court retains "continuing jurisdiction" over the alimony, custody and support questions, so that should there be any change in circumstances, such as an increase in Bob's earnings, then he could be brought back into court and the support payments increased. Bob is granted visitation rights with the children, specifically spelled out in the separation agreement, which is made a part of the divorce decree when it is entered by the Judge. He is granted the right to visit them on Saturday from 10:00 o'clock in the morning until 4:00 o'clock in the afternoon, and he can also take the two older children, but not the baby, on a trip. This order is subject to change by the Court as the children grow older and, when a child reaches the age of fourteen, he is allowed by law to make a choice as to the parent with whom he wishes to live, which the Court will usually follow.

Should any of the court orders not be followed by either party, then the lawyer must again be consulted. On affidavit of the party complaining, the lawyer obtains a contempt citation, which is served by the sheriff. This brings the offender into court for a hearing at which the judge gives a lecture, and if the failure or refusal is serious enough, the party can be fined or jailed.

The divorce is granted and the case is settled six months after filing. The time it takes to get a divorce varies radically between the states. In Nevada, for instance, a divorce can be obtained immediately upon filing if the six-week residency requirement is fulfilled. Most other states require a waiting period, sometimes three months or even one year, designed to enable and encourage the couple to reconcile if there is any inclination to do so. Other states grant an "interlocutory" decree which takes six months, or some other arbitrarily specified length of time, before it becomes final and binding. Divorce is usually a hurry-up deal to the parties. "I can't stand it another minute," they say. But the law intentionally seeks to temper the brash approach.

It has been said from the bench that "divorce is a luxury." It is true that few people can afford it, and yet the beleaguered souls survive, some of them surprisingly well, and many of them live to make the same mistakes again, though still not being able to afford their past mistakes. The "luxury" theory causes Legal Aid offices in many cities to reject all divorce cases. Legal Aid is one of our finest charities, supported by United Fund contributions in most metropolitan areas for those who can't afford to hire a private lawyer. There is constant pressure for these offices to enter the domestic relations field, and some draw the line only at mental cruelty, stating, in effect, that divorce on this ground is indeed a luxury, but when physical abuse, nonsupport or other grounds are present, it is a necessity.

Assume that instead of an automobile mechanic, Bob was a salesman in New York with education and a bit of wile in his makeup. He is enamored with a gorgeous secretary, and instead of waiting for Linda to drop the boom, he takes off for Nevada, stays there six weeks in order to satisfy that state's residency requirements, and divorces Linda. The Nevada court decrees that he will pay $100 per month for child support. This may be a perfectly valid divorce. Why? Because of a provision in the United States Constitution which states that "the several states shall give full faith and credit to the judicial proceedings of every other state." This is sometimes called "comity" between governments, and even though the residency requirements may be one year or more in the state in which Linda and Bob live, Nevada is entitled to set up its own residence requirements and its own grounds for divorce, and the other states will recognize its decrees.

But the Nevada divorce route may not be as simple as Bob thinks. There are a lot of traps. Linda was not personally in Nevada, available for service of process of the divorce papers. She was notified of the action by mail, but this is only "constructive" or "substituted" service. This is enough to give the Nevada court power to grant the divorce, but its rulings as to custody of the children, support payments, and division of property are a complete nullity. This is because the Nevada court did not have jurisdiction over these subjects. When Linda shows these mailings out of Nevada to her lawyer, he advises her not to make any appearance whatsoever in the Nevada court, either through an attorney or otherwise. Nevada has no power to make her appear and, if she did so, she would then be subjecting herself to the jurisdiction of the Nevada court for all purposes, which would be unwise.

Let us assume that after Bob secures his Nevada divorce, he then goes over the line to California, and there marries the gorgeous secretary, leaving Linda, who is in New York, with the house, the children, and the bills. Linda receives the $100 per month support which the Nevada court so magnanimously awarded her. But this does not begin to supply her needs. The inequities are apparent, since Bob is now earning $700 per month as a salesman in California.

What does Linda do? Her lawyer advises her to hire another lawyer in California to sue Bob for divorce in that state, asking a fair award for child support, alimony, and division of property. The California lawyer serves Bob with a Summons and Complaint for divorce in that state, asserting as grounds therefore adultery, desertion, nonsupport, and cruelty. Bob goes to his lawyer in California and says, "What's going on here? She can't sue me for divorce. We are already divorced!" The lawyer says, "That depends. Your Nevada divorce may or may not be valid but, in any case, her claim against you for alimony and support is something to worry about, because she has obtained personal jurisdiction over you even though she is in New York, but you didn't obtain personal jurisdiction over her in the Nevada court. You may be stuck, because you are in California and, therefore, the California court can enter valid orders against you even though the house, the children, and your wife are still in New York."

Bob's lawyer defends the divorce claim on "plea of former judgment." This is called *res judicata*, saying, in effect, "the thing has already been decided." Bob's lawyer obtains a certified copy of the Nevada divorce decree and files it in the California court, asking that court to give "full faith and credit" to the Nevada decree. Linda's California lawyer argues that the Nevada divorce is invalid because the facts show clearly that Bob went to Nevada for the sole purpose of getting the divorce; and if this is really the case, then California need not give "full faith and credit" to the Nevada decree. It is a question of domicile, not residence, says Linda's lawyer.

"Domicile" and "residence" are a couple of tricky little concepts calculated to delight the true legal eagle, that legalphile who loves to tinker with concepts of evasive meaning. Residence a state can fix and define, but domicile, no—this is a question of Federal-Court-made law under the full faith and credit clause. Why? One must first understand something about jurisdiction itself, often a neat little riddle of overriding importance. If a court does not have jurisdiction over the subject matter and the people involved in a controversy, then it has no power whatsoever to deal with the subject, and any order it might enter in that regard would be worthless.

Domicile is a much more stringent concept than residence. One may have more than one residence. One may be a resident of a motel for just one night, or a few days. Just a very brief residency may suffice, for example, for a valid marriage to be performed in a state, but domicile is supposed to describe the one place where the individual in reality intends to live, and the length of time that one may stay is only one factor. If Bob stayed for six weeks in Nevada but left his bank account back in the other state, if he didn't change his voter's registration, if he didn't change his car registration, or if he didn't take up employment of a permanent nature in Nevada, then, even though that state's six-week residency requirement is satisfied, it will not satisfy a sister state unless he was truly domiciled in Nevada, so the California court could well decide that the Nevada decree was totally invalid and ignore it. But even if the California court felt it should recognize the Nevada divorce, it would still have the jurisdiction to enter its own orders regarding alimony, support, custody, and property division.

As to property division, the California court has a problem because the house is not within its jurisdiction. However, it can enter an order awarding the house, even though it be within another state, to Linda. Then, if Bob refuses to give a Quitclaim Deed to Linda, placing the house in her name, free and clear of any ownership by him, he can be brought into the California court and fined or jailed for contempt. This proposition is sometimes called the divisible divorce, that is, the divorce itself is divided from all other questions involved. Divisibility takes the sting out of "race to the courthouse" problems where one spouse files for divorce in one state and the other in another state. If each state has jurisdiction over the marriage status by having one spouse truly domiciled within its borders, then "first in time first in right" is the rule. But here, for example, Bob's victory in choosing Nevada, a sympathetic forum to him, becomes rather academic and hollow when he finds out how limited Nevada's powers really are. Similarly, the spouse who tried to obtain some advantage by filing first within the state of matrimonial domicile will be sadly disappointed. This doesn't change the merits of anything, and the party who deserves to obtain the favorable orders will obtain them, regardless of who happens to become the plaintiff or the defendant.

All interstate divorce problems are based fundamentally on the requirement of due process of law as guaranteed by the Federal Constitution. One of the essential features of due process of law is that a person cannot be divested of property or rights of any sort without having the opportunity for a full hearing in the court seeking to adjudge those rights. Linda could have appeared in the Nevada court, but only to great disadvantage, and she was not required to appear because the court did not have personal jurisdiction over her. All the Nevada court had, and as we have seen even this point is questionable, is personal jurisdiction over one of the parties to the marriage, which is sufficient to give it power to dissolve the marriage status but not to bind as to any other issues.

For Better or for Worse • 193

"Full faith and credit shall be given in each state to the judicial proceedings of every other state" and "Nor shall any state deny any person due process of law" are both firmly engraved in the Constitution. They are of equal rank, but if recognition is sought for a sister state decree not based on due process of law, then the giant principles are at loggerheads. They ram each other like buck sheep at mating time. Who wins, which one gives way, where is the line drawn? In this instance, due process of law wins out, but one state is not entirely free to decide whether another state has granted or denied due process in its handling of a case. The United States Supreme Court lays down the rules and the state must follow.

A state will often recognize and enforce valid court decrees of a foreign country, as well as those of another state. This is based on "comity" alone as no full faith and credit provision exists between countries. Full faith and credit is mandatory between states, but comity is merely a courtesy or a gratuitous accommodation which one sovereignty will grant another, not as a matter of right but out of deference and good will. It has no binding force behind it, but it is done by one country in the hope that the favor will be returned by the other country. However, the Mexican mail-order divorce is totally invalid and will not be recognized because it has none of the essential aspects of due process of law.

What if Bob skips out of California to avoid that state's judicial process just as he left New York to avoid his family responsibilities? The various jurisdictional problems involved in family law make it readily apparent that a really intent and resourceful recreant can avoid his responsibilities without too much trouble. It is here that the criminal law steps in.

Willful nonsupport is a serious state crime, carrying a penitentiary penalty and subjecting the offender to extradition proceedings. The district attorney's offices in all of our large cities run a large number of criminal nonsupport cases through their files every year and runaway fathers are the subject of a high percentage of the fugitive-from-justice warrants floating around the country at any given time. Although nonsupport is a penitentiary offense, courts only resort to imprisonment as a last resort. Instead, they use the threat to force the father to do his duty toward his children. In the usual criminal case, the offender is brought back to the state and tried, but in a nonsupport case the last thing the state really wants is to have the deadbeat back within its borders. He couldn't or wouldn't fulfill his responsibilities when he was there before, and the courts realize that the chances are good that he would fail again if brought back. For this basic reason a number of the states have adopted Uniform Reciprocal Support Acts, which still have as their "kicker" the criminal penalty for nonsupport, but enable the state court where the father is found to supervise and enforce payments for his family living in another state. In a sense, the district attorney and court of one state act as agents for another state in enforcing support. This is a very fine example of interstate cooperation seeking to control a serious social and economic problem.

Divorce is the messy work of the law, not because the clientele is bad nor because the legal problems are unappealing, but because the people involved are so bitter, irrational, and frantic that it is no simple task for the lawyer to keep from getting involved emotionally in the intense feeling of the situation. Everything, big and small, is fraught with calamity, and miracles have to be accomplished immediately or else the entire world will surely end. Some lawyers are fairly accomplished marriage counselors and probably all lawyers make at least a token effort to effect reconciliation before going off to battle. But this is not the lawyer's job.

The divorce client must first receive an explicit definition and explanation of what the lawyer can and cannot do. Since we rarely contest divorce cases, the lawyer's work boils down to the handling of money, property rights, and child custody questions. When it is made clear to the client that the lawyer will not don a black mask and hire himself out as a personal torture artist, it is amazing how nimbly the client's mind then conceives the idea of using the property questions and the lawyer along with them as eye-gouging devices. Tragically, this attitude also frequently causes child custody battles in which the parents each fight for the last pint of the child's blood.

Property and money are the truly big issues in practically every divorce case. In fact, the decision to marry, which we leave to children, is, even in the lowest paid work brackets, about a $200,000 proposition. At least that much money and earnings are involved to sustain a marriage for life, and to carry on the responsibilities which necessarily flow from the relationship, whether or not it lasts. And when the litigants are just a cut above the bare survival state, where there is actually a little property about which to be concerned other than objects encumbered by installment bills, they then have a supply of cannon fodder with which to carry on a personal battle of retribution and recrimination. A couple will fight over a hideous chest of drawers or a wall mirror or a set of dusty books (that neither of them ever read), for no good reason except to stick needles into the other party. And yet property rights are often very substantial and a number of legitimate questions of dispute arise.

These questions are not triable before a jury. Rather, most states give the judge alone wide discretionary power not only to grant alimony and child support payments, but also to take the entire worldly fortune of both of the parties into his hands and then divide all of these things between them in some equitable way. Seldom does a single judge have more power and responsibility. If the parties cannot agree on a property division and settlement, then the judge must literally pick through the lifetime accumulation of material goods of both of the parties and, like a nursery maid, say, "You get this and you get that," right down the line, even to the potted plants and the Italian glassware. Of course, the parties, by this means, abandon any personal privacy and dignity that they might once have had, but to many this is far preferable to any procedure which would tend to spare the opposition from pain and suffering.

The property that the court is supposed to divide is the property which was accumulated during coverture. It matters not that the husband earned all the money to pay for the possessions, if this is the case. The wife is considered to have contributed equally by performing her wifely services. A husband's business property will not necessarily be divided unless the wife contributed directly through service in the business. However, if the husband is allowed to retain his business, it will then be encumbered with a steady, periodic alimony award to the wife. Property, money or stocks, which were acquired by one of the parties through inheritance or gift, are not subject to division and should be awarded to the recipient free of the other spouse's claim unless the other spouse had a great deal to do with the acquisition or retention of the gift

MARRIAGE LAWS*
As of July 1, 1963

State or other jurisdiction	Age at which marriage can be contracted with parental consent - Male	Age at which marriage can be contracted with parental consent - Female	Age below which parental consent is required - Male	Age below which parental consent is required - Female	Common-law marriage recognized	Maximum period between examination and issuance of marriage license	Scope of medical examination	Waiting period Before issuance of license	Waiting period After issuance of license
Alabama	17	14	21	18	★	30 da.	(a)		
Alaska	18(b)	16(b)	21	18		30 da.	(a)	3 da.	
Arizona	18(b)	16(b)	21	18		30 da.	(a)	3 da.	
Arkansas	18(b)	16(b)	21	18		30 da.	(a)		
California	18(c,d)	16(c,d)	21	18		30 da.	(a)	3 da.	
Colorado	16(c)	16(c)	21	18	★	30 da.	(a)		
Connecticut	16(c)	16(c)	21	21		40 da.	(a)	4 da.	
Delaware	18(b,d)	16(b)	21	18		30 da.	(a)		
Florida	18(b,d)	16(b,d)	21	21	★	30 da.	(a)	3 da.	
Georgia	18(b,f)	16(b,f)	21(f)	21(f)	★	30 da.	(a)	3 da.(g)	(e)
Hawaii	18	16(c)	20	20		30 da.	(a)	3 da.	
Idaho	15	15(c)	18	18	★	30 da.	(a)		
Illinois	18	16	21	18		15 da.	(a)	3 da.	
Indiana	18(b)	16(b)	21	18		30 da.	(a)	3 da.	
Iowa	18(b)	16(b)	21	18	★	20 da.	(a)		
Kansas	18(c)	16(c)	21	18	★	30 da.	(a,h)	3 da.	
Kentucky	18(b)	16(b)	21	21		15 da.	(a)	3 da.	
Louisiana	18(c)	16(c)	18	21		10 da.	(a)		
Maine	16(c)	16(c)	21	18		30 da.	(a)	5 da.	
Maryland	18(b)	16(b)	21	18				48 hrs.	72 hrs.
Massachusetts	18(c)	16(c)	21	18		30 da.	(a)	3 da.	
Michigan	(i)	16(b)	18	18		30 da.	(a)	3 da.	
Minnesota	18(d)	16(j)	21	18			(a)	5 da.	
Mississippi	17(e)	15(e)	21	21		30 da.	(a)	3 da.	
Missouri	15(c)	15(c)	21	18		15 da.	(a)	3 da.	
Montana	18(c)	16(c)	21	18	★	20 da.	(a)	5 da.	
Nebraska	18(b)	16(b)	21	21		30 da.	(a)		
Nevada	18(c)	16(c)	21	18					
New Hampshire	(k)	(k)	20	18		30 da.	(a)	5 da.	
New Jersey	18(c)	16(c)	21	18		30 da.	(a)	72 hrs.	

New Mexico	18(b)	21	18	16(b)		(a)	
New York	16	21	18	16(c)		(a)	24 hrs.(l)
North Carolina	16	18	18	16(b)		(m)	
North Dakota	18	21	18	15		(o)	
Ohio	18(b)	21	21	16(b)		(a)	5 da.
Oklahoma	18(b)	21	18	15(b)	★	(a)	(p)
Oregon	18	21	18	15	★	(r)	30 da.(q)
Pennsylvania	16(c)	21	21	16(c)	★★	(s)	3 da.
Rhode Island	18(c)	21	21	16(c)	★★		
South Carolina	16(b)	18	18	14(b)			24 hrs.
South Dakota	18(b)	21	21	16(b)		(a)	
Tennessee	16(c)	21	21	16(c)	★	(a)	3 da.(u)
Utah	16(d)	21	18	14		(a)	(p)
Vermont	18(c)	21	18	16(c)		(a)	5 da.
Virginia	18(b,d)	21	21	16(b,d)		(a)	
Washington	17(c)	21	18	17(c)		(o)	3 da.
West Virginia	18(d)	21	21	16(d)		(a)	3 da.
Wisconsin	18	21	18	16		(a)	5 da.
Wyoming	18	21	21	16		(a)	
Dist. of Columbia	18(d)	21	18	16(d)			3 da.

*Prepared by the Women's Bureau, United States Department of Labor.
★Indicates common-law marriage recognized.
(a) Venereal diseases.
(b) Statute establishes procedure whereby younger parties may obtain license in case of pregnancy or birth of a child.
(c) In special circumstances statute establishes procedure whereby younger parties may obtain license.
(d) Parental consent is not required if minor was previously married.
(e) Residents, 24 hours; non-residents, 96 hours.
(f) If parties are under 21, notice must be posted unless parent of female consents in person, but if female is under 18, consent of parent is required.
(g) Unless parties are 21 years or more, or female is pregnant.
(h) Feeblemindedness.
(i) No provision in law for parental consent for males.
(j) Parental consent and permission of judge required.
(k) Below age of consent parties need parental consent and permission of judge.
(l) Marriage may not be solemnized within 3 days from date on which specimen for serological test was taken.
(m) Subject to uncontrolled epileptic attacks, idiocy, imbecility, mental defectiveness, unsound mind, infectious tuberculosis and venereal diseases.
(n) 48 hours if both are non-residents.
(o) Feeblemindedness, imbecility, insanity, chronic alcoholism and venereal diseases. (Also in Washington, advanced tuberculosis, and, if male, contagious venereal disease.)
(p) 3 days if one or both parties are below the age for marriage without parental consent.
(q) Time limit between date of examination and expiration of marriage license.
(r) Venereal diseases, feeblemindedness, mental illness, drug addiction and chronic alcoholism.
(s) Infectious tuberculosis and venereal diseases.
(t) If female is non-resident, must complete and sign license 5 days prior to marriage.
(u) Does not apply when parties are over 21 years of age.

DIVORCE LAWS AS OF JULY 1, 1963*

State or other jurisdiction	Residence required before filing suit for divorce	Grounds for absolute divorce — Adultery	Mental and/or physical cruelty	Desertion	Alcoholism	Impotency	Non-support	Insanity	Pregnancy at marriage	Bigamy	Separation or absence	Felony conviction or imprisonment	Drug addiction	Fraud, force or duress	Infamous crime	Relationship within prohibited degrees	Prior decree of limited divorce	Other	Period before parties may remarry after final decree — Plaintiff	Defendant
Alabama	(a)	★	★	1 yr.	★	★	(b)★	5 yrs.	★			★	★				(c)	(d)	60 days(e)	60 days(e)
Alaska	1 yr.	★	★	1 yr.	★	★	★	18 mos.				★	★		★			(f)	1 yr.	1 yr.
Arizona	2 mos.	★	★	1 yr.	★	★	★	3 yrs.		★	5 yrs.	★						(g)		
Arkansas	1 yr.	★	★	1 yr.	★	★	(h)★	3 yrs.			3 yrs.	★			★				(i)	(i)
California	1 yr.(j)	★	★	1 yr.	★	★		3 yrs.			3 yrs.	★								
Colorado	3 yrs.(j)	★	★	3 yrs.	★	★		5 yrs.			7 yrs.	★								
Connecticut	3 yrs.(j)	★	★	2 yrs.	★	★	★	5 yrs.		★	3 yrs.	★			★			(k)	3 mos.(l)	3 mos.(l)
Delaware	6 mos.	★	★	1 yr.	★	★		2 yrs.				★	★					(m,n)		
Florida	6 mos.	★	★	1 yr.	★	★		3 yrs.	★									(o)	(l)	(l)
Georgia	2 yrs.	★	★	6 mos.		★					2 yrs.(p)	★				★				
Hawaii	6 wks.	★	★	1 yr.	★	★		3 yrs.			5 yrs.	★						(q)	(s)	
Idaho	1 yr.(j)	★	★	1 yr.(r)	★	★	★	3 yrs.				★							1 yr.(l)	1 yr.(l)
Illinois	1 yr.	★	★	2 yrs.		★						★								
Indiana	1 yr.(u)	★	★	2 yrs.	(v)★	★		5 yrs.	(t)★			★			★				6 mos.	6 mos.
Iowa	(y)	★	★	1 yr.	★	★		5 yrs.	★★	★		★		★	★		(z)	(q,w,x)		
Kansas	1 yr.	★	★	1 yr.	★	★	★	5 yrs.			5 yrs.	★	★						6 mos.	6 mos.
Kentucky	(y)	★	★		★	★	★	5 yrs.			2 yrs.	★	★		★				wife, 10 mos.	wife, 10 mos.(aa)
Louisiana	6 mos.(j)	★		3 yrs.							18 mos.	★			★			(ac)		
Maine	1 yr.(ab)	★	★	18 mos.	★	★	★	3 yrs.				★								2 yrs.(ad)
Maryland	5 yrs.(j)	★	★	3 yrs.		★					5 yrs.	★						(n)		
Massachusetts	1 yr.(j)	★	★	2 yrs.	★	★	★			★		★							6 mos.	6 mos.
Michigan	1 yr.(j)	★	★	1 yr.	★	★		5 yrs.				★						(o)		(af)
Minnesota	1 yr.(j)	★	★	1 yr.	★	★	★	3 yrs.	★		2 yrs.(p)	★	★	★				(g,ag)		
Mississippi	1 yr.	★	★	1 yr.	★	★		2 yrs.	★	★		★	★				(ae)		6 mos.	6 mos.
Missouri	1 yr.(j)	★	★	1 yr.	★	★		5 yrs.				★							6 mos.	6 mos.
Montana	1 yr.	★	★	1 yr.	★	★	★	5 yrs.				★							6 mos.	6 mos.
Nebraska	2 yrs.(j)	★	★	2 yrs.	★	★	★	5 yrs.				★							3 mos.(l)	3 mos.(l)
Nevada	6 wks.(j)	★	★	1 yr.	★	★	★	2 yrs.			3 yrs.	★						(w,ah)		
New Hampshire	1 yr.(j)	★	★	2 yrs.	★	★					2 yrs.	★								
New Jersey	2 yrs.(j)	★	★	2 yrs.								★								
New Mexico	1 yr.	★	★	★	★	★		5 yrs.				★						(f)		
New York	(ai)	★																(d)	(l)	(aj)
North Carolina	6 mos.	★		1 yr.			(h)★	5 yrs.			2 yrs.						(c)		(ak)	(i)
North Dakota	1 yr.(r)	★	★	1 yr.	★★	★	★★	5 yrs.			1 yr.	★		★	★			(n)		
Ohio	1 yr.	★	★		★★	★						★								

198

State									
Oklahoma	6 mos.(u)	★★★★							6 mos.
Oregon	1 yr	★★★★	★				(f,n)	6 mos.	6 mos.
Pennsylvania	1 yr	★★★★	★				(al)		(aa)
Rhode Island	2 yrs.	★★	★	5 yrs.(am)				6 mos.	(an,ao) 6 mos.
South Carolina	1 yr.	★							
South Dakota	1 yr.(j)	★★★★	★	1 yr.	5 yrs.		(al)		(ap)
Tennessee	12 mos.	★★★★	★★	1 yr.	3 yrs.				(aa)
Texas	3 mos.	★★	★	3 yrs.			(ar)	(ar)	(ar)
Utah	6 mos.,(as)	★★★		1 yr.	5 yrs.			3 mos.(l)	3 mos.(l)
Vermont		★		3 yrs.	5 yrs.	★	(at)	3 mos.(l)	2 yrs.(l)
Virginia	1 yr.	★★★★		1 yr.			(au)	(aw)	
Washington	1 yr.	★★★★★	★	1 yr.	2 yrs.		(d,av)	(aw)	6 mos.
West Virginia	2 yrs.(j)	★★★★	★	1 yr.			(ax)	60 days	60 days(ay)
Wisconsin	2 yrs.	★★★★	★	1 yr.				1 yr.	1 yr.
Wyoming	60 days(j)	★★	★	1 yr.			(az)		
Dist. of Columbia	2 yrs (j)	★		2 yrs.	5 yrs.		(ba)	6 mos.	6 mos.

* Prepared by the Women's Bureau, United States Department of Labor.
★ Indicates ground for absolute divorce
(a) No specific period required except 1 year when ground is desertion or defendant is non-resident, or 2 years if wife sues husband for non-support.
(b) To wife, living separate and apart from husband, as resident of the state for 2 years before suit, and without support from him during such time.
(c) May be enlarged into an absolute divorce after expiration of 4 years.
(d) Crime against nature.
(e) Court may forbid remarriage.
(f) Incompatibility.
(g) Crime before marriage.
(i) Also to husband in certain circumstances.
(j) Final decree is not entered until 1 year after interlocutory decree.
(j) Under certain circumstances a lesser period of time may be required.
(k) Female under 16, male under 18, complaining party under age of consent at time of marriage has not confirmed the marriage after reaching such age.
(l) In the discretion of the court.
(m) Habitual violent and ungovernable temper.
(n) Defendant obtained divorce from plaintiff in another state.
(o) Mental incapacity.
(p) Under decree of separate maintenance.
(q) Loathsome disease.
(r) Five years if on ground of insanity.
(s) Two years where service on defendant is only by publication.
(t) Unless at time of marriage husband had an illegitimate child living which fact was not known to wife.
(u) Five years if on ground of insanity and insane spouse is in out-of-state institution.
(v) If on part of the husband, accompanied by wasting of husband's estate to the detriment of the wife and children.
(w) Joining religious sect disbelieving in marriage.
(x) Unchaste behavior on part of wife after marriage.
(y) No statutory requirement for adultery or felony conviction; 2 years when ground is separation.
(z) Limited divorce may be enlarged into absolute divorce after 1 year for innocent spouse and after 1 year and 60 days for guilty spouse.
(aa) When divorce is granted on ground of adultery, guilty party cannot marry the accomplice in adultery during lifetime of former spouse.
(ab) No specific period required except 1 year if cause occurred out of state, and 2 years if on ground of insanity.
(ac) Any cause which renders marriage null and void *ab initio.*
(ad) Not more than 2 years in court's discretion.
(ae) Limited divorce may be enlarged into absolute divorce after 5 years.
(af) When divorce is granted on ground of adultery, court may prohibit remarriage. After 1 year court may remove disability upon satisfactory evidence of reformation.
(ag) Husband a vagrant.
(ah) Wife's absence out of state for 10 years without husband's consent.
(ai) No time specified. Parties must be residents when offense committed; or married in state; or plaintiff resident when offense committed and action commenced; or offense committed in state and injured party resident when action commenced.
(aj) Defendant is prohibited from remarrying unless after 3 years court removes disability upon satisfactory evidence of reformation.
(ak) When husband is entitled to a divorce and alimony or child support from husband is granted, the decree may be delayed until security is entered for payment.
(al) Incapable of procreation.
(am) Or a lesser time in court's discretion.
(an) Void or voidable marriage.
(ao) Gross misbehavior or wickedness.
(ap) When divorce is for adultery, guilty party cannot remarry except to the innocent person, until the death of the other.
(aq) To husband for wife's refusal to move with him to this state without reasonable cause, and willfully absenting herself from him for 2 years.
(ar) When divorce is granted on ground of cruelty, neither party may remarry for 12 months except each other.
(as) One year before final hearing, and 2 years if on ground of insanity.
(at) Intolerable severity.
(au) A limited divorce granted on the ground of cruelty or desertion may be merged with an absolute divorce after one year.
(av) Two years fugitive from justice; wife a prostitute prior to marriage.
(aw) When a divorce is granted on ground of adultery, court may decree the guilty party cannot remarry. After 6 months the court may remove disability for good cause. Remarriage of either party forbidden pending appeal.
(ax) Want of legal age or sufficient understanding.
(ay) In court's discretion, guilty party may be prohibited from remarrying for a period not to exceed 1 year.
(az) Living entirely apart for 5 years pursuant to a judgment of legal separation.
(ba) Limited divorce may be enlarged into absolute divorce after 2 years.

199

property. This becomes a serious puzzle, particularly when the gift property has lost its identity over the years by being intermingled with the couple's other assets.

Often the law and the courts seem bewildered by the volume of divorce litigation, but if the courts are unable to control the march toward divorce, or to fathom its real reasons, it is because they are given no real responsibility until the end is at hand. It is society's mess and the courts are hired only to mop it up. Yet, this narrow, though prevalent, view of responsibility has not satisfied all jurists. In an attempt to contribute to the solution of the basic problems some domestic relations courts have set up marriage counselling services as an arm or agency of the court. The parties avail themselves of the counselling service on a completely voluntary basis. The plan has met with fair success. Often it seems the parties do not realize the full legal and financial impact of their decision to part until they are faced with the sanctions of law.

A word about private marriage counselors or social workers. While marriage counselors are often listed in the classified telephone directory, this is the poorest possible way to choose one to help you. The title "marriage counselor" may be used with impunity by anyone in most states, regardless of training or the lack of it. For the names of trained and qualified marriage counselors near you, information will be supplied by the American Association of Marriage Counselors, 27 Woodcliff Drive, Madison, New Jersey. All members of this organization have either a master's degree in social work, or an M.D. or a Ph.D. in psychology, sociology or a related field of study or a three-year graduate degree from a theological seminary.

If you wish to consult a privately practicing social worker for diagnosis and perhaps for psychotherapy, you may write to: National Association of Social Workers, 2 Park Avenue, New York City and the NASW will send you its list of chapter chairmen for selection nearest to you. All social workers in this organization have at least a master's degree in social work. It is a very risky procedure to accept a friend's recommendation. Many people do just that out of inertia, timidity or embarrassment being reluctant to make formal requests for the names of authorized practitioners.

Much worthy talk, and some action, points toward the introduction of counselling by religious or other responsible professional representatives of society at much earlier stages in the marital relationship, but the strict and universal application of pre-marriage counselling in a state is deterred by the fact that a couple, whether they are really old enough, mature enough, or financially able, can easily go off to another state and enter a legally binding marriage. This is similar to the factor which tempers the strict enforcement of divorce prohibitions.

In a free society, the responsibilities are great upon the individual and no real solution can be invoked except to persist in bringing about, by education and enforcement of laws, an increased awareness of such responsibility. In this, the courts can do their part by at least maintaining as high a degree of dignity and decorum in their domestic relations divisions as in their other departments.

Chapter Eleven

ON THE JOB

If you were looking up some law concerning your rights as an employer or employee, your first shock would be to discover it indexed under the title, "Master and Servant." This anachronism might cause you to conjure up a vision of slave trading, complete with high leather boots, bull whips and cowering serfs. But in the text you would find a quite different story. The employment relationship is a freely made contract. And since we talk about contracts so often, maybe we'd better try to define the term, because, unless we keep in mind what a contract is, we might sometimes fail to recognize its existence.

A contract is nothing more than a mutual agreement creating an obligation on both sides. Let's illustrate this: You say, "Let's go fishing." At this point no contract has been entered into because I haven't agreed to go with you. It lacks mutuality. You say, "Let's go fishing," and I say "O.K." Here we have a mutual agreement but we still don't have a legal contract. Why? Because we haven't said where and when; the terms and conditions are not set, so neither side is obligated to fulfill the agreement. You say, "Let's go fishing in the morning at 6:00. I'll drive to your house and you be ready." I say "O.K., we'll go to Moon Lake." Here we have a legally binding contract. (1) There is mutuality of agreement. Our minds have met on all the essential conditions which have been stated in explicit terms; and (2) we have each promised to do something which we would not otherwise have to do if we had not chosen to enter into the agreement.

If you fail to drive to my house by 6:00 in the morning, as promised, then you have broken the contract and, theoretically, I could sue you for damages to compensate me for my time and trouble in getting ready. In this case, I could not very well sue you for "specific performance," that is to have the court force you to do what you promised to do, because the enforced performance would be valueless to me by the time the court could act. But I might claim loss of catch against you if I could present a reasonable amount of proof that I probably would have caught a certain number of fish if you had fulfilled your obligation. Similarly, if you drove to my house at 6:00, as promised, and I failed to be ready, you could sue me for damages, including your time and driving expenses and whatever loss you could show resulted from my breach. But let's add another element. Say the fishing season was not open, and our deal was, in effect, to go fishing illegally. In order to be binding, a contract must have a lawful purpose, so neither party could sue the other for breach of this agreement.

A word about formal and informal contracts. The difference is about the same as between formal and informal dances. The formal dance involves more trappings, but at the informal dance you are still dancing. Both types of contracts are equally binding. The informal contract is usually oral, brief and concise in its terms. For very good reason employers tend to favor this type of employment contract. They simply say, "O.K., you come to work and we'll pay you a certain wage." Here, all the employer does is promise to pay for your time and work. He has not promised to keep you on the job any particular length of time. This leaves him free to terminate your employment at will. Employers know that the minute somebody starts writing down and spelling out the terms of an employment contract, nothing can come of it except a sentence by sentence abrogation and gnawing away of their rights to hire and fire as and when they please and to freely govern and control their own business.

This natural and free right of employers still is the fundamental characteristic of the employer-employee relationship. However, in the last half-century or so a lot of people have been writing down sentences partially abrogating and diminishing the right. Many of these sentences, bitter to the employer and sweet to the employee, appear in union contracts which are given their validity by legislation.

The right freely to own, use and to enjoy property is guaranteed by the Constitution. Neither the federal government nor a state can deprive one of private property without due process of law and without just compensation. These simple but fundamental provisions are the essential die in which our capitalistic system is cast. The die has been reshaped and refined in many ways since the day it opened its jaws and emitted that first crude casting. Labor legislation is a noteworthy and basic refinement, but notwithstanding the critics of change, the original shape of the die still exists in recognizable and vital form.

The natural role of the worker is, and always has been, one of subservience. The story of the world is force and counterforce—power meeting power. And power always wins. The lone worker in an open labor market has no power at all as compared to an employer. Not unpredictably, therefore, the notion of absolute freedom in ownership of private property has resulted in serious abuses.

The great law of supply and demand operates in the labor market just as in every other market, and it is the one central and most important factor in any job or prospective job. This is what determines whether any particular job will exist or not, and this is the first consideration in governing how much a job will pay. All labor legislation does is set up modifications of the free choice and open market supply and demand aspect of labor. Basically the legislation is designed to force the application of some reason and humanity to that blind, vise-like grip over property which, if left unchecked, impels some towards cruelty and injustice to their fellow man. It is designed to ease the harshness in the law of supply and demand. None of the legislation is intended to abolish the property right. Rather, it all starts on the premise that the property right exists, and will continue to exist. It then asks itself, "How far should we go in altering the fundamental right to own, use and enjoy property in order to correct this or that untoward situation?" The major pieces of labor legislation are wage and hour laws, laws governing the right to unionize, workmen's compensation and unemployment compensation.

But before we go into labor legislation, let us look at the employment contract itself, because, contrary to some opinions, this is where the real deal usually is made, not in Washington or the state capitol, or in the headquarters of a huge international union. You may read in the newspaper about some big league baseball player who just signed a $70,000 contract for the next season. You might say, "Why don't I get a deal like that? Not so much money, of course, but why don't I get at least a guaranteed wage for the year?" Here the law of supply and demand steps in. That ball player or a sought-after football coach or a famous actor has ability, reputation and talent placing him in short supply. He can demand this guarantee as a condition of his going to work. But most of us are on the other end of the supply and demand picture. Our services are wanted, all right, but we can't claim to be unique, and therefore most of our jobs are on an "at will" basis, whereby either side can chop the thing off without severe penalties at any time.

But before you shed too many tears about your lowly lot, you should realize that the set term employment contract can have its definite disadvantages to the employee. Just as any contract, it's a two-sided affair and it is governed by its terms and conditions first agreed upon and put down in writing; therefore, if the employee cannot or does not wish to complete the term, or if he wants to squeak out because he has a better offer, the employer can hold him to contract and can even sue the employee for heavy damages arising out of his failure to complete what he said he would do.

You should recognize the distinction between an employee, an agent, and an independent contractor. Clyde Bomm owns and operates a small commercial radio station. He hires Fred as an announcer, and George as a salesman. Fred is paid a salary, but George is paid only out of commissions. Fred is an employee, and Clyde is his employer; George is an agent, and Clyde is his principal. Dora gives singing lessons in her home. Clyde hires her to sing on a particular show every week. Dora is an independent contractor. You will notice that all of these people were "hired" by Clyde, but each has a different status. The independent contractor is in business for himself. He hires out to do a particular job. His only responsibility is to do that job, and the person who hired him need only pay for the work as agreed.

Agency and employment can be very similar, in fact, an employee can often be an agent, too. The major distinction is that the agent is hired to represent the principal in dealings with others. The employee, on the other hand, merely performs work for his employer and doesn't represent anybody. An agency may exist for the accomplishment of just one particular task. If I ask you to go to the bank to deposit some money for me, and even if you do this gratis, you are my agent. No one need undertake a gratuitous task, but once undertaken, then the agent owes the same duties to the principal as if he were being paid. He is obligated to perform his task with diligence and honesty. But let's face it—most agency contracts involve a promise to pay by the principal. In this instance, the agent has the additional obligation of obedience to the principal. He must act not only diligently, but in complete trust and confidence, and if asked, he must be ready to account to the principal for all of his activities in the principal's behalf.

The principal must pay the agent's expenses incurred in the principal's business, and he must also protect and, if necessary, indemnify the agent for claims made against him arising out of his activities in behalf of the principal. All of these rights and obligations hold true even if they aren't spelled out either in written or oral contract form. They arise by the general or common law as applied to agency.

An employer is obligated to provide his employees with a safe and healthful place to work. He is obligated to furnish adequate tools, to pay the worker, to hire competent fellow employees, and to conform to all local, state and federal requirements for the employees' protection. Included in this, of course, is the requirement of withholding a portion of the employee's pay for income and social security taxes. The employee must, in turn, give obedience, good faith and the use of the necessary skills and competency for the job. Unless otherwise specified, either an agency or an employment contract can be terminated at any time by mutual agreement or by either of the parties. In many localities and in certain types of jobs, custom requires one to give two weeks' notice of intention to resign, and if the employer fires a worker, then he should receive two weeks' pay, but this is usually not a legal requirement.

Now as we get into the subject of labor legislation, we must remember that even though the statutes are very important and far reaching, not one of them repeals the super law governing the employer-employee relationship—the law of supply and demand. This is not a governmental law, but a law of economics; its only relationship to governmental law is that the government enables it to function by recognizing and protecting ownership of private property. Economists frequently explain this law, and the success of capitalism, by pointing out that it automatically elicits the services of millions of decision makers. You a member of the public decide what to buy and somebody in turn decides what to produce and whom to hire. It all rests neatly on the shoulders of those little decision makers, you and me.

It is only when our decisions fail to do right by humanity that the government steps in. Thus we have minimum wage laws, the federal law being appropriately entitled The Fair Labor Standards Act. This sets up a minimum wage of a dollar and a quarter ($1.25) an hour which must be paid in industries engaged in interstate commerce. Why interstate commerce? Why draw such a strange line? Why doesn't the federal government say that the minimum wage shall apply to all industries and be done with it?

This touches off another subject, a fascinating one for the legal buff. Suffice it to say that the reason is that the federal constitution gives Congress specific power to govern interstate commerce (which it does not bother to define), and leaves all things not specifically delegated to the Congress up to the individual states and the people. The puzzle, then, becomes: What is interstate commerce? It is operating a truckline by which merchandise is carried across state lines, and it is producing a product for distribution in different states. But is it working with raw materials which were shipped from another state? Is it building a dam which will produce electricity which will ultimately be transmitted across state lines, or not? The legal controversy about the meaning of this term in specific instances is a continuing matter. But most states have their own minimum wage laws applying to industries not controlled by the federal law. Minimum wage statutes are criminal laws—that is, they make it an offense against the government to pay less than the minimum and provide a penalty of fine or imprisonment, or both, for violation.

The first labor legislation concerned child labor. These laws prohibiting child labor exist in all states, along with laws governing the hours and conditions of work for all laborers. In some states women are given special treatment in the law which sets up certain requirements for female labor.

In addition to the problem of wages and hours, another area in which free property ownership and the law of supply and demand fails to police itself is in the field of accidental injury while on the job. Here the states did the job themselves, without coercion from the federal government. Workmen's Compensation Acts were first enacted around 1915 and have been passed in every one of the fifty states. Here are the fundamentals: First of all, we know that in law, for every wrong there is a remedy, and if one receives a personal injury through the fault of another, then he can sue for damages. This is tort or negligence law, and prior to the enactment of Workmen's Compensation Acts, general tort law governed injury on the job. But it didn't work well. Why? Well, first of all, the employer was the one always sued because he or one of his servants was the one alleged to be negligent and he was the only one with the financial responsibility to make the suit worthwhile. But one or more of three rules in tort law almost invariably stopped the worker cold in his tracks in court, no matter how serious his injury. These doctrines were called (1) assumption of risk; (2) fellow servant; and (3) contributory negligence.

So Joe hires out as a janitor in a foundry where the product is railroad car wheels. He leaves his broom in the wrong spot and walks where he isn't supposed to. An overhead crane operator jerks a cable, it breaks, and a wheel falls on Joe's head, killing him. Joe's widow sues the company, saying "You negligently caused my husband's death by having a defective cable and because your servant, the crane operator, was negligent in jerking the machine." The company answers in court, saying "(1) We're sorry, madam, but your husband didn't have to go to work in our foundry. When he did so, he assumed the risk of injury or death because it's a hazardous place. (2) In addition, the negligence you complain of, if in fact there was negligence, was committed by the crane operator.

If you want to sue anybody, you should sue him. The law is clear that an employer is not liable for injury to a worker caused by a fellow worker. And (3) We don't admit that the cable was defective. You'll have to prove that. But, even assuming that it was, your husband was not where he was supposed to be at that particular time. This is negligence on his part, therefore he contributed to his own fatal injury and you cannot recover under the law."

Most workers were excluded from any recovery by the neat operation of these rules, and on the other side of the coin, a minute percentage of injured workers hired lawyers who artfully managed to wend their way around these defenses, to the point where the matter was presented to a jury. The jurors thought they knew all about that dirty, dangerous factory, and how rich the owners were getting, and frequently returned ruinously high verdicts. The fact that tort law as applied to industry contains pitfalls both for the worker and for the owner may partially explain why this legislative reform took place.

The Workmen's Compensation Acts have worked very satisfactorily, and remarkably they are not criminal statutes. This is the real genius of the Acts; it would be well if we could more often find ways to draft needed regulatory legislation without always including some criminal penalty.

Workmen's Compensation Acts are not mandatory. Not at all. Either the employer or the employee, or both, may elect not to come under the Act. "That's strange," you say. Here is what lawyers call the "kicker," the real bite to the law: right at its start the law abrogates and abolishes the three favorite defenses. It says, "Mr. Employer, no longer can you claim (1) assumption of risk; (2) fellow servant; or (3) contributory negligence if you are sued by your worker." But then it adds, "Now look, friend, we're not going to put you out of business. All you have to do is take out some reasonably priced Workmen's Compensation insurance. If you do that, then we won't let your worker sue you in court for a million dollars for an injury, but we'll make him abide by our statute by which he will get some compensation for injury regardless of who is at fault, but he won't get rich out of it." The law then says to the workers, "Now, of course, you don't have to be covered by this if you don't want to, but if you don't, then we're going to give your employer back all those defenses he used to enjoy, which reduces your chances of ever getting any compensation for injury to approximately nil."

The Act is administered by a Commission with referees who conduct hearings and make awards. Only three comparatively simple factual determinations must be made. (1) Was the injury accidental? Yes or No. If Yes, it's compensable; if No, it's not compensable. (2) Did the injury arise out of and occur within the course and scope of the employment? Yes or No. If yes, it is compensable; if No, it is not compensable; and (3) What is the injury? These answers determined, the statute then sets out a formula saying exactly how much compensation will be received for injuries to the various parts of the body, plus a schedule of weekly disability benefits, depending on the nature of the injury. The worker is penalized by having his benefits lowered 50% if he was wilfully violating some specific safety rules or if he was intoxicated while on the job.

The philosophy behind the Workmen's Compensation laws is to accept the risk of injury as a cost of industry and to utilize insurance to spread the cost throughout industry and ultimately to the consumer. Of course, the compensation rates and the premium cost of the insurance vary between the states, but the death benefits, for example, exceed $15,000 in many states, making it a very important item for a family. What does the Act require of the employee? Merely that he report the accident to his employer if he is able, and that he file a claim.

Workmen's Compensation is not health insurance, and does not cover sickness apart from an accident. This leaves a large gap in the toll of industry on human life since some occupations have their own associated diseases. The classic example of an occupational disease is silicosis, a lung condition which besets mine, quarry and rock workers, caused by breathing silicone dust. This is not a "sudden and unexpected" accident, but arises over a long period. Thus all states have also passed Occupation Disease Acts, allowing compensation for disability arising out of certain listed and specified occupational diseases.

Another area in which the pure system of free property ownership and the law of supply and demand breaks down is in taking care of the unemployment problem. Just as in Workmen's Compensation, someone must make factual determinations and must exercise a limited degree of judgment and discretion in determining whether compensation will be paid in any particular case and if so, how much. Here an administrative body performs a judicial type function and the duty falls to a referee or a deputy referee in the Department of Employment. The issues are simple: (1) Is the person unemployed? (2) Is the person available for work and actively seeking work? And (3) Is the person out of work due to no fault of his own? An appeal route also exists for either the worker or his ex-employer, should either be dissatisfied with the ruling. The employer is concerned not just because tax dollars are being paid out but because the amount paid, in effect, comes directly out of his pocket in that it is charged against his account in the fund. A case may be first appealed to a referee from the deputy, thence to a commission, thence to the highest level trial court in the state, and next up to the appeals court. The record of testimony is made before the referee. The deputy acts merely on the basis of written questionnaires filled out by both sides.

Most businessmen believe in and approve of the unemployment compensation system. But practically every employer has suffered assault to his sensibilities by seeing some undeserving and shiftless lout receive something for nothing. Here is exactly what happens: A worker is laid off because he is no longer needed. He is unskilled, and his take-home pay came to only about $60.00 per week. He applies for compensation and signs his name to the statement "I am available for and am actively seeking work." He then begins to draw compensation, tax free, and without any transportation or other expenses connected with work, in the amount of perhaps $45- to $50.00 per week. This way he finds he has about as much money to spend as he had when he was working. Every week he has to go to the Department of Employment and tell them what he has been doing to try to find a job. At this precise moment both society and the individual worker, within each other and between themselves, are joined in an immensely significant moral issue.

Did the worker sincerely look for a job that week or not? If not, then not only has society lost one week of productive work, but the worker has lost character and dignity. There is no such person as a simple human being. No person's life and psychological make-up may be capsulized in a word, a phrase, or a sentence. We are all beset by complex drives, events, desires and pressures. So it is not by pure desire that we follow the course of least resistance. Nevertheless, that is our tendency.

If we did not already know it, William James gave us some important insight into the nature of the human being. The essence of character and morality is to show constant strength on little things. This in turn builds big strength on big things. And the same rule applies to a society. But who does society place in charge of its character in the decision of whether unemployment compensation will be paid to a person in any particular week? Somebody who is usually overworked and under motivated to express society's position with strength. The government, at this point, too often joins with the worker in the course of least resistance.

The clerk in the Department of Employment every morning faces a long line of people, and not one of them gets turned down because he wasn't sincerely looking for work; rather, whatever statement he wants to make, no matter how specious, is accepted at face value. "I called out at Grisley's, and they said they didn't need laborers," or "My brother told me they weren't hiring out at Fromp's." Determination of this one issue—availability for work—is too often glossed over, and yet it is the heart of the whole system.

Under the constitution, unemployment compensation is an exercise of the police power of the state. The state may protect the public health, safety, morals and welfare by paying compensation to those who are unemployed through no fault of their own, but payment of benefits to the undeserving is not a proper exercise of the police power of government. The challenge is not to write a new and better law but to administer more efficiently the one we now have. Every single dereliction is thrice destructive of society and the strength of our country. (1) It destroys an individual's incentive to work, (2) it produces ammunition for the wreckers who want to abolish all labor legislation, and (3) it pays out money without corresponding productivity which is an inflationary activity.

At the beginning of this chapter we explained what comprises a contract and that employment constitutes a contract between the employer and the employee. Further, a contract involves not only rights and obligations between its parties but it also creates obligations, and sometimes rights for other people outside of the contract —people who had nothing whatsoever to do with its formation. One prerequisite to any contract is freedom, that is, (1) the parties must be free to exercise their judgment and discretion in obligating themselves to the contract, and (2) they must be free to carry out its terms without interference. Freedom from governmental interference is a specific guarantee of the federal constitution. Article I, Section 10: "No state shall pass any law impairing the obligation of contracts." You might ask yourself, "Well, that's interesting. You and I agreed to go fishing, but the state said fishing was illegal at that season. Isn't the state impairing the obligation of our contract?" The legal answer to this is "No." (1) The state had already declared the seasons before we entered into our contract, and thus it was not impairing the obligation of an existing contract; and (2) like all other rights and freedoms, freedom to contract is subject to reasonable controls and limitations and must cease when it clashes with other specific powers and duties of the government. In this instance, protecting wild life by setting seasons is within the police power of the state to protect the public health, safety, welfare and morals.

It is patently clear that the federal government is a government of specified powers. No specific clause in the constitution gives Congress the power to interfere with the free exercise of the right to contract or to impair the obligation of contracts already made. Therefore the federal government does not have this power, nor may a private individual or group of people interfere with either the freedom to contract or the freedom to carry out and enforce a contract already made, so if you and I agree to go fishing and your brother, who is miffed because he was not invited, hides your fishing pole or lets the air out of your tires, or does something else to interfere with our plans, then we can both sue him for damages resulting from this interference because he has no right to interfere.

An important concept in the law is conspiracy which is a "joining together" or combination of the efforts of two or more people for the accomplishment of some unlawful end. In a sense, conspirators contract between themselves in that their minds meet and they each obligate themselves to do something. Just as a contract may be made between two or more, it may involve an unlimited number of people, so long as all of their minds meet, so that a conspiracy may involve either a small or a large group. By its very definition, conspiracy has an unlawful purpose so that the law will not only refuse to enforce the obligation between the conspirators, but will severely penalize the parties for making the agreement in the first place. The law recognizes that there is strength in numbers. If the goal of the conspiracy is to accomplish a criminal act, then the mere act of entering the conspiracy constitutes a crime, whether or not the criminal goal is accomplished. If the goal of the conspiracy is not criminal, but is solely to interfere with someone else's rights and freedoms, it is known as a civil conspiracy. In this event, the victim has a right to sue for damages and for an injunction against all of the conspirators.

An injunction is an order made by a court of competent jurisdiction: it requires and demands that someone do or cease doing a particular act. The courts enforce their injunctions by contempt powers, that is, if someone refuses or fails to obey such an order, then he is hailed into court. At this point the court is the custodian of the dignity of society. The offender is first given an opportunity to purge himself from contempt by doing what the court said he must do, and giving some satisfactory explanation of why he didn't do it before. If this is accomplished, then the contempt citation is dismissed. If it is not accomplished, then the individual is fined or jailed, or both, until such time as the dignity of the court and thus the dignity of the people is vindicated.

Ordinarily, a conspiracy to interfere with someone's employment contract would give rise to a civil rather than a criminal case. The federal government, however, and some states have passed anti-trust laws with criminal penalties attached. These are directed against monopolistic practices whereby a market is bottled up so that free enterprise and free competition no longer exist. In as much as our economic system is very complex and the mind of man is capable of thinking up endless angles, the anti-trust laws are very broadly written, denouncing as illegal, "every contract, combination in the form of trust or otherwise, or conspiracy in restraint of trade or commerce among the several states or with foreign nations."

From these several points in the fundamental law we see why

trade unions were long regarded as illegal. By definition, a trade union is: A combination or association of workers for the purpose of exercising power, coercion and restraint against employers in their employment contracts, in effect a conspiracy to interfere with contracts and to restrain trade.

In view of this fundamental law, the trade union movement in America had a long, rough and rocky road to success. Some courts were quick to recognize that collective bargaining is a legal activity by workers, and if it contravenes the fundamental principles above outlined, then it is an exception to those principles. For many years, however, particularly during the 1800's, much confusion prevailed in the law and many acts of labor unions (designed to show their power and achieve their goals) were enjoined by the courts. Strikes, boycotts and picketing were often held to be illegal.

However, in 1935 a milestone was reached when the National Labor Relations Act was passed. Pinned to the commerce clause of the federal constitution, its purpose is to give greater protection of the right of employees to organize and bargain collectively. To this end, it designates certain actions by employers as "unfair labor practices." When in 1947 the Act was amended, some actions by labor unions were designated as unfair labor practices. The Act does not impose criminal penalties; rather, it sets up the National Labor Relations Board as its administrative body. The Board can make orders against either employers or unions, which may be enforced in court through the contempt power. Basically, the Act gives life to trade unions by preventing employers from interfering with the activities of trade unions. It also allows unions to strike and to picket in order to enforce union demands for higher wages, better working conditions, pension plans, or whatever they are seeking. Obviously these activities which affect commerce are declared to be legal, and since they are legal, they are consequently considered not illegal under the anti-trust laws. Yet here, as you may suspect, we have a developing (and somewhat unsettled) area of law in which it is contended in certain instances that some activities by labor unions are so unreasonable and so obstructive they in truth do constitute criminal monopoly.

The right of workers freely to join together in labor organizations, and by the same token the right of those organizations to protect their existence results in a radically different version of employment contract than the simple agreement which employers favor—"You come to work and we will pay you a certain wage." In fact, a union negotiated labor contract, which then becomes the contract between the employer and every worker in his plant, may contain thirty or more pages, with every little detail indicated from working conditions, hours, overtime pay, pension plan, seniority, down to the type of restroom facilities the employer must provide.

Not every plant is unionized. Only when the workers have "elected" to choose a union, as their bargaining agent, will the union be in control. It is part of the duty of the National Labor Relations Board to supervise these elections in order to see that the vote is not unfairly influenced or coerced either by the union organizers or by the employer. Many employers have avoided unionism by voluntarily providing their workers with favorable wage scales augmented by profit sharing and pension plans. In most cases, if these benefits are extended, the workers do not want to have a union, but of course for its part the trade union movement can claim much credit for the favorable situation of good wages and fringe benefits where it prevails since the threat of unionism motivates the employer towards such generosity.

Another notable and developing area in labor legislation in many states prevents discrimination in hiring due to race, creed or color. While such legislation is in derogation of the normal free and open right of employers to hire and fire as they please, it has been held to be a proper exercise of the police power of the state, and will be enforced in a proper case, if it is clearly shown that the sole reason for refusal to hire a person was his race, creed or color.

As a whole, labor legislation has worked remarkably well, not only in fulfillment of our human and social ideals, but in building our economy through a broad base of purchasing power. It is true that our high wage scales place us in an unhappy competitive situation abroad and this is a major problem, but we may take encouragement from two developing factors. (1) We are still able to compete because of a high and efficient technology, and (2) The day may arrive when foreign workers enjoy a pay scale comparable to ours, which would narrow the world imbalance which now prevails.

Chapter Twelve

OF SOUND MIND

Wills and estates are happy subjects, in spite of the fact that they involve death, the event which initiates into operation this remarkable field of law. It is no more significant than the other great events of life—birth, marriage, the acquisition of property and of children. Wills and Estates are termed happy subjects, because in a sense, you can take your treasure with you in the peace of mind of allocation as you wish it. In America, you can make of yourself what you will by work and accumulation of property, entailing not responsibility alone but the happy opportunity to extend your efforts beyond your time of life.

The law recognizes and respects your dominion over property, and your will is exactly what the name implies—an intentional expression of power and dominion over that property. The term for making of a will, called a testamentary act, will help you to understand the subject. To make a direction as to what will happen to any certain piece of property after the death of the "testator" constitutes a testamentary act.

Henry Kard is old and infirm. He wishes to give his house to his wife and a thousand dollars to his niece. Rather than bother with a will, he just signs the house over to his wife and makes the gift to his niece, a month before his death. The effect of his action is exactly the same as if he had made a will. Was it a testamentary act? No. You and I buy and sell, make gifts, and do other things in the exercise of dominion over our property every day of our lives and what we do carries on after our death, but this doesn't make every act testamentary. (1) The gift to the niece and the conveyance of the house to the wife took place before, not after, Henry's death; and (2) Once done, these actions could not be changed by Henry, but if he had done them by a will, then he could have changed his mind before his death. A will is revocable in whole or in part, at any time, but an outright gift or transfer of property is not.

In the long history of the law, technicality and anti-technicality has swung back and forth like a pendulum. At one stage we see the strict requirement that all contracts must be in writing in order to be binding. We then see a swing-away from this view and a recognition of all contracts, whether oral or written. But in one area the law has never managed to slough off all technical requirements and this comes generally under the heading "Frauds." Every state has one or more Statutes of Frauds, better described as anti-fraud statutes. These require that certain transactions must be exhibited by a written instrument, the most common requirement being that a sale of land or real property must be in writing and the seller's signature must be acknowledged before a notary public. The reason for this is to avoid land ownership disputes whereby people could come into court and claim some oral, unwritten sale or agreement to sell which had been agreed upon years ago and disturb the peaceful possession and ownership of their land and property. The writing requirement prevents such frauds.

Similarly, the statutes setting up particular requirements for the making of a will are anti-fraud statutes. They prevent appearance in court to claim title to something from an estate, when the deceased person did not intend to give the claimant anything at all.

With minor exceptions, all wills must be written and must be signed by the maker in the presence of witnesses. The signing formality is called attestation, and it contains certain simple but extremely important requirements. The witnesses to a will need not have read its contents. Essentially they are doing three things: (1) they are listening to the maker declare this piece of paper to be his will; (2) they observe him apply his signature to it; and (3) they make a judgment as to whether he is of sound mind at the time of making the will. Any will prepared by an attorney contains an attestation clause.

"In witness whereof I have hereunto set my hand and affixed my seal, this 4th day of February, 19———.

HENRY KARD (signed)

Signed, sealed, published and declared by Henry Kard, the testator, as and for his last will and testament in the presence of us who, at his request and in his presence and in the presence of each other, have hereunto subscribed our names as witnesses.

CARL GIVEN Address: 25 DeKalb Avenue
EDGAR MARDO Address: 8240 Fiber Drive
STEVEN STITES Address: 692 Hale Parkway

It is possible that a will may be valid without this clause. However, in that event the witnesses would have to come into court and swear from their memory that the testator did, in fact, sign in their presence and that they each signed in his presence and in the presence of each other. If many years have elapsed since the signing of the will, it might be difficult to do this. The written clause provides a presumption that the proper procedures were followed. If a will contains more than one page, the testator will initial each page to avoid the possibility of a page being substituted with provisions which are not his.

What if the evidence is overwhelming and uncontradicted that a person made an oral will in the presence of witnesses without the formalities of writing and signature? The law will usually reject the proof regardless of its strength. And this is true in all anti-fraud type legislation. If the formal requirements were not met, then nothing happened legally. Some states recognize an oral will made under emergency circumstances at (or close to) the time of death of the maker in the presence of at least two disinterested witnesses. This is known as the "nuncupative" will. Some states recognize what is known as a "holographic" will completely written out in the handwriting of the testator and signed by him. In all of these matters the law exercises great caution against a result which is contrary to the testator's intention, and if there is any hint of fraud, coercion or undue influence exerted against the deceased by any beneficiary of the will, then the whole will may be rejected by the court.

What happens if a person does not make a will or if his will is determined to be illegal? He is then considered to have died "intestate" and the property will be distributed to the natural inheritors of his bounty according to the schedule and formula set up by state statute. These regulations usually provide that half of the estate be given to the spouse and half to the children. If there be no spouse or children, then to grandchildren, parents, and so on through uncles and aunts and cousins, nieces and nephews if no closer relatives are living. By statute in most states the spouse is entitled to a substantial share of the estate even if a will gives less. This is known as the widow's or widower's share, commonly one-half, and in addition, the wife is entitled to a sum (in some states set at $3500.00) in advance of all creditors, for her immediate support.

The making of a will cannot defeat the right of creditors of the estate. The statutes set up a definite list whereby creditors are placed in different classes of preference (A, B, C, D, etc.) so that Class A creditors will be paid first, then if there is any left, the next class, and so on.

You may ask yourself: Why trouble to make a will if the law will distribute the property as you yourself would choose? There are many answers. The main one is that the administration of your estate will be smoother, quicker, less expensive and less complicated if you have a proper will. If you are the parent of minor children, you should think about what would happen if both you and your spouse were killed, and you should provide in advance of any eventuality for a proper guardian. By a will, you can dispose of your property, and can also choose your personal representative who will act in a fiduciary capacity for you after your death. Ordinarily, this representative may be your wife or husband, even if she or he is the major beneficiary. You may provide that your executor act without a fidelity bond. In some instances such bonds are an unnecessary expense, but they are required by the law unless the testator directs that they should not be.

Almost every person has three types of property. Before you read on, you might think to yourself: "Now, what in the world does that mean—types of property? Is it house, car and clothes? Is it books, food and stocks?" No, this is not the sort of classification about which we are thinking. We have in mind the nature of your ownership, regardless of what the item may be, for estate law purposes, and these classifications are as follows: (1) solely owned property; (2) jointly owned property; and (3) insurance.

Any property which you yourself own outright can be called testamentary property, because it is the only property which you may dispose of by a will. Property which is held by you with your spouse or with anyone else in joint tenancy, with right of survivorship, automatically goes to the surviving owner without any estate proceeding or expenses. Joint tenancy property is generally free from claims of creditors of the party who dies. Because of the convenient and automatic features of joint tenancy, and because most married couples wish to own things fifty-fifty, this device is widely used. That which has written evidence of title such as a house and a car are held in joint tenancy. But there are some traps, particularly if an estate is large enough to be subject to state or federal inheritance and gift taxes. Under the federal law this is $60,000.00 and lesser sums apply under state tax laws. The entire matter of joint ownership in lieu of a will is fraught with dangers and problems. A person who is a party to joint ownership should seek the advice of a lawyer who can examine the entire situation and advise accordingly. One of the problems is the fact that many people place property into joint ownership and then forget by doing this it is in reality a gift to the other. Both the federal and state governments have enacted gift tax laws as an adjunct to their inheritance tax laws so that people cannot avoid the inheritance tax bite entirely by making gifts during life. Thus, a surviving tenant may find that his or her interest in property is subject not only to gift tax but long years of penalty and interest for not paying the tax when the joint interest was received.

A person may dispose by will only property which he owns. The direction as to disposal of a certain piece of property such as a diamond ring, a painting, a house, or whatever, is sometimes called a bequest, a legacy or a devise. These terms are practically interchangeable. Lawyers usually advise against making bequests of particular sums of money or specified pieces of property to certain individuals. Rather, they favor a fractional division of the estate to each beneficiary. The reason for this is that several years may elapse between the making of the will and the death of the testator. In the meantime, his property ownership situation may change entirely so that if he gives "One Thousand Dollars to Aunt Hannah, Fifteen Hundred Dollars to Cousin Sue, and my diamond ring to my brother Bart," and if he wrote the will at a high point in his opulence, the bequests may have been a mere pittance when made but, should his estate have been dissipated by high expenses for final illness, for example, then these token bequests, contrary to his intention at the time they were made, may become the largest share of the estate.

A will is not in operation until presented to the court for probate. Two questions may well come to mind at this point: (1) What is probate? (2) Who makes the presentation to court?

Presentation is more of a problem than is generally recognized. Many people imagine that the County Court or the Probate Court, whichever it is called, keeps a record of all the deaths in the County and sees to it that something is filed concerning the property of every person who dies. This is not so. The court only handles matters which are presented to it, and it does not go out and overtly seek any filings or business of any sort.

A person who is named as Executor in a will has a legal responsibility to present the will to the court for probate. However, a person may be named Executor without his knowledge. Some people are secretive about their wills, concealing them and telling no one about them. An Executor need not be told what the will contains but he should always be advised that he is being asked to act in this capacity.

It is a criminal offense for a person to secrete a will of another and although the cases in which dishonest and selfish motives may cause someone to defeat a will by merely hiding or destroying it are perhaps rare, the law has to be on guard against such temptation. The law cannot do everything and the testator should assist in seeing that the will actually comes into operation. This may be safely done in any one of three ways: (1) Most states have a statutory procedure whereby a will may be lodged for safe keeping with the probate court when it is written; (2) A will kept in a bank safety deposit box is generally guaranteed to fall into the hands of the court as banks keep careful watch of obituaries. They are required to maintain a liaison with the State Inheritance Tax

Department and safety deposit boxes of deceased individuals must be opened under a special procedure with the state represented; and (3) Many people leave the original executed will with their lawyers.

Since a will is by definition a revocable instrument which may be (and indeed should be) revised and changed as a person's economic and life situation develops, you can well imagine the many interesting legal problems which have arisen over the centuries and are recorded in cases concerning conflicting wills. Elmer Moody, a man of 60, executes a will leaving all of his property to his beloved wife Mary, and if she should not survive him, then one-half to his son, Elmer Moody, Jr., and one-half to the Widows and Orphans Fund, a fraternal organization. Being thoughtful, Elmer executes the will in "multiple originals," that is, he fully signs and has the witnesses sign the typewritten original and three carbon copies. The carbons then attain the same rank as the original because in law it is not the fact that a paper happens to have been the first sheet in the typewriter that makes it authentic but whether it was signed and acceped as written. Elmer supplies both his son and the Widows and Orphans Fund with originals.

When Elmer's wife Mary dies, he goes to another state to live with his niece Nancy Brooks who treats him very kindly for the last several years of his life. His son Elmer, Jr. after his mother's death, remains in the town where he was born, writes to his father infrequently, usually at Christmas and at Easter and finally he is negligent about even this and ignores his parent. During this period, Elmer, Sr. disappointed in his son's absence of affection, executes a new will, in which he gives all of his property to his niece Nancy, beginning the will in the usual way, "I, Elmer Moody, being of sound mind, hereby make and declare this my last will and testament and revoke all previous wills and codicils made by me."

When Elmer Moody, Sr. dies, his son and the fraternal organization take out their copies of the will and attempt to have it govern the distribution of the estate, claiming that his niece Nancy exerted undue influence on Elmer to get him to will all of his property to her, that he was suffering from senility and was not of sound mind at the time he executed the will to the niece. Nancy Brooks then submits to a long court battle to secure what is rightfully hers. This is an example of why most lawyers recommend only one original of a will be executed and if copies are kept they be unsigned, because it can be unwise and even dangerous to have excess signed copies around—in fact, it is an excellent idea when a new will is being drawn to bring the prior signed will and destroy it in the presence of the witnesses.

Three groups have a vested interest in the property of a deceased person: (1) the beneficiaries either under a will or under the statute if a person dies without a will; (2) the creditors of the deceased; and (3) the government, for tax purposes. Any member of any of these groups may cause estate action to be commenced, although people often die and no estate proceeding results because either there is no property or none of these groups or their representatives have knowledge of property.

Strictly speaking, the word "probate" means proving a will, but the word is used generally to cover all estate proceedings in a probate court. If a will was written, then the person charged with the duty of assisting the court carry out the directions of the will is the Executor. If a will was not written and the person died "intestate", then an Administrator will be appointed. These parties are the personal representatives of the deceased.

The Executor or Administrator's duty is to amass the assets of the estate and distribute them to their rightful takers. When this is accomplished, the estate is closed. The entire procedure generally takes from six months to two years. One of the many requirements is that a public notice be published in a newspaper telling creditors they must present their claims within a certain date or be forever excluded. For all of this work, the personal representative is allowed a fee set as a percentage of the estate assets and in addition, the attorney who represents the Executor and helps him weave his way through the maze of requirements is entitled to a percentage fee. Each of these fees amount to as much as 6% in a smaller estate and operate by a sliding scale down to 1/2 of 1% in huge estates. The testator can choose an Executor who he knows will be willing to serve without fee and can so direct. This is usually the case when the Executor is the major beneficiary.

We mentioned that life insurance is a form of property which generally is not part of the probate estate. This is because the life insurance contract contains its own distribution provisions and the company merely pays the money over to whoever is named beneficiary of the policy. An insured may name his "estate" as the beneficiary. In this case the company pays the money into the court for distribution, like all other assets. Quite often life insurance is the major asset a person leaves to his heirs.

A rather ill defined field of professional activity and advice has developed generally under the name "Estate Planning" and at least four different occupations can claim a legitimate place in the field. These are law, insurance, banking and investment. The term "estate planning" covers such a wide scope no one professional man can perform the complete service without the aid of the others.

Here is a brief example of how estate planning can work. Perry Gardner with a partner owns and operates a rug cleaning business. Together, they own three trucks, a stock of supplies, some office equipment and a substantial amount of business good will built up over the past four or five years by advertising and service. Perry is 43 years old. He has a G. I. insurance policy which will pay $10,000 on his death, plus two other policies totaling $25,000. If he should die without a will and without any pre-planning, then his partner will find himself in partnership with Perry's widow and children because they will receive half of the business. The partner will probably want to buy them out but then there will be a question of (1) how much Perry's share of the business is worth and (2) where the partner is going to get the money. Or the partner might want the widow to buy him out with the proceeds from her insurance policies, which she could not afford to do and would not want to do. Perry's widow will, of course, take care of the children, but their one-half of the estate by law will have to be kept in a special guardianship fund and supervised by the court until they become twenty-one. Thus we have an estate which will be in court for years and years with many difficult and expensive problems.

Perry's insurance man sees some of the dangers in this situation and tells Perry to go to his own lawyer. Perry's lawyer wraps the whole problem up in a rather simple manner. First he writes a will giving the whole estate to Perry's wife. By this, Perry is not disinheriting his children but he knows that his wife will have to take care of them anyway, and feels that she should have full control of the property without the court's say-so. Then he drafts a "buy and sell" agreement for Perry and his partner, and suggests that each of the partners buy a life insurance policy naming the other as beneficiary. These policies are for rather high amounts, and both partners agree that the proceeds will be used by them to pay the widow of the other for his interest in the business if he should die. The premiums for the life insurance policies are paid as an expense of conducting business.

If Perry wishes to go a step further, to assure a college education for his children, he will set up a trust with a bank and buy another insurance policy directing the proceeds to go into the trust if he dies; then the bank will protect the funds for years and years after his death and do exactly what he directed in the trust paper. In this way the court will not be involved and Perry has made great strides towards governing and controlling his own destiny and the destinies of his children.

As in all other fields of law, the way to come out on top rather than on the bottom, and the way to take full advantage of the opportunities afforded is for the individual to arm himself with a general insight into the law of wills and estates. For this purpose he can utilize professional counsel to its best advantage. And it is not the quantity of money but the quality of planning that achieves the best result.

Chapter Thirteen

PREVENTATIVE LAW

There are many misconceptions about the law on the part of laymen.

Some do-it-yourself types feel that they know a lot about law and can handle things all right themselves. A curiously frequent gem of legal knowledge among such persons, and something pronounced with great authority is: "If you disappear for seven years you are legally dead." This is not necessarily the case. Different rules apply in different states, and varying facts and circumstances must be proven; also the legal consequences of unexplained absence vary according to the rights and issues which may be involved; for example, whether it is grounds for divorce, or what to do with abandoned bank account funds, or whatever. Another great bromide is "If you pay a dollar a month, they can't do anything to you." The trouble with this group is that they want dangerously to oversimplify law and their personal confidence is bolstered beyond its due by a weird amalgamation of obscure bits of knowledge.

On the other side of the mountain of open light and wisdom is Old Fear Gulch, full of legal hypochondriacs who are afraid to do anything because all those lawyer fellows are so smart and trying to do everybody out of everything. But the person with just a little healthy insight into the processes of the law will realize that law is basically a means to govern the orderly and just interplay of people in society, that courts are not to be feared, and that if it is necessary to go to court, the system is there to find the truth and to do justice. Court is to be avoided if possible only because the processes through court are laborious and long.

A fairly complete law library contains upwards of ten thousand volumes, most of which are case reports from all of the states in the Union. You would find any of these books, taken from the shelf at random, to contain from one to two hundred entirely separate and disassociated cases, appearing in chronological order. At least one-third of the cases show that somebody became involved in an expensive controversy by not exercising a little wise prevention. On the other hand, situations often arise without fault or neglect on the part of anyone, but by reason of the natural and necessary flux and interaction of human lives and property. These account for one third. The other third cases will have some other type of error as their source. Many are negligence cases in which personal injury, or property damage, is sought against someone for carelessness.

Life itself places us in charge of our own destiny. Law, in general, lends itself neatly to a high degree of planning—in fact, this is the function of most lawyers. Trial lawyers are numerically few in comparison to the number of office lawyers who utilize their knowledge in solving problems in behalf of their clients and in an effort to avoid difficulties with the law. When a lawyer writes a contract, a deed, a will; advises on some course of action, he is exercising preventative law by showing how to make it binding, how to make it irrevocable, how to have the legal paper contain what you want it to contain. The lawyer can do this with great predictability, in fact probably with much more reliability than the medical profession can command in its day-to-day office practice. A doctor can give you an injection and tell you that it is "perhaps eighty percent effective," but a lawyer can write a contract that is one hundred percent binding, or he can draft a document that will, with virtually one hundred percent reliability, do what you wish with your property in the event of your demise.

The lawyer reduces thinking to paper so as to remove ambiguities, uncertainties, or outright errors surrounding a transaction not properly thought out. No businessman worthy of the name enters without legal advice into any important transaction. What about the average person? When does he know whether he needs a lawyer or not? If you think the answer to this question is "When you are getting sued or want to sue somebody," this is not exactly correct, for the handling of a suit is only a part of the lawyer's work.

A choice example of legal planning is the trust which an individual can set up to manage his property during his lifetime or after his death. It may include a person's entire estate, pointing it in the direction he wishes it to take. The trust thinks out in advance tax problems and virtually guarantees that not a dollar will be paid into the public treasury which does not need to be paid. This does not constitute tax evasion; it is a perfectly legitimate type of activity generally termed "tax planning." When set on its course, such a plan can take care of matters so smoothly a man's estate will barely feel a ripple upon his demise since everything necessary has been set up beforehand, spelling out exactly what will transpire. The difference between what actually occurs under good planning and what could, and does, occur without such planning is so marked and so extreme that the great good accomplished is a wonder to behold.

For instance, we have the matter of Norman Gilbert's business, a manufacturing concern, built into a fine organization over the years and solely owned by him. What happens when he dies? Well, if Mr. Gilbert writes a "simple" will giving his property to his wife, the problems involved will be overwhelming. Without her husband present to manage the business, Mrs. Gilbert is in great difficulty, and more likely than not the factory will have to be dismantled and the equipment sold. However, if Norman Gilbert plans his affairs properly by setting up a trust, selecting a bank or a responsible individual as trustee, then the business can be continued throughout the widow's lifetime, and conceivably up until such a time as the Gilbert children are grown and able to take control of the business themselves.

Many matters which present serious legal problems give a deceiving appearance of being fairly simple. This explains why law lends itself to unauthorized practice and to home brewed remedies, which become a boon to the legal profession. Whereas a small amount of revenue is lost to the legal profession by these practices of unauthorized laymen, the trouble created repays lawyers many times over in fees to litigate and straighten out needlessly botched up situations. In fact, the difference in cost between prevention and cure is so great if people consistently exercised preventative law, lawyers would have very meager practice remaining to them. There is little doubt if the public gave them the full opportunity to practice preventative law, lawyers in a few years time would perform so well they would work themselves right out of their profession. There need be little concern for the destiny of lawyers, however, human nature being what it is, this situation is quite unlikely ever to occur.

The kings of modern day retail marketing know, understand and utilize a basic rule of human psychology: People are impulsive: They decide, act and buy on impulse. They see something which looks good to them. If they happen to have the money, they will buy it whether they really need it or not. The Scottish novelist Robert Louis Stevenson (1850-1894) knew human nature when he said "Everyone lives by selling something." The housewife who makes up her grocery list and then adheres to it, when she shops will cut her marketing budget by 25%. Banks are known to process millions of small checks every week because people curb their natural impulses to buy by carrying only a small amount of cash and a personal check book. Similar impulse psychology applies to the great decisions and events of life.

The extreme opposite of impulsiveness can be just as devastating to happiness. Some people react so severely against impulsiveness they turn their lives into a cold cave of fear. Naturally, the achievement of a proper balance between these forces comprises our lifetime efforts, the success or lack of success in achieving a balance distinguishing the successful from the unsuccessful people. It is not the amount of money or good fortune which may come into one's life that makes for happiness. It is rather the equilibrium achieved between desire and reality. For the most of us, a limited amount of money is one of the grim realities we must from time to time reckon with. Another reality is the law. If you do not reckon with it, it will reckon with you on its own not your terms. And this does not mean just stopping your car when the light is red and not stealing other people's property. Such prohibitions are a small part of law. It means conducting your own life rather than having somebody else conduct it for you because you have become entangled on the wrong side of the law.

You may hear an advertising announcement on the radio or TV: "Come in and consult our financial counsellors. Consolidate your debts into one easy budget payment." Should you accept this offer the result will mean the addition of interest to your existing debts and the extension of your debts for more years into the future. It means that the vacuum cleaner you bought will ultimately cost you in interest not twice its value but three times its value. An ambitious and successful young man was asked why he wanted to make so much money. "Aren't you making too much of this money-making proposition? Is money that great?" "No," he replied, with wisdom beyond his years. "It's to be able to do what you want to do, to guide your own destiny rather than have someone guide it for you."

The financial "wizard" who may call himself a "counsellor" is in business to make money, interest money at the highest rate within the law that the market will bear. His counseling is "free" but like most things, it is worth exactly what you pay for it. The lawyer, on the other hand, is available to you for a truly professional, personal service. Your lawyer becomes an extension of yourself. At the moment you consult him and in respect to the problem you bring, you are then learned in the law. If you see him for an hour and he saves you ten thousand dollars by his advice, his charge is nevertheless usually a nominal fee set on a time basis.

Many commercial establishments seek to create the image of professionalism in their advertising—"Your Service Station Attendant is a Professional." Anybody who receives a commission from selling something is not a professional in the sense that a lawyer or a doctor is. Such a person is always an extension of himself and of the commercial enterprise he is furthering. You are not buying a valuable part of him and his time; he is selling to you. This is the real distinction. You can actually buy the services of a lawyer and his knowledge but you cannot buy a shoe salesman; you can only buy the shoes. Do not let them muddy your thinking about the difference between sales and true professional service. Bear it always in mind.

Now obviously, I realize that as you merrily follow your impulses through life you cannot consult a lawyer at every turn—in fact, you would not want to. You are going to have to use some horse sense based on a store of general knowledge as to when a lawyer is needed. Perhaps we can pinpoint some warning signals.

The first warning signal is money. No matter what the situation is, if any substantial sum of money is being exposed or is changing hands, whether in family or out of family, with friends or with strangers, this factor alone, for obvious reasons, is a warning signal. A great law professor used to point out that whether a case involves $50 or $500,000, the principles are the same but the noises are different.

A second warning signal might be called "non-reputation." What does this mean? It's the Little Red Riding Hood omen, "Don't talk to strangers in the forest." This and impulse are a deadly combination. Probably your two most expensive investments are a house and a car. When buying a new car, few people consult a lawyer and few have reason to be sorry afterwards. Why? Because new cars are sold by established and authorized dealers of large and reputable companies, and even though you may have to pay a high price for the slick buggy, the lawyer could not do any better if he were buying it for himself because the whole transaction is established by custom and reputation.

This is less true if you go to Happy Joe's Used Car Lot. The most hazardous of all purchases is from the man or woman who rings your doorbell. No matter who you are, whether you live in a trailer court in southern California or on a shaded drive in Westchester County, New York, one day you are going to be staring at the happy grin of a plausible sort of fellow who begins talking about a wonderful thing for you, something you knew you needed all along, and only at this moment, do you realize it is absolutely essential for your happiness. Whether this be a set of books, a fall-out shelter, dancing lessons for a new lease on life, the principle is the same. You never saw the salesman before. Do not sign on the dotted line ever unless you absolutely know what you are doing.

A common scheme to sell merchandise, from coffee pots to house siding, is to involve the prospective purchaser in a little business promotion partnership. "You get credit for every one of your friends we sell to so that you'll end up getting this for nothing." The transaction actually involves your signing a paper which constitutes a mortgage on whatever you are buying and a promissory note with heavy interest attached. That signed paper is a negotiable instrument. What does this mean? It means that the paper can be handed to somebody else and thereafter you are not dealing with the original affable person who so deftly handed you his pen and gleefully watched you sign your name to it. No. You had never seen him before and will not see him again.

What did he do with that little autograph of yours? You did not know you were so famous, but your autograph might sell for $500.00 or more, depending on what you signed. This paper is then "discounted"—this means that it is sold for cash to a finance company, a savings and loan institution, or even a bank, at less than its face value. With this money, the salesman pays for the merchandise which you bought from him and retains the balance for his commission. You will then receive from some outfit you never heard of before in your life, a welcome letter in the mail, with payment book enclosed. This company has you by the nape of the neck until all the money, plus the interest, is paid up.

So what if your Central Home Vacuum System, or whatever it happens to be, doesn't measure up? Legally the purchaser of this negotiable instrument can claim to be totally innocent of any fraud or irregularity in its inception. The bank is a "bona fide purchaser for value," and if you have any reason why you think you should not pay up, you are talking to the wrong fellow. Legally they can say to you as follows: "You signed it. We thought your signature was good. We thought you were honest and we had no reason to believe that you wouldn't do what you promised to do in writing, so we paid good money for this piece of paper, relying on your written promise. We don't know anything about your vacuum cleaner, there's nothing about that in here. All this says is that 'For value received, you promise to pay a certain sum of money.' If you have some complaint, you can always try to find that fellow you dealt with. He's your boy, not us. We're innocent. This thing you signed is as good as money, in fact we paid good money for it."

In this regard, the bank is legally absolutely correct. As a matter of fact, the note could be sold again and again, and somebody else you never heard of could be following you for the last few payments. Your note is like a dollar bill which is actually sold every time it changes hands. This illustrates only one of the many reasons why you should (1) know with whom you are dealing, and (2) know what you are signing, before you sign your name.

Probably your greatest possession is your house. Most people know that the subject of real estate bespeaks legal problems. What many people do not know is that the real "deal" is made not at the "closing," but when the contract to buy is signed. The chain of title problem is only one part of real estate. The real problems are created by the people to the transaction themselves. This will be discussed in greater detail in the real estate chapter, suffice it to say here that real estate is a warning signal. Where was that warning signal again? *Before.* That's right, before, not after you sign that agreement to buy or sell.

Another red flag is a serious accident of any type, whether this involves personal injury or property damage. While it is true that law can not prevent the accident, preventative law can keep the wrong legal result from attaching to the accident. The timing problem is simple, yet it is often misunderstood. The answer to it is: Immediately. That is, immediately upon occurrence of the accident, proper steps should be taken to protect legal rights.

This does not necessarily mean telephoning a lawyer right away. It does mean getting names of witnesses, taking a picture of the scene, if possible, not saying the wrong things to the investigating officer, and preserving any physical objects which would be significant or illustrative in a later reconstruction of the occurrence. What is important? The answer to that is: Everything. You should keep in mind that facts cannot prove themselves.

This brings us to another warning signal and another rule in preventative law. How is your record keeping? You know there is one great characteristic about a sheet of paper—it has perpetual existence. Until it is destroyed it exists and what is written on it constitutes evidence of something that has happened. Not so for the human memory. Oh, yes, courts will listen to people grub into the dark recesses of their minds trying to pick up mental imprints of some events of the past, but for obvious reasons, recorded evidence outranks the memory every time.

In the law of evidence there are two interesting concepts which are very relevant to the argument for a written record. These are "past recollection recorded" and "present recollection revived." In other words, if a witness' memory is faulty and some record was made of the transaction, then his attorney can take out the paper, show it to the witness, and say "Does this revive your recollection?" If it does, then the witness can testify directly from his own revived recollection. If it does not revive his recollection, the witness can state he knows it must have been recorded correctly at the time, and then the paper itself is accepted into the record. In a very real sense, all business records are potential evidence. The person who has kept records is the one who is going to win in court.

Justice is not an abstract, plucked out of the air when the need arises. It must be constructed and built by human effort, the best construction material available is recorded fact. People realize they must keep some kind of record for income tax purposes. They know they are in partnership with Uncle Sam who will insist on a good accounting. You are also in partnership with your spouse, for example.

It is not here inferred that married life be conducted with a view to what would happen in event of separation or divorce; still if it should occur, the court, in decreeing a property division, may have to go back many years to reconstruct the financial aspects of the marital union in order to determine allocation based on respective contributions of the partners. If records are not kept, then there is no way for the court to make just distribution. For example, if a wife has received several thousand dollars in gifts from her rich uncle which money has gone into the marriage, she may not receive credit for it unless she can clearly show how much the gifts amounted to and to what extent her Uncle's generosity may have relieved her husband from his primary responsibility to support his wife and children.

We have already emphasized that signing on the dotted line may be fraught with danger, that, in general, all contracts should be carefully watched. Another good warning signal in preventative law comes under the general term "bailment." This is a form of contract. Even if you have never heard of bailment before, you have without doubt been involved in it many times. It occurs when something of value is turned over to someone for safe keeping. This does not only apply to depositing money in a bank. Bailment is involved when you deposit your car with a garage for servicing, when you leave your soiled shirts with the laundry, or your television set in the repair shop. In such instance, you are the "bailor," the one trusted is the "bailee." Important rights and duties attend the individual transactions.

Another bailment is involved when you leave your car in a parking lot. Have you ever noted the form of language on the ticket given to you by the attendant? It is true you have not signed your name on any paper, but this is not the only way in which you can become bound by the writing of somebody else. By accepting the stub of the parking lot in exchange for having your car watched, you may be agreeing with the statement of the lot concern that your car is not worth more than $100 because it is not unusual to see a provision that such a sum is all the parking lot company can be made to pay for loss of your car, unless of course you can prove they were negligent. If when you return and your car is not in the parking lot where you left it, how can you show what happened?

We know that a will is necessary if we wish our desires to be fulfilled after death, which is inevitable. People also know they should buy some life insurance, which is another good warning signal in preventative law because your insurance should be associated with your estate thinking. Your will and your insurance policies should therefore be written in recognition of each other.

Another inevitable in life is the fact of your neighbors' having children. Children are legally a little different from other people. If you have a swimming pool or a trampoline in your backyard, you should be cautious. An inexpensive liability insurance policy may help you, but it is wise to read the policy over carefully, or have your lawyer do it for you. An interesting sidelight on the general problem of other people's children is the "attractive nuisance" doctrine. If a person leaves the type of thing on his own property which he, as a reasonable and prudent person, should realize would ordinarily cause children who are very curious by nature to want to inspect it, the property owner may be in difficulty.

There is no doubt about the fact that the children are trespassing, yet curiously enough, ownership of property is not an absolute right. The law says that your "property must be used in such a way as not to endanger or infringe upon the rights of others." So if a child climbs up on your antique windmill or plays in your toppled-over shack (which you intended to remove but didn't) and some timber gives way, causing injury to said child, and if you had reason to believe that the neighborhood children would find your oddities attractive to them, the fact is you are legally liable for the injury the child suffers. This danger may be avoided by (1) checking out your premises to see if such a potential exists; (2) being on hand to tell the children they cannot play on your premises and (best of all) (3) insurance coverage.

Preventative law is your best protective agent. It is for a very good reason that the medical profession advocates an annual medical check-up to prevent illness and disease. The American Bar Association is accepting the medical lead in advocating a periodic legal check-up. You will invariably stand to benefit by such diligence.

Chapter Fourteen

CRIME AND PUNISHMENT

The true measure of a civilization is the manner in which it treats its criminal offenders. Few people would protest this premise. Most Americans fondly believe they are part and parcel of the finest civilization which ever existed. Yet they are possessed of many negative impressions about the quality of administration of criminal justice. Criminal law suffers from poor public relations which stems in part from poor performance, and in part from a poor press. In "press" we include the public image makers—the reporter, the writer, the dramatist.

Criminal law is essentially deep, intense, alive and profound in subject with a nucleus, a matrix, which may be captured in a few words: Criminal law is the disciplinarian of a civilization. It operates in this way: Society finds certain acts intolerable, lists them as prohibitions then undertakes to the best of its power to enforce the rules it has laid down. Criminal law is moralistic. It expresses society's concept of right and wrong. Government in a democracy is formed as the agent of the people to establish and enforce society's rules and regulations.

Most criminal laws are imposed and enforced by the states. Each state has its constitution and its own set of criminal laws. Laws are made and enacted by the legislature. We have noted that courts can make precedent, which has the binding effect of law, by writing decisions in particular cases. However, even the supreme court of a state cannot define a crime and set a penalty therefor.

The entirety of a state's current statutes may very well be encompassed in eight to twelve hefty volumes. Buried in these tomes, you will somewhere find the basic criminal code, perhaps occupying less than one-fourth of one of the volumes. In the criminal code are set forth criminal court procedures and the classic crimes of murder, rape, robbery, burglary, theft, forgery, etc. The balance of the statutes are concerned with the operation of the various departments and institutions of the government itself, the regulation of various businesses, professions, organizations, institutions and the protection and definition of sundry property and personal rights.

The criminal code is fundamentally prohibitory in nature; the balance of the statutes are regulatory in nature, yet the legislature never forgets it is dealing with human beings who in most cases cannot be relied upon to do what they are told to do, unless they are forced to do it. It is for this reason that every legislative enactment is "mandatory" rather than "advisory." It is precisely for this reason that you will find scattered throughout the many volumes of state statutes a number of criminal laws and penalties which are not a part of the basic criminal code. To be specific, let us consider the barber licensing law. This state statute sets up certain standards and requirements which must be fulfilled before an operator can obtain his license to engage in public barbering. Such a law is a regulatory law. What happens if a man ignores this law and sets up his shop without a license? We find a "stinger" entitled "Barbering Without a License—Penalty." This states: "to engage in barbering or offer oneself to the public as a barber without being first duly licensed is a misdemeanor (crime) carrying a maximum penalty of 30 days in jail, or $300 fine, or both. Each day of the violation is a separate offense."

Some regulatory statutes do not require, and thus do not have, criminal penalties for their enforcement. They control and govern by the granting or withholding of certain privileges. For example, a corporation must act like a corporation in order to be a corporation. If it does not, then it loses its status as a corporation and its owners, while not suffering criminal penalties imposed by the state, will suffer private claims enforced against them.

Your state government is in charge of most criminal enforcement and within the broad but essential limitations of the Fourteenth Amendment to the Federal Constitution, the state, through its legislature and courts, can define crimes, try offenders and impose penalties as it sees fit.

The Fourteenth Amendment, which was passed immediately after and as a result of the Civil War between the states, provides: "All persons born or naturalized in the United States and subject to the jurisdiction thereof are citizens of the United States and of the state wherein they reside. No state shall make or enforce any law which shall abridge the privileges or immunities of citizens of the United States; nor shall any state deprive any person of life, liberty or property without due process of law nor deny to any person within its jurisdiction the equal protection of the laws."

Government has an enormous power, and you may not appreciate the full magnitude of that power until you experience, or see someone else experience, the heavy sanction of its criminal law. The federal Constitution is the state's superior officer. It tells the state govenment that while the State can, and should, prosecute criminals in order to maintain the peace, the State must do so by the rules. In protection of the rights of individuals against abuse of governmental power, the federal constitution treats all governmental levels the same. The federal, state and local governments come under its sanctions. In addition, each state constitution upholds personal liberty.

Our American Constitutions treat government as you might treat the man next door after he has abused your hospitality—"Look, Jim, I still like you and I think we can get along, but you have rather persistently shown your inclination to interfere with our peace of mind in certain directions. I have therefore established some specific do's and don'ts for you. I would like you to understand that these are the terms on which we meet and maintain our neighborly relationship and if these terms are not complied with, we will not meet. First: You do not put your feet up on my sofa. Your kids do not leave their tricycles in my driveway. You do not get drunk and try to hug my wife, etc., etc."

The Constitution says to the government, "Look, my friend, you have made mistakes too many times for me to be able completely to trust you any more. I realize that you have a great responsibility. You must maintain order and you must perform services. You must

Crime and Punishment • 241

protect us from our enemies. I also realize you must have the requisite power to do all of this. However you have abused that power too often in too many ways for you to be entitled to a free reign of power. Therefore, you must understand in order to maintain our mutually beneficial relationship there will be certain things you will not do."

In our imaginative monologue, the Constitution may continue to lecture the government in this wise: "One thing I have not liked is this: You have desired control over such freedoms as religion, speech, press, and assembly. I think this may be the result of an inferiority feeling on your part in that you are not too certain about your own religion, if any, and so you want to over-react and suppress any variant. And then, of course, speech and press may involve criticism of you. And then about people getting together for a meeting. It is true they may discuss you adversely and disagree with you, but you will have to tolerate their right of assembly."

The Constitution continues its harangue to the government: "There is another thing you have been doing of which I do not approve. You barge into people's private homes without any right to do so and rifle through their private papers and possessions. And it is not just the one time you have done this in a given instance, but it is the fact that having gone into the home in this manner with impunity you have intimidated people so that they do not feel secure about keeping things around their own house for the reason that they are no longer sure you will not again come in to repeat the affront to their privacy. People are sensitive, you know. I don't think it is your province to go elbowing your way through the door into a man's house. So this particular activity for which you have a proclivity will have to stop."

The Constitution has more to clarify so continues the lecture to the government.

"Now, I realize there may be treason and other serious crimes being perpetrated behind closed doors, and you must have the necessary power in this regard, so we will add a stipulation here which you must in all fairness recognize as reasonableness. I know it is fairly general and I would prefer to be more specific with you but I am afraid if I were, we would become greatly involved in error. We will therefore just say this: 'That all people shall be secure in their persons, houses, papers and effects against unreasonable searches and seizures.'

"One guideline you might like to have, and I think it is only fair that I give it to you, is this: Not always, but unless it is too much of an emergency to do so and whenever possible, you ought to get a warrant for your search from a judicial officer who is elected or appointed to his high position and who is detached and impartial and can be relied on to have a fair concept about what is reasonable and what is not in any particular fact situation. So much for that one."

Constitution continues: "I have noticed that you have been hasty in incarcerating people. I have seen you sidestep the law. You just have a person arrested and jailed in the clink and there he is—no charge, no judge, no hearing. That kind of activity must stop, and I am not concerned whether the person is guilty as sin or whether it is a traffic case, a robbery case, a murder case or a treason case. This person is entitled to a hearing, you understand? And he will have a hearing before an impartial judge who in his judicial capacity has knowledge of the law and a respect for it. In other words, you, the state, do not deny people due process of law."

Constitution now brings up the subject of persecution: "Often in your history, you have been eager to persecute people. You may become angry with a particular person, and if you prosecute him once and lose the case, you will be dissatisfied and want to try him again. Well, this is one of our constitutional prohibitions. Only one trial is permitted within the Constitution. If you lose it, your opportunity is ended. A person can be put in jeopardy only once for one particular crime.

"And then there is the evil of oppression of which you are not free from criticism. You have been known to jail people. And whether you are in possession of evidence or not, you charge them and then they cannot get out on bond. Now, I know your courts cannot operate if a person can just take off under no constraint to return for his trial, so you require him to put up bail, that is, he puts up his property or he hires somebody, like a surety company, to put up property for him, and this is his bond that says he will appear in court when he is supposed to and if he does not appear he can be charged the penalty of whatever the amount of the bond happens to be, plus some other penalties. However, you must abandon the idea of setting bonds so high that the person cannot command property to cover it or pay a surety company to put up the bond for him, which is in effect subjecting him to penal servitude before he has been given a trial and the due process of law we have discussed. So here is another constitutional prohibition."

The Constitution has other statements to make: "I am aware that you have taken the liberty to move into and quarter soldiers in people's private homes, and you have tried to prohibit people from bearing their own arms to protect their rights so that they are powerless against your armed power. These injustices must also stop. In other words, you do not preempt a private home for a barracks—in fact, you do not even for a moment deprive anyone of his private property without due process of law, and you do not prohibit the citizen from bearing his own arms.

"These are a few of the principles which the government is to bear in mind and respect the validity thereof. I think we can live in a peaceful atmosphere if you live by these rules. To insure integrity the lines of power and authority are balanced so that the people will be involved in decisions. In other words the lawmakers are elected to serve for a limited number of years, and your executive officers will also receive their positions by election of the people. Now the people are in the ascendancy and the lines of power and authority are channeled to you from the people rather than the reverse. The state and every governmental entity therefore exists by virtue of its people under our democracy."

In order for government to remember the above mentioned specific prohibitions leveled by the Constitution and escape the temptation to trespass on prohibited areas of activity, and to fill the gap between elections, the people are given an independent judiciary so that the requirements of the Constitution will be guarded, and applied to each individual case no matter who is involved or what the situation happens to be.

Below we list the fundamental rules of American criminal justice:

1. The accused must be informed of the nature of the accusation against him, and this must be specific and clear enough to enable him to prepare a defense.

2. Except in capital cases, generally limited to murder in the first degree, kidnapping and treason, the accused must be allowed his freedom from jail pending trial by putting up a bond guaranteeing his appearance in court when required, and the bail cannot be excessive.

3. The accused is entitled to a speedy trial.

4. The trial must be public.

5. The accused is entitled to an impartial jury chosen from the locality where the crime was committed, the district being previously ascertained by law.

6. The accused is entitled to a lawyer upon his arrest and at all stages to aid him in his defense.

7. The accused must be afforded due process of law. This means fair treatment and a fair trial in every particular.

8. The accused is presumed to be innocent and this presumption rests with him throughout the trial unless and until it is overcome by evidence sufficient to prove his guilt.

9. The burden of proof is at all times on the state and the accused need not prove his innocence.

10. Each and every one of the material elements of the charge must be proven by the state by clear and convincing evidence beyond a reasonable doubt.

11. The accused cannot be forced to take the witness stand and testify either for or against himself. Nor can a pre-trial confession be used against the accused unless it was absolutely voluntary. Ours is the accusatorial and not the inquisitorial system.

12. The accused has the right to confront the witnesses against him face to face, and to have those witnesses cross-examined by his lawyer.

13. The accused has the right to compulsory process whereby witnesses in his behalf may be forced to come into court and testify.

14. Evidence against the accused may not be gathered by unreasonable search and seizure of his private home and effects and then admitted into evidence against him in court.

15. There shall be only one trial against a person for each offense.

16. The accused has the right to appeal to a higher court.

17. If an accused cannot afford a lawyer or the costs of an appeal,

then the state must pay these costs and supply the accused with a lawyer and an appeal.

18. If a person is convicted of a crime he shall not be subjected to cruel and unusual punishment.

19. Any person detained against his will has the right to petition the court for writ of habeas corpus to determine whether his detention is lawful and he shall be heard promptly on such petition.

20. No accused shall be found guilty by a bill of attainder. This is an act of a legislative body directed against a particular person seeking to find him guilty of a crime without a trial in court.

21. No accused shall be tried, convicted or punished under an ex post facto law, that is, the crime and the punishment must be defined and published by the legislature prior to its commission and the legislature cannot enter after an act by the accused and define a crime to fit the act.

Lawyers who specialize in criminal cases occupy a difficult position in society. They perform a fine service by bringing to life our constitutional limitations on governmental power and making real the rights we would all demand if we were accused of a crime. Yet many lawyers feel that the public fails to sort out the difference between this high service and guilty association with the criminal element. The public is probably entitled to something better than this presumption of ignorance.

A crime is what the legislature says it is, and in its responsibility under the police power of the state to protect public health, safety, welfare and morals, the legislature may, within reason, designate practically anything as a crime. But this does not mean that fifty different states have deviated in as many different directions. No. All states (except Louisiana) have inherited the English common law; the criminal code is a statutory codification of the common law. There are variations, of course, but the similarities far outweigh the dissimilarities between the states.

The word "crime" is defined as a violation of a public law, in the commission of which there is a joint operation of act and intention. With few exceptions, the government must prove both the act and the specific intent to do the thing prohibited. Larceny, for example, is the taking away of the property of another with intent permanently to deprive the owner of his property. The taking alone would not convict a person. Proof of specific intent to steal must be present.

Some crimes may be committed by criminal negligence. An example of this is manslaughter, or negligent homicide. In this there is no specific intent to take the life of another. But if a person is so reckless, willful and wanton as to do an act which might well kill another, and does, like driving 90 miles an hour in trying to evade a policeman, for example, then the law makes this a crime, based only on the act and the general intent to do the reckless, willful and wanton thing.

Another type of crime which requires only a general intention to do what is prohibited, but not specific intent to commit a crime is statutory rape, in which a man over eighteen years of age has illicit sexual intercourse with a girl under eighteen years of age. Assuming she has consented to the act, and the man's intention was not one of forcible rape, yet the law deprives her of the power to consent until she is eighteen years old, and therefore makes his act a crime. It is still a crime if the man did not know she was under age.

In no case does proof of the act alone suffice to prove the crime. At least some evidence of a mental process showing intention must be presented. This evidence can be shown either by an expression of intention or by facts and circumstances surrounding the commission of the act. In other words, a mentally competent person cannot be heard to say that he did not intend to do what he actually did do. Intent is often presumed from proof of the act itself.

This is the morality of criminal law. The moral proposition is that man is a free acting agent, capable of and responsible for controlling and directing his own actions through the exercise of mental processes. Therefore, one type or another of criminal insanity or mental incapability forms a part of every criminal law system, for if one does not possess a mind to control his actions, then the moral proposition that one should control his actions cannot apply.

A man is charged with the felony of assault with a deadly weapon. It appears that he stabbed a co-patron of a tavern with a table knife. When he appears in court, his lawyer shows that he was so drunk he did not know what he was doing. He is acquitted because the state failed to prove the felonious intent to injure another person with a dangerous weapon. The legislature learns of this lapse and other instances in which persons are acquitted on the drunkenness defense and it passes a law which states: "Drunkenness shall not be an excuse for any crime." The State Supreme Court then applies the older, higher and more fundamental law that intention must form a part of every crime and thus waters down the "no excuse" pronouncement of the legislature. The Court presents a statement something like this: "The jury may be properly instructed that a statute of the state provides that drunkenness shall be no excuse for a crime, but they should be instructed further that evidence of drunkenness may be considered by them on the question of whether or not the accused, at the time of the commission of the crime, could form the criminal intent required."

A person pleads not guilty by reason of insanity. The jury is then instructed that an accused shall not be held responsible for his criminal acts if at the time of the commission of the act he was so diseased of mind that he could not distinguish between right and wrong, or, being able to so distinguish, could not refrain from the wrong. This test states the moral proposition that a person is accountable for what he can control and not accountable for what he cannot control.

Psychiatrists and social workers approach the legislature and convince some committee that the right-wrong test is not right. These professional practitioners win their point if the legislature says that a person should not be convicted of a crime even if he could have consciously refrained, if he happens to be suffering some disease or defect of mind which caused him somehow to do the prohibited thing. It is said that such a test of criminal insanity would be easier to administer. But what is overlooked is that the entire purpose of criminal law is to force people to do right—both sick people and well people. "I am sick" is already the excuse for too many things in this world, and there is grave doubt whether the would-be reformers of criminal insanity law fully understand and appreciate that they are meddling with a supporting cornerstone of society's structure.

Crimes are divided into felonies and misdemeanors. A felony is a serious crime, the punishment for which may be imprisonment in the penitentiary or death. Misdemeanors constitute all crimes that are not felonies. Running through a red light, for instance, is a misdemeanor, because the penalty is a fine or a county jail sentence, or both, and a person cannot be sent to the penitentiary if convicted.

What does the law do with the kingpin in a criminal venture, the fellow who plans a robbery and then sends part of the gang out to commit it? The mastermind is in his own apartment when the act occurs. Did he commit robbery? Yes. He is an accessory before the fact. He is charged as a principal and is subjected to the same or even stiffer penalty than the actual perpetrators. An accessory before the fact is one who aids, abets, assists, counsels or advises in the commission of a crime.

An accessory during the fact is one who, seeing a crime being committed, stands by without interfering or doing anything to prevent it. One is not required to risk life or injury to prevent a crime, therefore, one who passively views a crime of violence is seldom charged as an accessory. But if a bank teller sees another teller stealing the bank's money and fails to report it, he may be charged with a criminal failure to interfere. This is a misdemeanor. The accessory, during the fact, cannot be charged as a principal perpetrator of the offense of stealing as he could be if he had counseled and aided in the crime.

An accessory after the fact is a person who, knowing a crime has been committed, either harbors the criminal or conceals his knowledge from the authorities. This is also a misdemeanor and is distinctly different from the principal offense.

If two people get together and break into a building with the idea of stealing some money, they both will be charged with two different crimes—one, burglary, and two, conspiracy. The crime of conspiracy exists when two or more persons agree, conspire or cooperate to do an unlawful act. Both persons could be convicted of both crimes, or the crime of burglary and not the crime of conspiracy. But if one is acquitted of the crime of conspiracy, then the other must also be acquitted, unless there may have been a third person with whom he conspired. Two or more people are always

Crime and Punishment • 249

required for conspiracy. Likewise, two people can conspire to commit a crime, and then never actually commit it, or be apprehended before they commit it. However, the conspiracy itself is a crime and the persons may be convicted for the act of entering into the conspiracy even if the offense was not actually perpetrated. Conspiracy to commit a felony is in itself a felony. Conspiracy to commit a misdemeanor is a misdemeanor.

As in intent, proof of conspiracy concerns itself with mental processes. These can be proven directly by statements of the conspirators overheard by people who subsequently become witnesses, such as "Let's go break into that building." "O. K." Or conspiracy may be proven circumstantially, that is, if two people act in concert to commit a crime, this in itself is evidence that they conspired, although not conclusive evidence.

A crime may be committed by intentionally doing a prohibited act, or by intentionally failing to do a required act. It is a crime to fail to file an income tax return or to fail to support your children.

A single state may have on its books two hundred or more different crimes including traffic offenses and offenses for practicing various controlled occupations without a license, plus the classic crimes of murder, robbery, rape, burglary, larceny, forgery, perjury, etc. Crimes fall within the following classifications: (1) crimes against persons; (2) crimes against property; (3) crimes against the administration of justice; (4) regulatory crimes. A person is conclusively presumed to know the law since "Ignorance of the law is no excuse." It is surprising that more people do not get into difficulties considering their heavy responsibility of citizenship. Every crime committed is not reported and prosecuted since someone has to register a complaint and the evidence has to be gathered.

The District Attorney does not ordinarily seek out prosecutions but merely makes himself available for complaints from police officers or private citizens. Anyone can sign a criminal complaint, and in most states the District Attorney can file a criminal case merely over his signature, a grand jury indictment not being required.

One of the most constant and prevalent problems of any District Attorney's office is to avoid the use of state power to collect private debts. People come to his office with any matter that is tinged with criminality and insist that a case be filed. If they can achieve this, they will then use the threat of the penitentiary to force a person to pay them money due. When they get the money, they want to drop the criminal case they initiated. However, this is not their choice to make and they themselves may incur a criminal charge for the reason that: It is a crime to take payment from anyone with the promise not to press a criminal charge as consideration for the payment. This crime against the administration of justice is called "compounding a felony."

But the most interesting and problematical factor on the prosecution's side of the criminal law is how to reach the big operator and at the same time protect the small. Most people who become seriously involved with the criminal law are the unintelligent who because of poor environment and limited natural gifts blunder their way into trouble. May it be said to their credit that most of them are realistic and manly about their plight. Their stupidity lies in failure to find a lawful pursuit and outlet for their energies.

By the same token, a great deal of the work involved in criminal apprehension and investigation takes no more talent than to be able to see the obvious. The person who blunders his way into crime as readily blunders his way into conviction. He is the perpetual amateur. The penitentiary is full of people who submitted to the natural temptation to confess. You know that even though a person may not be forced to confess or forced to testify against himself in court, he may very readily waive his constitutional right by voluntarily telling all. If he does this then his confession can be used against him in court.

The many stringent limitations on the state's power to prosecute are set up to protect the innocent and to convict the guilty. They delineate a balance between the rights of the public, power of the state and the rights of individual. They necessarily view the accused as a comparatively weak and defenseless prototype, and indeed he usually fits the pattern.

What of the exceptional criminal? The problem is not unlike that of the exceptional child. The schools plan studies for a prototype which encompasses perhaps 95% of all children, but the very bright or the very backward child simply does not fit the mold.

The backward criminal is convicted with sure fire regularity; the exceptionally resourceful and intelligent criminal usually gets himself regularly acquitted. Remarkably, the lone criminal with a high I Q does not always fit into the high exceptional category. The reason for this is that since he is usually a loner he does not have the resources to confound the prosecution. The resourceful criminal is the organized, gentleman-type criminal. He operates the rackets and profits from vice as if it were a business. If he is charged with a crime, he hires the finest lawyer and makes available vast funds for his successful defense. To such a criminal, our criminal system, and particularly the jury trial requirement, presents many opportunities to frustrate the prosecution.

The burden of proof is always the responsibility of the state. Furthermore, every person on the jury has prejudices and weaknesses which can be used by the criminal's lawyers, to the advantage of his defense. An articulate and skillful defense attorney can usually convince at least some members of a jury that proof "beyond a reasonable doubt" means much more than it actually does. A prosecution witness, for example, may be unable to state precisely what time of the day he saw a certain occurrence, a human (and immaterial) discrepancy in the state's proof (in a sense adding credibility to the state's case because it is normal to have only a general and not a precise idea of time). This factor in the hands of a skilled advocate can be a fatal defect: "The witness is not sure of the time, so how can he be so positive it was my client he saw running out of the jewelry store?"

The federal government at times aids the states in coping with the exceptional criminal. Perhaps the racketeer may be smart enough successfully to evade state prosecution and then find himself involved in a case of income tax evasion. The Federal Bureau of Investigation has seldom suffered bad public relations because its agents are well trained and well paid.

The major function of the criminal law is to govern the ascertainment of guilt or innocence. Punishment of the guilty is almost a separate subject, but a fascinating one.

Criminal punishment in America is limited generally to: (1) imprisonment; (2) death; (3) fine; (4) loss of privileges such as the right to vote, the right to hold office, the right to certain freedoms. The Constitution prevents "cruel and unusual" punishment, and this excludes everything except the above categories.

Regardless of the philosophy behind punishment, one premise is unassailable, that offenders of equal guilt should suffer approximately equal punishment. In some of the courts in the early frontier of the West, the penalty was within the discretion of the jury with no guidelines set down. An unusual punishment appears in the records of an 1861 Miners' Court in Central City, Colorado, which shows that a jury of six men was impaneled to try one John Rush on the charge of burglary. When the defendant was found guilty by the jury, he was sentenced by the jury to have the right half of his head shaved, the left half of his beard shaved, and to leave the mountains within twenty-four hours.

As the law progressed, sentencing was removed from the province of the jury to the judge. In a typical state the penalty for robbery, for example, is from two years to life. The judge does not rely solely on the evidence given at the trial, but is supplied with a carefully compiled personal history of the convicted man. Since the judge is trained and experienced, this is supposed to assure a proper sentence and some uniformity of sentences. However, no matter how qualified judges are, they differ from each other just as people in any other group differ. Each judge tends to emphasize as being important different factors in the crime as well as the punishment which fits it.

In one case there were three men varying in age from twenty-four to twenty-six. All had juvenile records and in their adulthood each was previously convicted of serious crimes. This youthful trio went on a crime spree across the country. They were finally apprehended while committing the robbery of a gasoline filling station. The men were charged with the same crime but separately tried before different judges because of the statute which holds that if one co-defendant confesses, and the other does not admit to the confession, then the persons charged are entitled to separate trials. All three were convicted. Within a period of four days in the same city, before different judges, one man received a sentence of from 20 to 30 years in the state penitentiary; another from 8 to 10 years; the third 2 to 3 years. Each of these judges was honest and sincere, but greatly divergent in his ideas about sentencing. How the penitentiary warden can control the morale of inmates with this type of disparity in meting out sentences—is a mystery to everyone including the warden.

Sentencing by the indeterminate sentence system used in California removes discretion from the court. If an offender is convicted of a certain crime he is sent to the penitentiary. A professional board periodically studies the convict's entire record and determines when he may be ready to return to society. The nature of the offense committed is one of the many factors taken into consideration. This more humane system affords better protection to society. Experienced penal officials know sooner or later there comes to almost every convict an awareness of having offended society by his crime and a sincere resolution to reform. It is salutary to have an official in the penitentiary endowed with sufficient discretion to take advantage of this glimmer of awareness on the part of a prisoner before it recedes. If a sentence has been set years ago by a judge who could not foresee the convicted man's reformation, then all concerned are bound into an unfortunate mold which does not fit the reality of the particular situation of such an individual.

Organized society needs no prodding to protect itself from criminals. It does so by instinct, but always needs the help of its best talents to do it well. The natural tendency is to over-react against crime, yet the criminal law should not be a system of licensed revenge. It must be resourceful enough to convict the exceptional and yet humane enough to protect the innocent and to help the erring victim of environment and circumstances.

It has been truly said that a civilization is measured by the manner in which it treats its criminal offenders. Every failure in the criminal law, either on the side of over or under enforcement, is society's failure and every success is society's success.

Chapter Fifteen

HOME, SWEET HOME

Land represents more wealth to more people than anything else in the world. The reason for this is its inherent usefulness. In law, land (and everything more or less permanently attached to it) is known as real property. Everything else which is owned is known as personal property. The term "real" comes from the nature of legal actions about land, that is, a person suing in court claiming some right to land wants the real property itself, and not money or some substitute therefor.

Real estate law reflects the immutable characteristics of land itself. Every piece of land in the world is unique, immovable and indestructible. Land has four dimensions: (1) East-West; (2) North-South; (3) Up and down; and (4) Time. We are inclined to take the term "ownership" for granted and think of it as absolutely private. This is largely true as to personal property. You can buy, use, preserve or destroy anything you like, but land ownership is less absolute. It has rights, privileges and duties. Land is held by title, which is the evidence you have of your ownership. Newlyweds, Joyce and Dick Stark, agree to buy a new home and take title to their home several weeks later. In the meantime, all arrangements are made for the "closing of title." The arrangements may be complicated or simple, depending upon the case, but the essentials are: (1) the buyer must be supplied with evidence of the seller's right to sell; (2) the land must be described; and (3) the financial arrangements must be made.

Every county maintains a recorder's office where evidence of ownership of the land in the county is maintained as a public record. This has two major purposes: (1) to prevent land disputes, and (2) to keep track of ownerships for the purpose of taxation. Every piece of land has a history of ownership since the beginning of its occupancy, and public records are perpetually kept to show every ownership. Title is transferred by a deed which must be in writing and acknowledged before a Notary Public. The requirement that the deed be recorded is enforced by the stipulation the courts will not recognize the buyer's right to the land unless his title is recorded. An unrecorded transfer will be enforced between the buyer and the seller, but not as to anyone else. The writing requirement is set up by what is known as the statute of frauds, which holds that no oral sale of real estate is allowed. This is to prevent confusion and fraudulent claims to an interest in land. The public record controls so there can be no dispute as to who owns what.

Modern photocopy techniques have aided greatly in keeping the public records which are strictly chronological, with every paper filed going in the volume at a certain page. In former times, every instrument used to be laboriously copied by hand; now they are photographed, and some counties use microfilm. Titles and abstract companies utilize the public record and perform a service by keeping track of what happens to every parcel of ground. These firms make up what is called an abstract of title, which is a sheaf of papers showing everything that has happened to any particular piece of ground since the beginning. They either sell the abstract to the owner so that he can present it to the buyer and the buyer has his attorney examine it, or the abstract company examines the document itself and sells a title insurance policy guaranteeing that the title is good. The abstract must show an unbroken chain of title, and every link in the chain must tie in securely with every other link. It is the attorney's duty to determine if there is some possible break in the chain which could cause difficulty.

In the case of Joyce and Dick's property, we would find that it was first owned by a government—which government would depend on where it is located. The land in the thirteen original colonies was owned by the King of England, and he granted it to his various subjects who came to the new world. When the United States was formed, the private ownerships that existed at that time were, under a long recognized rule of international law, recognized by the new government, and whatever vacant or unoccupied land still existed within the colonies belonged to the original states. But as to the rest of the United States, with the exception of Texas, the federal government itself took title to all vacant and unoccupied land as it was received from other governments or merely by claim. Part of the land was granted by the United States to state governments for schools and other purposes, and to railroads to encourage their development, and other parts were homesteaded, granted or sold to private individuals. Much public land still remains in the name of the United States and the various states. When Texas became a republic, it also recognized such private ownerships as had existed under the Mexican government, but this republic took title to all vacant and unoccupied land, then when Texas became a part of the United States, the state government retained ownership of the land. Thus the first entry in an abstract will show a grant by a government to a private individual, then every other entry will show succeeding sales or inheritances or transfers of title down through the years.

Basically the examining attorney's job is to see that every right, title or interest in the land that once existed was somehow extinguished. Otherwise, there always exists some possibility that a person who once owned the land, or his heirs, might come back and claim ownership. Proper title examination requires great technical knowledge, not only of the present day requirements for transfer of realty, but the requirements as they existed at all stages in the past. There are endless possibilities to find defects in a title, but just one example would be that Joyce and Dick's lot was, sixty years ago, part of a farm which was bought by one J. Walsh. Ten years later it was sold by one Jay Walsh. The question then is whether J. Walsh and Jay Walsh were one and the same person. If not, conceivably the heirs of J. Walsh could still claim they owned the land. This might constitute a "cloud" on the title, requiring a title suit to correct the defect. Such a lawsuit follows a special procedure designed for just such problems. The present owner is named as plaintiff and all names that can be picked out of the abstract of title and all heirs and descendants of those people who can be discovered by a reasonable inquiry are named as defendants. In these suits it is often impossible to find anyone who can be personally handed the suit papers, so it is permissible to publish notice of the suit in a newspaper and to include as defendants, in effect, all the rest of the world. Thus, say Joyce and Dick Stark were buying the home from Jill and Terry Barr, with the Happy Homes Realty Company acting merely as sales agent. Before Joyce and Dick's attorney would approve the title, he would require that the Barrs correct the defect. The suit caption would read:

IN THE DISTRICT COURT

Terry J. Barr and Jill T. Barr,

    Plaintiffs,

vs.

Jay Walsh, J. Walsh, Claude Walsh, Henry Walsh, Susan Garbotski, and all unknown persons who claim any interest in the subject matter of this action,

    Defendants.

Quiet title Action.

The attorney included the names of Claude, Henry and Susan inasmuch as his investigation determined they were the three children of J. Walsh. The action claims the plaintiffs are the owners of the real estate, that the defendants may claim some ownership and ask judgment to be entered quieting title in the plaintiffs, and barring the defendants named and everyone else in the world from claiming any interest in the real estate. If no one answers the publication within thirty days then the Barrs can secure a judgment, clearing their title and forever excluding the defendants or anyone else from challenging it. At this point of the proceedings the Barrs are in a position to convey to the Starks clear title to the property.

Courts have few jurisdictional problems when real estate is involved because they have power over the land within the territory of their jurisdiction. The source laws of real estate are: (1) the Constitution of the United States, particularly the Fifth Amendment, which explicitly recognizes ownership of private property; (2) the

Constitution of the State; (3) statutes, local, state and federal; (4) the common law of England; and (5) court-made law. Each state establishes its own property law system, and within the confines of the Constitutional requirements, which basically state that "no private property shall be taken for public or private use without just compensation," the legislature can govern and control property as it sees fit by enactment of statutes. In most states real estate lawyers have encouraged legislation which will obviate hypertechnical requirements in examinations of titles, so that very old defects or ones of minor significance may be ignored.

We have inherited much of our terminology, both in real property and the law of inheritance, from western Europe, where for many centuries the feudal system of government prevailed. Kings owned all land. Private individuals possessed land in exchange for military services to the king. This arrangement was called "feudal tenure." The word "tenure" is a cousin to our word tenant, or a renter who has the right to temporary possession.

The word "landlord" refers to the feudal lords, appointed by the King to govern particular territories. The lords received power over the royal land in exchange for which they rendered their services to the King by protecting the King's domain from invaders and usurpers. In their turn, the landlords gave to others called "tenants" the right to possess smaller parcels in exchange for the tenants' services to the lord in fighting the King's feuds. As the centuries passed, people demanded more and more rights as against the King. "Feudal tenures" were therefore bought and sold and by inheritance passed on from generation to generation finally maturing into actual ownership rights. The European system of feudal tenure was never known in America since it was abolished by law in England prior to any substantial American colonization.

A piece of land can be designated as a relatively flat area on the surface of the earth, or it can be regarded in its true sense, as a three-dimensional geometric form beginning at a point in the center of the earth and extending up to the sky. In law, an owner of land owns everything below and everything above. This concept has vegetated a number of interesting legal problems, for the reason that there are aspects about land not nearly as solid and as immovable as the pure, geometric description may suggest. Winds blow, crops grow, airplanes fly, oil, gas and water flow, and wild animals do not respect property lines.

Who has the right to kill, to keep or to butcher for the table a wild deer that runs across a person's property? In the first place, the state has the right to govern where, when, and under what circumstances any wild life may be taken. Therefore a property owner must abide by the state game laws. A municipality or a state has the power to govern where, when and under what circumstances a gun may be fired. If it is the hunting season and you shoot and kill a deer on the land of Farmer MacGregor, he can claim the deer, for he owns everything on his land.

If the tree which grows on your neighbor's land obstructs your view of the beautiful lake, unless there are zoning restrictions or restrictive covenants against such trees obstructing the view, you have no right against the tree. If, however, your neighbor's hedge overlaps onto your property, do you, then, have the right to cut it down? Yes, inasmuch as that part of his property is actually on your property and you have rights over such portion of his hedge. If your neighbor decides to spray-paint his house and the wind blows some of the paint onto your car, you can sue him for this because he has used his land in such a way that it caused damage to you, his neighbor. The applicable maxim in law is: Every person must use his own land in a way which does not damage the peaceful use and possession of another's land. The basic law involved here is that of nuisance, which is as complicated as the infinite number of fact situations which may conceivably arise. A primary example of nuisance in relation to property ownership: A man buys a lot and builds his house. Next door another man buys a lot and erects a glue factory, the operation of which produces noxious odors. In such a case the law will require the factory owner to cease and desist such operation or operate in such a way that noxious odors are not emitted.

What rights do you as a property owner have against airplanes flying overhead? This situation touches on the province of the United States government which has for the purpose of air traffic control declared itself sovereign owner of air space for normal and necessary flight patterns over the United States. This is considered by the courts as a "reasonable governmental limitation" on your ownership of property. However, an airplane may still be a nuisance and if continual flying overhead disturbs the peaceful use of your property, you may get an injunction against the airline, the city, the pilot or whoever is responsible to cease and desist or get damages for the nuisance.

Water law, and oil-and-gas law are two separate and voluminous legal topics. Needless to say since the law recognizes what it calls the "fugitive and migratory" nature of fluids and gases, it contrives to cope equitably with the many obvious problems arising while at the same time recognizing private ownership not only as the right of the owner to "peaceful use and possession" but the right likewise to profit from "valuable substances found in or on the land."

In addition to the general law of nuisance, there are many both public and private restrictions and controls in regard to the use of land which not only restrict but also protect land-owners. It is of interest to note that by unanimous consent, land-owners (in a designated area) may set up restrictive covenants to designate what may or may not be done for all time in the future on the land. This action is often taken by one individual who owns a large tract of land which is subsequently divided and subdivided into many ownerships. If the covenants are "reasonable, practicable and constitutional" they will be enforced by the courts and can be set aside only by the unanimous consent of all the land-owners of such a tract. Many attractive residential areas are pre-planned and controlled in this manner. There is nevertheless one covenant which cannot be enforced by the courts. This is the creation of a restriction against certain races purchasing land since it has been held unconstitutional for the courts to lend their governmental power to enforcement of such a stipulation.

In the cities of our nation, public control of land use is extremely comprehensive. Part of this control is encompassed in building and use codes which provide for minimum safety standards in construction, wiring, plumbing, etc. Use restrictions, which include smoke control, also affirmatively provide for rules on trash disposal and snow removal from sidewalks.

We now reach the modern law of zoning which is one of the most engrossing of subjects. A city is divided into districts and each district comprising the whole has certain restrictions as to the type of use, size of buildings and density of population. Zoning laws are absolutely necessary for proper city planning for the reason that metropolitan real estate in its normal development assumes such amazing economic proportions. It is only natural that a tract of land which is zoned for business use will be perhaps ten times as valuable as the identical land if designated for residential use. A person who is in business is primarily interested in profit whereas residential owners are primarily interested in maintaining the residential character of their neighborhood. Consequently, the integrity and good judgment of the city fathers are continually challenged by these conflicting interests of a city's citizens which resolve into zoning disputes.

In residential areas density of occupation is controlled by requiring a minimum size building lot for a single family dwelling, with requirements that the front, back and side setback lines of the building be a certain number of feet. In apartment house zoning, the height of a building is restricted on a particular size lot, which prevents apartment houses from being too close to each other with no air space between.

Some of our cities have exerted efforts to prevent density of construction in office buildings, by requiring that parking space be provided in ratio with the square feet of office space built. Zoning on all of these points is pitted not only against economic pressures but against legal obstructions as well.

Very often a world traveler returning to the United States extols the city planning of many of the handsome cities of Europe, their pure, symmetrical beauty as viewed particularly from the air in comparison to the hodge-podge that many of our American cities have become. He wonders why America, which is a wealthy country, has many unsightly cities while a comparatively underprivileged country such as Spain for example is neat and orderly, at least in its modern planning of new construction in its cities. The answer to that is: Our free economic and political system has some deficiencies in relation to the purities of planning.

Zoning has had a difficult constitutional history from its inception for the reason that the Constitution abhors the idea of confiscation. Government cannot unreasonably restrict private use or, in the furtherance of its public projects for highways, parks and other improvements, take land without just compensation to the owners. Thus the pure, neat and clean ideas of planners are continually being opposed in the courts. The over-all plan may appear to be good, but when a private property owner is subjected to some economic disadvantage he objects vociferously that it is not "for the public good" as claimed by the government because it is confiscatory to his property. As often as not he wins his case in court.

While government may take private property for the public use of highways and other necessaries, each property owner is entitled to a jury trial as to determination of the amount he will be paid for his land.

Would it be more simple and less expensive under dictatorship where such problems could be peremptorily handled? Probably— yes. The price we pay for many of our freedoms and for our incentive system of private land ownership is a degree of complication in settling of protests between private land ownership and the government in our planning. Recently in a prosperous American city, zoning officials determined that, since there were no subway or other effective rapid transit services, the downtown area should be developed with sufficient parking area to allow reasonable ease of driving in and out. They therefore stipulated: parking space will have to be provided commensurate with the amount of office space in buildings erected. The Supreme Court of the state held that such planning was not within the "police power of the state" in that it had "no reasonable relationship to the public health, morals, welfare and safety." Taking advantage of the decision, the business community immediately constructed many skyscrapers in close proximity to each other without providing parking lots or parking buildings to service the needs of occupants and visitors to these great buildings. The reason for this serious omission was purely a matter of mathematics and not because the builders were unaware that such parking space would be direly needed. Land costs so much per square foot. The more office space provided on a piece of land, the greater the profit. Two or three years later, however, the law of economics confounded the city planners. The parking business itself became so profitable businessmen began to demolish old buildings to provide the parking required.

The result—a more attractive and useful downtown than the fondest dream of the zoning planners.

Real estate has always borne a heavy, and sometimes inequitable tax burden. The State has jurisdiction over all of the privately owned land within its borders and sets up a system of assessment. Every County has an Assessor, either an elected or appointed official, whose duty is to set an assessed valuation on every piece of real estate. Thereupon the State allows the various local governmental units the power to impose a tax of a certain percentage of the assessed valuation. In some instances, the State itself will impose a real estate tax, requiring local officials to collect it, and to pay it over to the State. Real estate taxes are termed "ad valorem"; the amount paid is termed the "mill levy."

If you own a house worth $20,000, the market value is only one factor for the assessor. He uses a comprehensive formula set up by the State which takes into consideration your lot size, the number of square feet in your house, the number of bathrooms, the type of construction, type of roof, garage space, and numerous other factors. You may find that your assessed valuation seems to bear little relationship to the market value. Perhaps it will be $6,000. Then the State authorizes the City to assess a mill levy. Since a mill is one-thousandth part of a dollar, the City assesses 40 mills, which would mean that you would pay $40 for each one thousand dollars of assessed valuation or $240. The School Board imposes another 30 mills, so you pay an additional $180 for schools. Then the State assesses another 5 mills. This costs you $30. You then have a 75 mill levy on your house and a $450 tax bill.

Every city home buyer should be acutely aware of location, not only because this is a major factor in pleasure, utility and continued value of the home, but because so many of our cities have outgrown their boundaries. Many residential areas are across the border in neighboring counties; county governments often fail to provide good metropolitan services. The explanation for this is that the county system of government was originally planned for a basically agrarian and town type of development, which plays havoc with good city planning.

This costs many people a great deal of money in taxes without receiving any real benefit in return. It is possible that the owners across the street from your house, which has a 75 mill levy on it as above described, might find that their house and land is in another county and they are required to pay 100 mills, or $600 tax analyzed as follows: School 35 mills; County 22 mills, Recreational District 6 mills; Sewer District 8 mills; Fire District 5 mills; Water District 13 mills; State 5 mills; Special Improvement District 6 mills. And they may well wonder what benefit the tax dollars bring because they see little, if any, evidence of services out of these small governmental units.

To take up the matter again of Joyce and Dick Stark buying a home, they will have to be sure of what they are receiving for their money before they pay it for a deed. A clear chain of title is only one of the several factors with which they must be concerned. Another is the description to their property. This should be clearly spelled out before they sign any contract to buy and a careful double check is always in order. Land description is a study in itself, and the methods used vary widely. The idea is to reduce to paper the actual space and shape that a piece of ground covers on the surface of the earth.

In the time of George Washington, who was a land surveyor by profession as well as a very large land owner, and even before his time, land in the eastern seaboard area was described by metes and bounds. Some landmark, such as a rock or a stream, or even a tree, would be selected and the description would wander in various directions from landmark to landmark until an enclosed area was achieved. Many of these descriptions still prevail, but they have inherent weaknesses, mainly due to human error. Adjoining properties often do not join, or sometimes they overlap.

On May 20, 1785, the Continental Congress of the United States passed a law establishing a system for the survey of the public lands of the United States. The Federal Survey has been of incalculable value in avoiding confusion and contention in development of the country. For the purpose of land description, this dissected the country into great squares six miles in width which were called townships. Each township contains thirty-six sections, a section being one mile square, or 640 acres. Sections are again divided into half-sections and quarter-sections, a quarter-section being 160 acres, which was the typical homestead. This survey explains the geometrical patterns one finds in the rural parts of central and western United States, and the section lines are still perpetually used to describe lands.

Joyce and Dick's property is probably described even more simply than by section or quarter-section lines. It may be as follows: "Lots 7 and 8, Block 4, Hillside Heights, according to the recorded plat thereof." What does this mean? At some time in the past, a real estate developer owned perhaps 25 acres of land. He desired to divide it up into appropriate home sites. To facilitate this, the State or the County or City where the land is located, allows him to file a plat which is simply a map, showing where the acreage is located according to section lines, and laying out lots, blocks, streets and intersections with measurements on the map. In this way, the plat is a perpetual reference to the property lines, otherwise the property descriptions would have to be spelled out in detail:

> "A parcel of land in Springfield County, Town of Hillside, located within the North East 1/4 of the South West 1/4 of Section 28, Township 4 North, Range 42 West of the Fifth Principal Meridian, described as follows: Starting at a point on the East line of Section 28, 1843 feet North of the South West corner of said Section 28; thence East 1522 feet to a point known as the point of beginning; thence North 135 feet; thence West 94 feet; thence South 135 feet; thence East 94 feet to the point of beginning."

But even when the lots are simply spelled out by reference to a plat, it is usually advisable to have a survey made to show that all structures conform to property lines, zoning and covenant standards.

The maxim, "Caveat emptor" (the buyer beware), pertains in real estate more strongly than in any other type of property. The buyer assumes ownership which is subject to all restrictions or burdens on the property that are indicated from the public record or from a reasonable inspection. Ordinarily, the buyer cannot return and claim something is wrong with the house or the land because he is presumed to have been aware of everything about his purchase, both good and bad. But there are two major exceptions to this. One is hidden defects, and another is wilful misrepresentation or fraud. The presence of these exceptions is enough to upset any legal transaction. Real estate people are well aware of the difference between fraud and mere sales talk. Fraud has to be a definite misstatement of a fact the intent of which is to (and actually does) motivate the sale. An example: "Have you ever had any trouble with termites?" The seller or his agent answers: "No, never. There are no termites in this country. You couldn't possibly have any trouble like that." One week after the buyer moves in, the floor timbers collapse from termite damage. This would be fraud; the buyer could get his money back. But usual sales talk, which is largely the mere expression of opinions, does not constitute fraud. "This is a lovely neighborhood. You'll be happy in this fine house," etc.

Now about the financial problems. With the exception of their marriage, Joyce and Dick Stark have never made a greater decision in their lives. The prospect of owning a house has a way of exciting one to quick action. There is a firm idea that this particular house will not be there by tomorrow. Many purchase contracts executed by young couples unseasoned in the ways of real estate, are signed in a flurry of excitement engendered by prospective ownership, but there are many factors which neither the buyer nor seller should take for granted. For one thing, the contract may not be a contract at all. Rather, merely an option to buy. This depends entirely upon the wording of the instrument. Unless the purchaser specifically agrees to buy, he can later change his mind by forfeiting his deposit. The deposit is sometimes called "earnest money," and it should be enough to be in earnest. A seller makes a mistake in allowing his property to be tied up with an option. Sometimes these are written with as little as ten dollars down, and the "buyer" can exercise the option perhaps years later. During this period, the property is tied up and any other potential purchaser would have to be turned away.

As a practical matter, purchase contracts are often more binding on the seller than on the buyers. Contingencies of necessity are inserted about the buyers being able to obtain a certain type of loan. There are three common types of mortgage loans: (1) Federal Housing Authority; (2) Veterans Administration; and (3) Conventional. In the first two types, the federal government guarantees the lender that he will not have a heavy loss in case the borrowers fail to pay, and because government moneys are being exposed to a risk, the federal agencies set up rather stringent requirements: the loan is not to be out of proportion to the actual market value of the home; the borrowers are to have sufficient income to make the payments. These loans are popular because the lending institution will require a lesser down payment, inasmuch as they are not taking the whole risk. Veterans loans are the most liberal, often allowing a buyer to move in without any down payment.

Conventional loans are merely a private transaction; banks, however, are controlled in the size of the loan based on the true value of the property. The interest rate on government backed loans is usually lower. It often takes several weeks for all of the procedures required to set up one of the government type loans. This delay may cause a heavy loss to a seller. This is true because during the time a prospective buyer is endeavoring to get a loan lined up the seller must keep up his mortgage payments, taxes and other expenses. If the buyer cannot qualify for the loan because of an insufficient income or some other reason, the seller has to begin all over again. The major problem on any house sale is to find a buyer with enough cash to make a decent down payment.

A seller can experience another grave problem. Many sellers try for a few fitful weeks to sell their own house but they soon find that although they believe real estate brokers charge heavy fees for their service, they perform an important service few people are able to perform by themselves. Before a broker will expend any effort, he must have what is called "a listing." This guarantees him his stake in the sale. It constitutes a contract as binding as any other contract and it is in writing.

The broker asks the seller, "What do you want for your house?" Answer: "$21,500." "Fine," the broker says, as you sign your name to a three months listing. Does this guarantee that you will get $21,500? No. Nor does it mean that the broker will really try to obtain that price. He works on a percentage, perhaps five to ten percent of the sale price, so his desire is to complete a sale, not necessarily at the highest price obtainable, but at any price. If his commission is 6%, and if the house sells at $21,500, the broker receives $1,290. If the house sells at $20,000, he still receives $1,200. Even though his percentage amounts to a great deal of money, it does not make him a large enough stakeholder really to care what the sale price is. Yet while his listing is in force, the seller's expenses go on and neither the seller himself nor any other broker can sell the house.

Also, a broker can sometimes collect a commission even though a sale is not consummated. His duty is to achieve a meeting of the minds between a buyer and a seller. Once he has done this he has earned his commission, and if the parties decide to back out later, he can still collect the fee either out of the deposit put up by the buyer or directly from the seller.

The seller might find himself with other heavy expenses besides the brokerage fee. Sometimes he has to pay a loan fee in order to help the buyer secure the mortgage. This may not seem just, yet that is the way it works. This loan fee might be up to 3% of the mortgage, and if the mortgage amounts to $18,000, for example, it becomes a matter of a $540 expense.

Sometimes a sale can be made without the cost, expense and delay of making a new mortgage. The buyer will "assume" the seller's mortgage and pay the difference between the mortgage and the sale price as down payment. The mortgage company certainly has no objection to this. Why? Because the seller is still obligated on the mortgage and they have acquired a new person who is also obligated. If this is to constitute the deal, the crucial terms are set forth on the day the contract to buy is signed. The language used is of utmost importance. The buyer should try to avoid promising to "assume and agree to pay" the mortgage, but should just agree to take the property "subject to the debt." The seller, on the other hand, would always prefer to have the buyer agree to pay the mortgage. This does not remove the seller's responsibility to the lending company but it does make the buyer jointly obligated.

According to local custom and law, mortgages take different legal form in different parts of the country. However, there are always two parts: (1) a note, and (2) a legal instrument signed by the borrower and recorded in the public records giving the lender a stake in the property so that if the note is not paid then the lender comes into possession of the property.

What is a house? Nobody thinks that the furniture forms a part of the house, yet there are items more or less permanently installed which some people would consider to be a part of the house and some would not. In law, fixtures are a part of the real estate. Clearly, a light fixture, a sink, a tub, a door handle, a screen, a storm door, built-in kitchen appliances, and a cupboard are fixtures. But what about draperies, venetian blinds, television antenna, curtain rods, carpeting and the like? People sometimes wish to make a separate sale of stoves, dishwashers, refrigerators, washing machines and other equipment which are particularly suited to the house in which they are situated. Such items should be written down in advance because personal property is conveyed by a separately made out bill of sale.

Then what about taxes, insurance, water bills and other such constant liabilities? These have to be pro rated to the date of transfer, that is, the seller pays everything while he still owns the place, and the buyer pays everything thereafter.

There are three typical types of deeds: (1) the warranty deed; (2) the quitclaim deed; and (3) a combination of the two, sometimes called a special warranty deed. Buyers should insist on a warranty deed, especially if this is customary in the area. By this, the seller guarantees or warrants that he has the right to sell what he is selling, and will make up any loss to the buyer if there is some mistake about it. By quitclaim deed, on the other hand, the seller merely says, "I relinquish any claim to this property. I am not guaranteeing anything." The special warranty deed is similar to the quitclaim deed except the seller adds a warranty that since the day he has owned the property, he has not done anything to make the title less secure than it was when he came into possession of such title.

Real estate can experience other mishaps besides faulty transfer. For one thing, we have what is known as the "mechanic's lien." The word lien puzzles some people who hear it for the first time. While it is pronounced like l-e-a-n, it does not refer to what the tired ditch digger uses his shovel for. It is a charge against property for some service performed to repair or improve the property. If a plumber comes out to fix your leaky faucet, he can not only make a charge against you, if you do not pay him, he can also make a charge against the property. Liens are filed in the public record. If they are not paid, the property can be sold to pay such liens. This is a note of caution for a buyer inasmuch as plumbers, carpenters and lumbermen have a period of time set by statute, perhaps ninety days up to six months, within which to file their lien. If the house is new, or if recent improvements or repairs have been made, it is entirely possible that a lien could be filed after the transfer of title, even if the public record does not show any such encumbrance at sale time.

The buyer should either obtain a surety bond protecting him against mechanics' liens, or he should inspect all unpaid bills, deduct this amount from the price and see that they are paid himself, or at the very least, he should require the seller to furnish an affidavit that there are no known lien claims against the property and making the seller promise to protect the buyer against any such claims that might be made. With all of these problems, and more, involved for both the buyer and seller, it should be obvious that competent legal counsel is needed at the time of a real estate transaction.

Within the four dimensions of land there are a number of possibilities besides a mere sale of a particularly described piece of land and the improvements on it. How is it, for example, that the telephone poles can run across the back of your lot? This is done by "easement." The telephone company has a limited right to use a portion of your land for a particular purpose. How did they get this right? This is an interest in real estate just as surely as your ownership is; it must have been granted to them by some owner in the past and the grant must also appear as part of the public record, otherwise the telephone company cannot use your land in this way.

What if Farmer Jack owns the property between the road and the property of Farmer George? Jack will not let George drive across his property. Does George have to go twelve miles out of his way to get to town? He does not. George can go to court and enforce "a way of necessity" across Jack's land for the reason that nobody can utilize his own land in such a way as to deprive another of the beneficial use of his land. Will George have to pay Jack for the way of necessity? Yes. The Constitution says that no property will be taken for public or *private* use without just compensation. Does Jack have the whole say on how much will be paid? No. Both George and Jack are entitled to a jury to set the price.

Despite all its limitations, land possession is still true ownership.

Some of the basic principles pertaining to oil drilling illustrate the nature of land ownership better than anything else. Typically a rancher grants an oil "lease" to a company. Here the word "lease" is a misnomer. Actually what the rancher is doing is selling his oil and leasing the right to the oil operator to go on the land in order to recover said oil. As we know, a lease is a rental agreement granting a mere right to temporary possession. Since the land-owner owns everything beneath his land, he can actually separate what is below from what is on the surface and sell it separately.

Similarly, a city lot owner could sell a piece of air space, since he owns everything skyhigh. If a city man builds a tall building and does not want an equally tall building to be constructed next door to his which will block off his windows, he may go to the land owners next door and say, "I'll buy your air space." If a price agreement were reached, the air space or "property" would be described as a "cube," say, commencing 50 feet in the air, going up another 100 feet, and covering the same area as the lot below. Then no skyscraper could be built next door without the permission of the purchaser of this air space. In a similar way the rancher could sell oil rights at all depths between 500 and 5,000 feet below his land to one company, and separate rights to a different company to all oil to be found from 5,000 to 20,000 feet below his land.

Compared to other types of property, land is indeed perpetual and indestructible, and yet there are exceptions to this premise. If oil is taken out, then the land has been destroyed to the extent of the oil removed and it can never be replaced. This is called "wasting," and it is the basis of the controversial oil depletion allowance. Oil producers are allowed a healthy tax deduction because they are using up something that can never be replaced. Of course in a sense, everything is "wasting." You are not "wasting" your time in the usual sense by reading this book, but you are using up your lifetime and you can never replace the time used. Yet it is one of life's injustices that the government does not give you a depletion allowance on your mind and body. Be that as it may, real estate is not only physically unique and valuable but it forms the basis for a large, important and interesting field of law. The more you know about it, the more value and comfort you can derive from its use in your lifetime.

Chapter Sixteen

SUMMING UP

In these pages, you have been in and out of courtrooms, observing the administration of justice. You have learned of the many legal ramifications involved in an accident, you have followed the progress of a murder trial, and have been a spectator in many other cases. As John Selden (1584-1654) English jurist and scholar, wrote over three centuries ago: "Ignorance of the law excuses no man; not that all men know the law, but because 'tis an excuse every man will plead, and no man can tell how to refute him."

Many maxims of the law, its knowledge and philosophy have been reviewed and discussed herein. To concentrate some of the basic facts about jurisprudence, we have included a list of questions and answers of particular value to all interested in the subject of the law as it affects them in the many phases of their lives. Laws are written for your protection and for the protection of others as well, and it is up to you to know and to observe them.

1. Q. What is a court?
    A. An agency of government established to administer justice in specific cases.

2. Q. What is a case?
    A. A lawsuit, a cause or a grievance stated by one party against another wherein a court is asked to use its governmental

power to determine the worthiness of and then enforce the claim stated.

3. Q. What types of cases are there?
   A. Civil and criminal.

4. Q. What is a criminal case?
   A. A charge by the government against one who is said to have committed a crime.

5. Q. What is a crime?
   A. The violation of a statute which defines the prohibited conduct and sets a penalty.

6. Q. What is a statute?
   A. An enactment of the legislature.

7. Q. Who presents a criminal case to court?
   A. The District Attorney or the grand jury on complaint of a citizen.

8. Q. What is a grand jury?
   A. A jury of citizens with power set by law to investigate cases and return indictments.

9. Q. What is an indictment?
   A. A criminal charge presented to a court by a grand jury.

10. Q. What is a petit jury?
    A. A jury of citizens empaneled to try a case.

11. Q. Is a person accused of a crime always entitled to a jury?
    A. Yes.

12. Q. What is a civil case?
    A. Any case not criminal.

13. Q. How does a civil case come to court?
    A. A lawyer presents it by filing a complaint with the clerk.

14. Q. What is a complaint?
    A. A document prepared by a lawyer which states the grievance of his client.

15. Q. Must you have a lawyer to go to court?

A. No. You can plead your own case. This is called pro se—"in your own behalf."

16. Q. Can you appoint anyone besides a lawyer to represent you?
A. No.

17. Q. How does a person know he is being sued?
A. A process server hands him a summons.

18. Q. What is a process server?
A. A person hired to deliver legal papers.

19. Q. What is a summons?
A. A paper stating the name of the court, the names of the parties to the lawsuit, the type of grievance involved, and the date by which it must be answered in court.

20. Q. Who are the parties?
A. The plaintiff and the defendant.

21. Q. Who is the plaintiff?
A. The person making the complaint.

22. Q. Who is the defendant?
A. The person against whom the complaint is made.

23. Q. What happens if the defendant doesn't answer?
A. Default judgment can be ordered against him.

24. Q. How does the defendant answer?
A. By filing his answer with the clerk.

25. Q. What is a judgment?
A. An order of court deciding the outcome of the case.

26. Q. What are the three essential parts of a judgment?
A. (1) findings of fact; (2) conclusions of law, and (3) order.

27. Q. What is a default judgment?
A. One granted for failure of a person to answer.

28. Q. Can a person be sued and not know it?
A. Rarely. Wherever possible, personal service is required. Personal service is always required if a defendant can be found within the jurisdiction of the court.

Summing Up • 275

29. Q. Must a summons be served on the defendant personally?
A. No, it may be served on an adult member of his family or office staff.

30. Q. Where does the court acquire power to grant judgments?
A. From the government of which it is a part.

31. Q. What is the jurisdiction of a court?
A. The geographical area and type of case over which the court has power.

32. Q. How is this power determined?
A. By the constitution and legislation of the government.

33. Q. What is the duty of the court?
A. To determine truth and apply law.

34. Q. How does a court determine truth?
A. By considering evidence—the group of facts relating to a case.

35. Q. Does every trial have a jury?
A. No. The right to a jury may be waived.

36. Q. What are the respective functions of the judge and jury?
A. The judge decides the law and the jury decides the facts.

37. Q. Where are the facts?
A. Knowledge in the minds and memories of people from personal observation or in the form of physical objects.

38. Q. How are the facts presented to court?
A. The people who know the facts become witnesses and testify as to what they know, under oath.

39. Q. Can a witness be compelled to testify?
A. Yes, by being served with a subpoena.

40. Q. What is a subpoena?
A. A court paper issued by the clerk stating when the witness must appear in court.

41. Q. How is a subpoena served?
A. It is handed to the witness by a process server.

42. Q. What if a witness doesn't appear?
    A. He can be jailed or fined, or both, for contempt of court.

43. Q. What is testimony?
    A. Statements made by witnesses under oath in response to questions.

44. Q. What is an oath?
    A. A solemn promise before God to tell the truth.

45. Q. What if a witness does not choose to swear before God?
    A. Then he takes an affirmation where he merely swears and affirms that he will tell the truth.

46. Q. Is the promise of an oath or an affirmation binding?
    A. Yes. Lying under oath is perjury.

47. Q. What can happen to one who commits perjury?
    A. Perjury is a crime subject to penalty—fine or imprisonment or both.

48. Q. Does a witness need to be represented by a lawyer?
    A. No.

49. Q. Is it legal to coach a witness?
    A. It is illegal to encourage a witness to say something that is not true, but it is perfectly proper for a lawyer to prepare a witness by discussing the case and making suggestions as to emphasis, demeanor, and the like.

50. Q. What is subornation of perjury?
    A. A serious criminal offense against the administration of justice consisting of the procurement of a false witness.

51. Q. When may a witness refuse to answer a question?
    A. When the answer might tend to incriminate the witness.

52. Q. What happens if a witness cannot remember exactly what happened?
    A. The witness is only obligated to tell what he honestly remembers.

53. Q. May a witness express an opinion?
    A. Generally the witness acts merely as a conduit of informa-

tion whereby he gathers facts through his senses and then, without comment, relates what he saw, heard and observed. The jury, and not the witness, decides what the facts are. Yet, a witness may express an opinion when there is no other practical way to relate his observations, such as "the car was going fast, I would say about 75 miles per hour." Also expert witnesses may express opinions.

54. Q. What is an expert witness?
    A. A person trained and experienced in a special field of knowledge not common to most people. An expert need not have personal knowledge of the facts of the case but may express opinions based on facts presented to him by questions.

55. Q. Is the jury bound to accept an expert's testimony?
    A. No. The jury can take an expert opinion for what they feel it is worth and may accept or reject it, just as any other witness's testimony.

56. Q. What is law?
    A. A collection of rules.

57. Q. Who makes the rules?
    A. The people.

58. Q. How are the rules made?
    A. Through governmental processes. When a government is formed, a convention proposes a constitution which is then ratified by the people. The constitution makes certain broad rules and provides a system for making more rules of law, as needed, by legislation and by court decisions.

59. Q. Where is the law found?
    A. In books containing the constitution, the statutes of the legislature and the decisions of the courts.

60. Q. How does the court find the law?
    A. The lawyers present the law to the judge and the judge reads it, or the judge may make his own study.

61. Q. Is there a specific rule of law to fit every case?
    A. No. Each case is different.

278 • SO YOU'RE GOING TO COURT

62. Q. Then what rule applies?
A. (1) A more general rule which covers the case, though not specifically, (2) a rule on a similar case, or (3) a rule from another jurisdiction.

63. Q. Is a juror expected to know the law?
A. No. The judge instructs the jury as to what the law is pertaining to the case.

64. Q. What if a juror doesn't agree with a proposition of law as presented by the judge.
A. By his oath the juror must follow the law whether he agrees with it or not.

65. Q. What happens if a juror refuses to follow the court's instructions?
A. Theoretically he could be penalized for contempt of court, but jury deliberations are private and seldom is their conduct inquired into.

66. Q. What if the judge disagrees with the jury's verdict?
A. He must accept the verdict whether he agrees with it or not.

67. Q. What is a directed verdict?
A. An order by the court that the jury return a certain verdict.

68. Q. Why have a jury if the judge can direct a verdict?
A. Until all the evidence is presented in court, there usually is no way to know if the case is worthy or not. The judge directs a verdict only if the case is so one-sided that reasonable minds could not differ on the outcome.

69. Q. What if there is no doubt that the defendant caused an accident but much doubt as to whether the plaintiff's injury is serious?
A. The judge directs the jury to find the defendant liable but submits the question of damages for the jury to decide.

70. Q. What if the judge is mistaken in his evaluation of the law of a case?
A. Then an appeal court will reverse the decision.

71. Q. What if a jury is mistaken in its evaluation of the facts of a case?
    A. The verdict stands. The jury is confined to an area of reasonableness, and it cannot be said that a "mistake" was made about facts upon which reasonable minds can differ.

72. Q. Can a jury verdict ever be reversed?
    A. Yes. The rule of reasonableness applies at all times. If a jury verdict is so unreasonable that it had to be the result of prejudice, passion, confusion or a failure to read and understand the court's instructions, then it will be overturned.

73. Q. How is it possible to tell if a jury verdict was based on pure reason or passion, prejudice and confusion?
    A. Usually it is not. The jury is presumed to be reasonably intelligent and properly motivated. Most verdicts give no clue as to their basis. But certain types of verdicts show impropriety on their face. For example, where the amount of damages awarded is so excessive or inadequate that no reasonable person could so find.

74. Q. How is the jury foreman chosen and what are his duties?
    A. He is elected by the jury. He presides over the jury deliberations and, in the grand jury, he administers oaths and questions witnesses.

75. Q. What happens if a jury verdict is erroneous?
    A. If it appears that the jury did not understand the court's instructions, the judge may clarify his instructions and send the jury back for further deliberations. Ordinarily, however, the verdict is set aside and a new trial ordered.

76. Q. What is a mistrial?
    A. Where something goes awry to make it clear that a fair trial is not going to take place, the judge will halt the proceedings and order a new trial at a later date before a different jury.

77. Q. Can a petit jury make its own investigation of the case?

A. No. In fact this is a good example of how a mistrial might occur. Should the judge find out that a juror decided to "drive by the scene and talk to a few people" a mistrial would result because the jury must decide the case solely on what is presented in court.

78. Q. What are the various restrictions on discussing the case during trial?
A. The jury cannot discuss the case either among themselves or with anyone else until they enter into deliberation. The witnesses may be excluded from the courtroom and told not to discuss their testimony with anyone except the lawyers. The lawyers may discuss the case between themselves or with the judge when both are present. The judge cannot discuss the case with the jurors, witnesses or with a lawyer unless the opposing lawyer is present.

79. Q. May a juror discuss the case after the verdict is in?
A. Yes. There are no restrictions, but a juror does not have to talk with anyone unless he wants to.

80. Q. Why do we have juries?
A. Every lawsuit is important because justice is important to people and the factual elements of practically every case are subject to divergent opinions. These may be resolved only by bringing together a group of people who will fairly apply their common sense and the broad base of human experience they bring with them.

81. Q. Why wouldn't it be better to have trained people decide cases?
A. The outcome of a case is only part of justice. Professionals invariably give the impression of being predisposed about certain types of cases and they cannot maintain the confidence of all litigants.

82. Q. Why are juries doubly important in criminal cases?
A. Under our democratic form of government, the people must have a voice in who is sentenced, especially since the death penalty or imprisonment is involved.

Summing Up • 281

83. Q. Can any facts be presented at a trial?
A. No. Presentation of evidence is strictly governed by a vast and complicated body of rules known as the law of evidence. This seeks to keep the jury from being misled.

84. Q. Why do the attorneys so often confer in secret with the judge at the bench or in chambers?
A. Usually they are discussing a point of evidence or procedure and the discussion itself might mislead the jury.

85. Q. Why does a witness have to go to court if he has already given his statement to an investigator? Why can't the statement just be read to the jury?
A. This points up one of the most important rules of evidence. The statement is hearsay and forbidden in court because (1) the witness was not under oath when the statement was given, and (2) there is no opportunity to cross-examine an absent witness.

86. Q. What is the purpose of cross-examination?
A. To challenge a witness's testimony and show weak spots, if possible.

87. Q. Can a witness be cross-examined about anything in the world?
A. No. Only the matters brought out on direct examination may be gone into.

88. Q. What does the court do when it has found the facts and the law?
A. The jury applies the law to the facts and enters a verdict; then the judge enters judgment based on the verdict.

89. Q. What happens then?
A. The losing side files a motion for new trial and if this is denied then time is allowed to appeal to a higher court.

90. Q. If the case is appealed, is it tried anew in the higher court?
A. No, the higher court examines the record of the case and determines if the law was correctly followed or not.

91. Q. Does the appeal court decide the facts?

A. No. If based on proper evidence, the appeal courts accept the trial courts' decision on the facts.

92. Q. What orders may the appeal court enter?
A. It may affirm or reverse the decision; if it reverses, it may enter judgment as it decides or remand the case back to the trial court for a new trial.

93. Q. Who decides if a case will go to the supreme court of a state?
A. The attorney on the losing side. Any litigant has the right to appeal.

94. Q. Isn't the poor man at a great disadvantage because of appeals?
A. Often he is, but if he has a judgment it draws interest while the appeal is pending.

95. Q. Can any case go to the United States Supreme Court?
A. Any case can be presented but few are accepted; the United States Supreme Court can refuse to entertain an appeal unless it is shown that the case should be decided by it.

96. Q. Do lawyers have an obligation to the public and to the clients to limit the number of appeals?
A. Yes. A lawyer is under oath to pursue only causes he feels are honestly debatable under the law of the land.

97. Q. What if an appeal is not taken?
A. Then the court enforces the judgment.

98. Q. How does a court enforce a judgment?
A. By various means—punishment by fine or imprisonment for contempt, garnishment, sheriff's sale of property, et cetera.

99. Q. What is contempt of court?
A. Failure to show proper respect, or disobedience of an order of court.

100. Q. What is justice?
A. To a court it is the fair determination of a specific dispute.

101. Q. When can the judge direct a verdict of guilty in a criminal case?

A. Never. No matter how clear the evidence of guilt may appear to the judge, only a jury can find a person guilty of a crime.

102. Q. Can the judge direct a verdict of acquittal in a criminal case?
A. Yes. This occurs when the evidence is insufficient to support a conviction.

103. Q. When can the state obtain a new trial after an acquittal?
A. Never. A person can be put on trial only once for one crime.

104. Q. Can an accused obtain a new trial after being convicted by a jury?
A. Yes, when either the trial judge or an appeal court finds some irregularity or unfairness in the trial.

105. Q. What happens if an accused is patently guilty, but unfair means were used to gather the evidence against him?
A. He goes free. Courts have no way to assure fair trials except to overturn unfair ones.

106. Q. Are not the rules very one-sided in favor of the defendant?
A. Yes. The state has no redress in the event of a criminal trial unfair to it.

107. Q. Why is the defendant favored?
A. Because the constitution so provides. Individual freedom is more highly prized than state efficiency in convicting every guilty party.

This presentation of the basic concept of the law has emphasized the individual's rights and obligations. When you require the services of an attorney, or go to court for whatever reason, your increased knowledge will help you to appreciate that the sole purpose of the law is to see that justice is done and justice is a virtue to be shared by all.

No man can know all of the law, not attorneys nor even judges. The journals of the law since ancient times are more voluminous than all of the other written records throughout history. These questions and answers are intended to provide you with only the fundamental knowledge of the law so that you can be apprised of its weighty responsibilities in maintaining order in a highly complicated society. In a democracy, no man is a law unto himself. We all live and work together for the common good and if this book proves to be an aid toward that desirable destination, it has fulfilled its purpose.

Glossary

Abstract of Title—A compiled history of the ownership of land.
Accessory—One who unlawfully aids a criminal.
Acknowledgment—The certificate of a Notary Public or other authorized official that a person has signed an instrument as his free act and deed.
Action—a lawsuit.
Administrator—A person appointed by a court to manage the property of an estate.
Admissible—Refers to evidence which is allowed in court as pertinent to the case.
Admission—A statement or concession by a party which is relevant to his adversary's claim. Can be made in or out of court.
Adversary—Contested; the opposite party in litigation.
Adverse Witness—One on the other side of a lawsuit.
Advocate—A lawyer as he argues his client's cause in court.
Affidavit—A written statement of facts, the truth of which is sworn to under oath or affirmation.
Affirmation—A solemn and formal pronouncement that a statement is true; substituted for an oath where the person making it does not choose to swear before God.
Agent—A person authorized by another (called the principal) to act for him.
Alimony—Support money a husband is ordered to pay to a wife after separation.
Alternate Juror—Extra juror called in case one of the regular jurors becomes ill or incapacitated.
Amicus Curiae—Latin "A friend of the court." A counsellor who offers aid to the court on a case in which neither he nor his client is directly involved.
Annulment—A legal action to declare that a marriage was

void from the beginning because a party was under age, mentally incompetent to consent to marriage, or because of some other defect in the marriage contract.

Answer—A court paper in a civil lawsuit served on plaintiff or his attorney in answer to the summons and complaint in which the defendant gives his side of the lawsuit.

Appellate Court—A higher court which reviews cases on appeal to determine if they were properly tried.

Arbitrator—A private, disinterested person chosen by the parties to a dispute for the purpose of deciding the issues.

Argument—Statements by an attorney in support of his client's case.

Arraignment—Where an accused is told in court of the crime charged against him.

Arrest—To restrain a person or deprive him of his liberty by legal authority.

Assignment—Transfer of a right from one person to another.

Attachment—Taking property by legal process for the payment of a debt.

Attestation—Witnessing the signing of a will and signing as a witness.

Attorney—One who acts for another.

Attorney-at-Law—A lawyer.

Attorney-in-fact—One who has been given power to act for another; need not be a lawyer; see Power of Attorney.

Bail Bond—An obligation signed by someone promising to pay the amount previously set by the court as bail if a defendant in a criminal case fails to appear in court when required.

Bailiff—A court employee charged with helping to maintain order.

Bankruptcy—The legal procedure under the federal laws which can be used when a person becomes totally unable to pay his debts.

Bar—The entire body of attorneys and counsellors at law; this is a figurative expression from the "bar," railings or dividers in court separating the place lawyers usually occupy.

Bench—Where the judge sits in court; also the entire body of judges.

Bequest—A gift by will.

Bill of Attainder—A legislative act pronouncing a person guilty of an alleged high crime and imposing sentence on him; forbidden by the constitution.

Bill of Particulars—A paper filed in court to explain the details of a case, in amplification of the other pleadings.

Bill of Rights—The popular name for the first ten amendments of the United States Constitution.

Binder—A preliminary agreement (in insurance and real estate).

Brief—A lawyer's written presentation of his case to an appeal court.

Burden of Proof—The task required of a party to a lawsuit to prove his claim.

Case—A court action, cause, suit or controversy.

Case Law—Rules of law created and established by the published opinions of courts.

Cause—A case, claim or lawsuit, on which plaintiff relies for recovery from defendant.

Certiorari—A review procedure by which a high court examines the actions of a lower court or of a governmental agency.

Challenge—Right of a party to a lawsuit to object to a juror during selection of jury before the trial.

   For Cause—Objection on the ground that the juror is disqualified for some reason.

   Peremptory—Without stating any reason.

   To the array—Objection that entire group of jurors were improperly selected.

Chambers—The judge's private office in the courthouse.

Chancery—A judicial system developed to administer "equity."

Character Witness—One who verifies a person's reputation for truth and veracity or as a law abiding citizen.

Charge—The judge's instruction to the jury.

Chattel—Any item of personal property as distinguished from land which is real property.

Chattel Mortgage—Document executed and delivered by owner of personal property, pledging the property to secure repayment of a loan.

Circumstantial Evidence—Indirect evidence. Proof of facts which tend, by logic, to prove other facts.

Citation—A writ issued out of a court of competent jurisdiction commanding a person to appear before it and perform some duty described therein, or to show cause why he should not.

Civil Case—A lawsuit between private parties.

Civil Rights—Usually refers to those personal rights guaranteed by the Federal Constitution.

Class Action—A suit brought on behalf of other persons similarly situated.

Closing of Title—This takes place when buyer of some real estate pays money due under the contract in exchange for a deed to the property.

Client—A person who hires an attorney.

Codicil—An amendment or addition to a will, executed with all of the formality of a will.

Commitment—Order of a court directing a person to be kept in custody in a penal or mental institution.

Common Law—The entire body of English law which forms the foundation of the legal system of our states (except Louisiana). Also, judge-made law of the states.

Commutation—reduction of punishment or sentence after conviction for a crime.

Comparative negligence—Principle in law which allows one who was somewhat negligent to recover for his injury against another person who was more seriously negligent in an accident.

Competent evidence—Proof in proper form to present in court. Example: testimony by an eye-witness is competent evidence; a newspaper story about the same event is incompetent hearsay.

Complainant—One who instigates a prosecution against an alleged criminal.

Complaint—The plaintiff's written claim in court.

Compounding a crime—The offense of agreeing not to prosecute if a criminal will make reparations.

Condemnation—Legal process by which authorized governmental agency takes private property for public use.

Confession—A defendant's statement that he committed the crime with which he is charged.

   Of Judgment—A contract provision whereby a debtor under certain conditions gives creditor right to claim judgment for the debt.

Confiscation—Act of taking private property as a penalty and a forfeit for public use.

Conflict of laws—A branch of law concerning the many problems where laws of different governments touch the same controversy.

Consideration—The thing of value that one party gives another party to a contract.

Consignment—Delivery of merchandise to consignee to be sold and proceeds, less commission, returned to *consignor.*

Conspiracy—An agreement between two or more people to cooperate in commission of an illegal act.

Constitution—The fundamental law of a government by which it is organized.

Contempt—Willful disdain or disobedience of a public authority.

Contract—A mutual agreement, supported by consideration, to do or not to do a certain thing enforcible in a court of law.

Contributory negligence—Negligence of an injured party which helped cause the injury; sometimes precludes any award for the injury.

Conveyance—Document transferring ownership in real property.

Corporation—An artificial person or creature of law established by governmental authority as a legal entity for specified purposes.

Corpus Delicti—Latin: "The body of a crime." The group of facts which support a criminal charge. (Evidence of the dead body in a homicide case is only one part of the corpus delicti.)

Corroboration—Evidence from two or more witnesses saying the same thing about the same event.

Counterclaim—A case against the plaintiff by the defendant.

Court—A body of government charged with the administration of justice in particular cases.

Court of Record—A trial court in which all proceedings are recorded by a court reporter, the person who stenographically records a trial or hearing in a court of record.

Covenant—A written promise; often applies to a restriction on property use contained in a deed or lease.

Criminal case—A charge by the government against an individual instituted to punish an infraction of the criminal laws.

Cross-examination—Questioning of a witness by the lawyer who did not present the witness in court.

Custody—The care and keeping of anything; applies, also, to a court order granting a parent or other person the right to live with, control, educate and guide a child.

Damages—Compensation for a loss or injury.

Decedent—The term denoting deceased person whose estate is involved in a will or estate proceedings.

Decree—A final decision and judgment of court.

Deed—Document which transfers ownership to real estate.

Default—Failure to appear or plead in court when required.

Defendant—Party in a lawsuit sued by plaintiff.

Defense—The reasons of law or fact put forward by one claimed against in a lawsuit as to why his adversary's claim should be denied.

Deliberations—A jury's consideration of a case in order to arrive at a verdict.

Deposition—Testimony of a witness to a lawsuit, called deponent, under oath but before the actual trial and usually outside of the court; also written testimony or "deposition upon written interrogatories."

Devise—Grant of real estate by will. Recipient is the *devisee.*

Dictum—A side comment in a court opinion not essential to explanation or determination of the controverted issues.

Direct Evidence—Proof of facts by witnesses who saw acts performed or heard words spoken.

Direct Examination—Questioning of a witness by the lawyer who called the witness to the stand.

Directed Verdict—Decision by the judge on the outcome of a case where the evidence is so one-sided that the jury cannot be allowed to decide.

Discovery—The legal system whereby a lawyer can find things out about his opponent's case before the actual trial.

Dismiss—When a case is thrown out of court.

District Attorney—The elected or appointed public officer who acts as lawyer for the government in prosecuting criminal cases in court.

Divorce—Dissolution of a marriage for some reason, proven in court, which the state law says is sufficient grounds for divorce.

Domicile—A person's permanent home.

Double Jeopardy—Prosecution more than once for a single offense; prohibited by the constitution.

Due Process—Regular and orderly administration of justice by a proper court in accordance with the established rules.

Duress—Wrongful threat, pressure or fear applied to deprive a person of the power of his free will.

Easement—Right of a landowner to use a part of his neighbor's land for an access road, water course, power line, or the like.

Eminent Domain—Power of government to acquire private land or property for necessary public use with just compensation.

Equity—Natural right or justice. The Golden Rule—the rule of doing to all others as we desire them to do to us. "To live honestly, to harm nobody, to render to every man his due." Justinian. Also a flexible body of law to produce justice where rigid rules would not.

Glossary • 291

Escheat—Turning of property over to the state where no heirs can be found.

Escrow—Where a deed or other important paper is kept by an independent party until a certain event when it is supposed to be turned over to someone else.

Estate—Used mainly in reference to the property of a deceased person; also describes ownership of lands or other property.

Estoppel—One cannot take a certain stand and then change to the detriment of others.

Evidence—The facts proven in a lawsuit. Also, the field of law governing presentation of facts in court.

Execution—Collecting a judgment or carrying something out to its completion.

Executor (feminine: Executrix)—A person appointed in a will to take care of property and carry out the will terms.

Exhibit—A paper or other physical object which tends to prove facts in a case.

Expert—A witness, learned in a specialized field of knowledge, who is allowed to give opinions in court.

Extortion—Offense of taking money or property by threat or duress under pretext of authority.

Extradition—The procedure whereby an accused criminal is transferred from the state where he is arrested to the state where he is charged.

Fee—In one sense, the charge of a lawyer for his services. In real property, "fee" designates a type of land ownership where the owner is free to dispose of the property as he wishes.

Felony—A serious crime where the punishment is a penitentiary sentence and conviction deprives *felon* of some civil rights.

Fiduciary—Describes the high trust and confidence required of one who promises to take care of another's property.

Foreclosure—The procedure of a mortgage holder to take the property when the mortgage loan isn't paid.

Forgery—Making, altering or counterfeiting in writing with intent to deceive.

Fraud—An intentional perversion of truth in order to deceive another and take his property.

Garnishment—A method of collecting a judgment debt by intercepting money owed to the debtor by some other party.

Good Will—The intangible value of a business in its ability to attract customers.

Grand Jury—A body of citizens who investigate to determine if crimes have been committed and, if so, to charge the persons apparently guilty.

Grant—Transfer of real property or interest therein by which *Grantor* transfers to *Grantee*.

Guardian—One who has a legal duty to care for a minor child and his property until the age of twenty-one.

Habeas Corpus—An application to a court complaining of unlawful imprisonment or restraint.

Hearsay—What a witness says he heard another say—second-hand evidence.

Heir—One who inherits property.

Holographic—A will in the handwriting of the testator.

Homicide—The killing of a human being by the act of another human being.

Impeachment of Witness—to question the veracity of a witness by contrary evidence or evidence that he is unworthy of belief.

Indemnity—Reimbursement by insurance for loss sustained.

Indictment—A criminal charge made by a grand jury. For federal crimes this is the only way one can be charged. In States, the complaint of a citizen and the signature of the District Attorney is all that is required.

Infant—A person who has not yet attained the age of twenty-one.

Information—A criminal accusation made by the District Attorney rather than through Grand Jury indictment.

Injunction—An order of court directing a person to do or refrain from doing a certain thing.

Insanity—Inability to comprehend duty and refrain from wrong conduct.

Instructions—The judge's charge in which he explains the law of the case to the jury.

Intent—The design, resolve or determination with which a person acts.

Interrogatories—Written questions to be answered under oath by a witness prior to trial. See *Deposition*.

Intestate—A person without leaving a will dies intestate.

Jeopardy—The defendant's danger of conviction and punishment during a criminal trial.

Joint Tenancy—Where persons own an equal interest in property, real or personal.

Judge—An elected or appointed public officer who presides over a court.

Judgment—The decision of a court between plaintiff and defendant.

Judicial Notice—Courts accept certain well known facts as true without formal proof. (Chicago is in Illinois; water freezes at 32° Fahrenheit.)

Jurisdiction—The authority of a court to hear particular cases.

Jury, Petit—A group of citizens assembled in a court and sworn to decide the facts of a case.

Last Clear Chance—The doctrine that the person who has the last opportunity to avoid injury is responsible even though others were careless in creating the dangerous situation.

Law—The body of rules of conduct and order established and enforced by the government.

Lawsuit—A case in court instituted by one party to compel another to do him justice.

Lawyer—A person learned in law, licensed to represent people in court and advise on legal matters. Sometimes called an attorney and counsellor at law.

Leading Question—One which suggests the desired answer.

Lease—Agreement by which owner of real estate called landlord or *lessor* rents to a tenant, or *lessee,* on payment of *consideration* called *rent.*

Legacy—A gift of personalty made by will, also called a *bequest.*

Legal Age—The minimum age required by law for a person to do some act. Example: Age 21 to contract.

Levy—To take property for payment of a judgment.

Liability—Being subject to a legal obligation.

Libel—Statement in writing which defames and injures the reputation of an individual.

Lien—A claim on property for a debt.

Limited—Sometimes abbreviated "Ltd.", means the organization is a corporation and its debts are limited to the property of the company and will not be paid from anyone's personal wealth.

Litigant—A party to a lawsuit.

Majority—The years after a person's minority—21 and over—when one is legally responsible for all of his acts.

Malice—An evil condition of mind devoid of social responsibility and fatally bent on mischief.

Manslaughter—Taking a human life without malice or intent.

Marriage—A contract of a man and woman to be husband and wife, concurred in and enforced by the state.

Master—A court representative appointed to do some act, such as sell property ordered sold under a decree.

Material—Evidence having important bearing on the merits of a case.

Misdemeanor—A crime or offense lower than a felony and punishable by fine, or imprisonment in some jail other than a penitentiary.

Moot Court—Pretended trials by students for practice.

Mortgage—A contract pledging real estate as security for the repayment of a loan.

Motion—A formal application to a court asking the judge to make some ruling.

Motive—A reason for action. Note: Intent and Motive are different things.

Murder—Killing of a person by another person with deliberate and premeditated design to cause death.

Naturalized Citizen—One who is an alien by birth but becomes a citizen through legal procedures.

Negligence—Lack of reasonable care to protect people and property from harm.

Negotiable Instrument—A check, note or other written instrument, the value of which can be transferred from one person to another.

Nolo Contendere—Latin. "I will not contest it." A plea by the defendant in a criminal case throwing himself on the mercy of the court.

Non Compos Mentis—A general term expressing all manner of mental diseases and derangements.

Notary Public—A person licensed to administer oaths and acknowledge the signing of documents.

Nuisance—A wrongful use of one's property so as to interfere with another's use and enjoyment of his property, which constitutes a *tort*.

Nuncupative Will—An oral will made before witnesses in a person's last illness. (Note: Not valid in many states.)

Oath—A solemn pledge binding one to God, conscience, and law for a promised act. Note: The customary requirement of raising the right hand is said to be based on an early English practice of punishing convicts by making them handle hot coals with their bare hands. Thus, their scars would be exposed in the oath taking process.

Objection—A lawyer's protest to the judge about some event in a trial, usually concerning a question or statement of the opposition.

Offense—Breach of the criminal laws.

Offer of Proof—Where a lawyer explains or shows the trial judge, in the record of the case but outside the presence of the jury, what he intends to prove on some point so that the judge, or an appeal court, can decide its propriety.

Opening Statements—Near the start of a trial where the lawyers on each side explain their position and outline their proof.

Opinion Evidence—A witness gives his conclusion about an issue; this is generally not allowed except by expert witnesses.

Opinion of the Court—The judge sets forth the factual and legal reasons for his decision.

Order—A formal direction of a court, backed by the power of government, that something be done or not done.

Pardon—A governor's release of a convict from punishment imposed by sentence of a court.

Parol Evidence Rule—A written contract controls by its terms, which cannot be altered by bringing out the conversations leading up to signing of the contract.

Party—One who sues or is sued in court.

Perjury—Lying under oath.

Personal Property—Every type of object capable of being owned except real property. Sometimes called *personalty*.

Pettifogger—An unprincipled or dishonorable lawyer who engages in mean and small business or who tries to obstruct justice with petty and ill-founded arguments of form over substance.

Plaintiff—One who complains in court against another.

Pleadings—The court papers in which the parties to a case explain their positions.

Police Power—The burden of government to promote the public health, safety, welfare and morals.

Polling the Jury—Part of trial procedure whereby each juror is individually asked in open court whether the unanimous verdict is, truly, his verdict.

Power of Attorney—A written authority by one person allowing another to act for him in specific situations.

Prayer—That part of a pleading in which the court is asked to grant certain relief or do a specific thing. Example: "Wherefore, the defendant prays that plaintiff's complaint be dismissed."

Premeditation—A prior determination to do an act which is later done; usually applies to criminal acts.

Preponderance—The weight of evidence as being more believable and convincing than that of the opposing party.

Presumption of Law—A rule requiring judges to draw certain inferences. Example: A person is presumed innocent of a crime unless and until proven guilty.

Pretrial Hearing—A separate hearing where the lawyers and the judge try to plan and simplify the trial, to be held some weeks or days afterwards.

Prima Facie—Latin—"at first sight." Enough evidence to support a claim until contradicted by other evidence.

Privileged Communication—Confidences which a court cannot inquire into, such as between husband and wife, attorney and client, or physician and patient.

Probable Cause—Good reason to think a crime has been committed by the one accused; sufficient to accuse, but not to convict, which requires proof beyond a reasonable doubt.

Probate—Proof that a will is genuine and valid. Also, the type of court and procedure followed for handling property of deceased persons.

Probation—One convicted of a crime may be granted probation rather than sent to prison if his being at large would not endanger society and guidance might help him reform.

Procedural Law—That which prescribes the method of enforcing one's rights in court, as distinguished from substantive law, which sets out what those rights are.

Process—The procedure for getting the defendant into court.

Promissory Note—A written promise to pay money to another.

Proof—The establishment of a fact by evidence presented in court.

Proof Beyond a Reasonable Doubt—The strength of evidence required to convict one of a crime—that which precludes any reasonable hypothesis of innocence and creates an abiding conviction of guilt.

Prosecution—The court proceeding used by the government against people accused of crimes.

Prosecutor—A lawyer hired by the government to pursue criminal cases in court.

Proximate Cause—A somewhat technical term describing how a person's negligence connects with another's injury for a court to recognize a claim. "Proximate cause is the efficient cause from which an injury flows in unbroken sequence without any intervening cause to break the continuity."

Public Administrator—An official who protects estate property when no family member or other person is available to do so.

Public Policy—Where enforcement of a contract or allowance of a claim would tend to endanger the public morals or undermine the public good, then a court will refuse relief on grounds of public policy.

Quash—To make void, or set aside for insufficiency of grounds.

Quit Claim—A deed releasing all claims against a property but without any guarantees.

Quantum Meruit—The reasonable value of services rendered

Quiet Enjoyment—Describes what an owner of real property may demand.

Real Property—Also called realty, real estate. Land and buildings, crops or other immobile things attached to the land.

Rebuttal—Evidence to offset that presented by the opponent.

Receiver—A person appointed by the court to hold property to be disposed of by court order.

Referee—An officer appointed by a court to hear argument and testimony and to report back his findings.

Refreshing Memory—Where a witness looks at his notes, pictures or other memoranda to bring past events into recollection.

Relevant—Evidence which logically connects with the issues in a case.

Replevin—The type of legal action you would undertake to regain possession of your property if it was wrongfully taken away from you.

Reply—The plaintiff's answer to the defendant's case.

Res Judicata—The rule that once a case is decided in court it cannot be adjudicated again between the same parties.

Residence—A person's place of abode, which need not be permanent or exclusive. (A hotel guest is a resident, even for one night.) Distinguished from *domicile*.

Respondeat Superior Principle in law which transfers liability to a principle for negligent acts of his agent. E.g.: An employer must pay for harm caused by want of care by his worker.

Res Ipsa Loquitur—Latin: "The thing speaks for itself." A rebuttable presumption that the defendant was negligent when something within his exclusive control causes injury and the accident is one which ordinarily would not occur: absent negligence.

Retainer—Denotes both the act of hiring a lawyer and the fee paid for obtaining his exclusive services.

SS—Abbreviation of the Latin word *scilicet*—"to wit" or "Let it be known." Used in affidavits where the place of swearing is stated.

Seal—An imprint on a document to certify its authenticity.

Search Warrant—A written order of court to search a certain house or other building for specific goods alleged to be unlawfully within.

Seisin—A term derived from the English feudal system designating possession and ownership of land.

Self Defense—The right of a person to repel force by force.

Separate Maintenance—Where married parties live apart but don't actually divorce, a court can order the husband to pay support for the wife and children.

Separation of Witnesses—On request, the judge will order witnesses not to discuss their testimony with other witnesses and to stay out of the court until their turn to testify.

Service of Process—The proper delivery of a summons, subpoenae, writ or other court paper.

Sheriff—The elected chief law enforcement officer of a county.

Sovereign Immunity—The rule that you can't sue the government without its consent. This has been modified in some types of claims.

Specific Performance—Where a court orders a contract performed by its terms.

Stare Decisis—The policy of courts to follow the rules laid down in their previously decided cases.

Statute—An act of the legislature, written and published, declaring, commanding or prohibiting something.

Statute of Frauds—A statute requiring that certain types of transactions—notably, sales of land—be in writing in order to have any legal force at all.

Statute of Limitation—A legislative act which limits the time when a plaintiff may bring a lawsuit; differs in each state for any particular type of case.

Stay of Execution—A judgment is stopped for a limited period of time, sometimes to allow the loser to appeal.

Stipulation—An agreed arrangement or settlement between the parties or their attorneys.

Subpoena—A court paper commanding a witness to come into court and give testimony.

Substituted Service—Where a party cannot be personally served because he is outside of the state or his whereabouts are unknown, service by mail or by publication in a newspaper is sometimes allowed.

Summation—The final argument or closing statement of a lawyer to the jury.

Summons—A court paper telling the defendant he is being sued and advising when he must answer in court.

Surety—The person who promises to make good the obligations of another.

Supplementary Proceedings—Steps taken in court to collect a judgment.

Surrogate—Judge in court where estates of deceased persons, guardianships, and the like are administered.

Talesman—Bystanders who are summoned as jurors when those regularly called prove insufficient in number.

Tenant—One who has some legal right in real estate, such as a renter or a part owner.

Testator—(feminine: *Testatrix*)—One who makes a will by which he or she leaves or disposes of his or her property.

Testimony—Spoken evidence given by a witness under oath.

Title—The evidence of property ownership.

Tort—A civil wrong committed by one person interfering with the rights of another, making grounds for suit in court.

Trespass—An illegal encroachment injuring a person or his property, or coming upon the land of another without permission.

Trial—A judicial examination of a cause for the purpose of deciding the issues in dispute.

Trial Court—A court where trials are held.

True Bill—A statement by a grand jury that they are convinced of the truth of a criminal accusation they have made.

Trust—An arrangement by which property is transferred to a person (called the trustee) so that he can take care of it for the benefit of another (called the beneficiary).

Ultra Vires—Acts beyond the scope of a corporation's charter powers.

Unanimous Verdict—Where all jurors agree; this is required for all cases in some states and in all states for conviction of a crime.

Unclean Hands Doctrine—Holds that one who asks a court for fair and equitable treatment must have given such consideration to others involved in the case.

Undue Influence—Any improper threat or persuasion which destroys one's will or consent to govern his own actions.

Unjust Enrichment—A legal doctrine sometimes used to prevent one from profiting inequitably at another's expense.

Usury—Charging more interest than the law allows.

Vendee—Buyer or purchaser.

Vendor—Seller.

Venire—The writ used to summon jurors to court.

Venue—A geographical location where the facts arise or where a case is tried.

Verdict—The decision of a jury.

Viewing the Scene—The judge takes the jury to look at the scene of a case.

Void—"Without any legal or effectual force to bind."

Voir Dire—"To speak the truth." Preliminary examination into the qualifications of a juror or a witness to act as such.

Voluntary Quit—Where a workman gives up a job so as to deprive himself of unemployment compensation benefits.

Waiver—The intentional abandonment of a legal right.

Ward—A minor (infant) child or a person of unsound mind who is in the care of a guardian.

Warrant—A writ or precept of a court directing that a certain act, such as an arrest or a search and seizure, be done by an officer competent to do so.

Warranty—A promise related to a contract.

Waste—Permanent damage to real property.

Will—A legal declaration as to what a person wants done with his property after death.

Conditional Will—A disposition which depends upon the occurrence of some uncertain event (e.g., I give my country estate to my nephew, John, if, but only if, he marries Pennybeth Davis and has at least one son.).

Witness—One who testifies as to what he has seen, heard or observed in a judicial proceeding.

Workman's Compensation—Payment for injury on the job.

Writ—A written order of court to a public officer or private person that something be done in aid of the administration of justice.

Zoning—The division of a city into districts and regulation of the type of buildings and uses of land in the different districts.

About the Author

ROBERT W. SMEDLEY received his B.A. degree in 1950 from the University of Colorado and from 1951 to 1953 attended the Columbia University Law School, New York City, returning for his LL.B. in 1954 at the University of Denver College of Law.

A practising attorney in Denver, Colorado, the author was a public prosecutor on the Denver District Attorney's staff from 1956 to 1961 before re-entering private law practice.

Mr. Smedley believes that the public should be informed on the law and is opposed to the mantle of secrecy which cloaks so much of the legal profession. This, he says, benefits neither lawyer, client nor the public. The layman is entitled to know about the practice of the law by which he is supposed to live and to be familiar with the responsibilities of lawyers, judges and the people who go to court.

The author was born in Denver in 1927. Mr. Smedley's grandfather Dr. William Smedley was the first of the pioneering family to live in Denver. He arrived from Chester County, Pennsylvania in 1870, founded the Smedley Dental Group and served as Superintendent of the Denver City Schools. (A school in North Denver is named in his honor.) The author's father, Dr. V. Clyde Smedley is a practising dentist in Denver and his mother, Anne Wheeler Smedley, is a retired Denver school teacher.

A contributor of articles to law magazines and newspapers, Mr. Smedley won particular commendation for his article in the May 1954 issue of the Labor Law Journal "A Plan for Union Democracy" and in the January-February 1961 issue of Case and Comment titled "The ABC's of Trial."

He is a member of the Denver Bar Association, the Colorado Bar

Association, American Bar Association, Exchange Club of Denver, Phi Alpha Delta legal fraternity, Masons, City Club of Denver, and Arbitrator of the American Arbitration Association.

Mrs. Robert W. Smedley is the former Phoebe Ann Ellis of Arlington, Illinois and Hamilton, Ohio. Her late father was Erle Ellis of Chicago and her mother, La Nelle Andrews Ellis, is the present Mrs. H. R. Grosvenor whose husband is Manager of the Hamilton Journal of Hamilton, Ohio.

Mr. and Mrs. Robert W. Smedley and their two daughters Cara Ellen, six, and Melissa Ann, three years old, live in Littleton, Colorado.